THE WIDENING STREAM

THE *Widening* STREAM

the Seven Stages of Creativity

David Ulrich

Shelburne Falls, Massachusetts. David Ulrich, 1975

BEYOND
WORDS
Publishing
I N C

Beyond Words Publishing, Inc.
20827 N.W. Cornell Road, Suite 500
Hillsboro, Oregon 97124-9808
503-531-8700
1-800-284-9673

Editor: Jenefer Angell
Managing editor: Julie Steigerwaldt
Copyeditor and proofreader: David Abel
Cover design: David Ulrich, Dorral Lukas, and Angela Lavespere
Interior design: Angela Lavespere
Composition: William H. Brunson Typography Services

Printed in the United States of America
Distributed to the book trade by Publishers Group West

Library of Congress Cataloging-in-Publication Data
Ulrich, David, 1950–
    The widening stream : the seven stages of creativity / David Ulrich.
      p.   cm.
    Includes bibliographical references.
    ISBN 1-58270-081-8 ISBN 1-58270-079-6 (pbk.)
    1. Creative ability.   2. Creative thinking.   I. Title.
  BF408 .U47   2002
  153.3′5—dc21

                              2001056557

The corporate mission of Beyond Words Publishing, Inc.:
  Inspire to Integrity

CONTENTS

ACKNOWLEDGMENTS

This book began as short essays to my students. Their sustained efforts, as well as the depth and breadth of their work, created the need for this commentary. They challenged me to clarify my concerns and responses—and kept my back against the wall. They helped ignite my passion for writing and deserve my grateful acknowledgment. I offer my sincere wish for their continuing creative growth.

Many people have contributed to the development of ideas found in this book. I am deeply indebted to Dorothea Dooling and Minor White for their wisdom and lucid guidance, shedding just enough light on my path of discovery and learning for me to begin to find my own way. To Nicholas Hlobeczy, for his tireless efforts toward awakening the creative spirit in himself and others, I offer my profound gratitude. The following individuals gave invaluable suggestions and feedback during the early stages of preparing the manuscript: Pamela Beverly, Kathleen Carr, Hilary Harts, Joe McNeely, Franco Salmoiraghi, and Nicole Wales. To them I owe my heartfelt thanks.

Without the staff at Beyond Words Publishing, this book would not be in your hands. Special thanks to Cynthia Black for her encouragement and vision. And my warmest *aloha* goes to Jenefer Angell, editor extraordinaire, who challenged me in so many ways to get it right, make it clear, and let it sing. For her firm yet flexible and open counsel, I am deeply appreciative.

To Julie Steigerwaldt and the entire Beyond Words family, I give many thanks for their dedication to excellence and their patience in initiating me into the mysteries of book publishing.

INTRODUCTION

What is the nature of the creative process? And how do we understand what is needed to fully engage this fundamental human activity? Most of us are drawn to participate in some form of creative expression, such as art-making, writing, dancing, cooking, or any of those daily activities that ask for a transformation of materials and energies. The urge to create—to use our minds, hearts, and hands in unison; to work with materials; to express ourselves and our observations, our deepest longings, our greatest aspirations, our joys and sorrows—is one of the basic human impulses. Every person holds the potential to enter the stream of discovery and invention. Each of us contains a vast wealth of inner resources that invite us to participate in the process of creation.

Many people long to fulfill their creative potential, yet reliable guidance is hard to find. Most current books on creativity fall into one of two categories: self-help books, which provide a limited, oversimplified, and idealistic view of the process; and books on the psychology or philosophy of creativity written by specialists in the humanities or sciences, which are highly complex and not easily accessible to the average reader. Over the years, however, several classic works have assisted me immeasurably in understanding and developing the ideas found within these pages. Among these noteworthy investigations of the creative process are Rollo May's thoughtful and descriptive *The Courage to Create*, written from the perspective of modern psychology;

Art & Fear by David Bayles and Ted Orland, an insightful series of observations on artmaking, designed for artists and students; *Writing Down the Bones* by Natalie Goldberg, an instructive contemporary exploration of creativity viewed through the lens of the writer's craft; and the undeniable tour de force of this small body of guidebooks, Rainer Maria Rilke's *Letters to a Young Poet*, which has inspired generations of readers.

The most significant contribution to my ongoing inquiry into the nature of creativity came from a comprehensive anthology titled *The Creative Process: Reflections on Invention in the Arts and Sciences*, edited by Brewster Ghiselin, published in 1952. Though outdated in language and tone (with some essays dating back more than a century), and lacking more recent insights from the field of transpersonal psychology, it remains a primary source on the development of the creative impulse, rendering most contemporary treatments incomplete and imprecise by comparison. Consisting of essays by a notable group of artists and scientists (including Albert Einstein, Vincent Van Gogh, Carl Jung, D. H. Lawrence, W. B. Yeats, Henry Miller, and Katherine Anne Porter), the principal value of this book lies in the rich diversity of voices heard throughout its pages, and the striking similarity among contributors' observations on the evolving stages of growth within the creative process. Reading it provided me with the stunning realization that creativity, perhaps the most ingenuous and liberating impulse arising within us, contains clearly identifiable stages of development.

And this seems to be a universal experience. Since my first encounter with Ghiselin's book over thirty years ago, I have repeatedly witnessed the unfolding of these stages in my own work as a photographer, heard similar insights reported by students and colleagues, and read numerous accounts by artists and scientists of their congruent views on the organic, developmental steps of creativity and innovation. In this respect, *The Creative Process* provided a touchstone for my observations, and I am deeply indebted to its wisdom.

The Widening Stream, in turn, was conceived as a synthesis of the perspectives found in these preceding books, and intended to provide an accessible overview of the stages of the creative process. Since I know of no other book that fully outlines these universal, evolutionary steps of creation, I have tried to offer both the results of my own experience and a summary of the collective understanding of many who have gone before me. My intent is to help guide individuals through the process and, at the same time, acknowledge its inherent mystery. I walk a fine line—a veritable razor's edge easily dulled by clamorous best-selling voices that promise instant success and life-changing eight-week transformations. The deep resonances of the creative impulse unfold over the scope of a lifetime, challenging our propensity to reach for the quick fix, the easy answer. I will not, cannot, oversimplify the topic and reduce it to a mere recipe or formula. Creativity must remain an inquiry; it defies logic and arises from a deeper region than the ordinary mind's domain, forever eluding our systematic Western mode of thinking. Through these pages, I wish to open a rich field of exploration in which readers may discover their own unique paths, their own successes, joys, and challenges. This book exemplifies the Zen-like finger pointing toward the moon, offering a means of awakening and investigating one's own creativity—without claiming to hold the answer to the luminance of the moon itself.

The ideas developed throughout this book are deeply related to my own working questions as an artist, teacher, and seeker; many evolved from an especially rewarding and challenging class, titled *Photographic Tools and Creative Expression*, which I taught at Hui No'eau Visual Arts Center in Maui, Hawai'i. It was an unusual class: most of the students were older than college age and were prepared to work passionately toward realizing their creative aspirations.

Most had faced the vicissitudes of life enough to have cultivated both diligence and humility. In twenty-five years of teaching art, I have all too often observed and lamented one unfortunate result of declining standards in education: many students initially view the creative process in an overly simplistic manner. They enjoy some success with the early stages of the process, which ask for spontaneity and freedom of expression. But they often shirk the rigorous work involved in the later stages, which requires self-discipline, an unflinchingly sincere and evolving self-knowledge, and a long-term commitment to themselves and their chosen medium.

Moreover, it is truly surprising to me that many young artists believe that they already, and seemingly by instinct, fully understand the process of creativity. It is not viewed as an inquiry; rather, they feel capable of accomplishing it through their ordinary mind alone, without the enlarging dimension of the deeper parts of their nature. This is a reductionist attitude—one that is unfortunately promoted by many popular books on creativity—in which students attempt to bring larger truths and ultimately unknowable dimensions of being down to their level, squeezing them into their own still-limited framework in order to understand them.

One of the many paradoxes of creativity is that we cannot know it fully, yet we can deeply experience it within ourselves. The creative process, as with all natural processes of growth and evolution, proceeds along a lawful line of development but does not always follow a linear progression. Like a river's journey, it contains broad currents of free-flowing movement, meandering streams that fuel its course, vigorous rapids and spirited falls, passages through perilous narrows, areas of inert stagnation, clear pools of polished stillness, and finally, a place of union with the sea, merging with the source.

The Widening Stream examines the full development of the creative process through seven definable and equally important stages. These cannot be grasped by the intellect alone, divorced from experience. Each stage requires our full attention, and each asks for its own particular blend of the energies of our bodies, minds, and feelings. It is only through a wide and deep engagement with the process, undertaken with a sense of "not-knowing," that we may begin to understand it. The stages serve to help us locate our place, find our way. Lacking taut boundaries, they should be viewed as a continuum in which each stage anticipates the next, seamlessly blending from one into the other in a natural, evolving process. As signposts, they mark our progress much like the definable passages in our lives from childhood through old age.

This book is divided into two parts. The first traces the seven stages of the creative process and how their secrets unfold as a result of an individual's work and discoveries. This part is intended to function as a tool for navigation, assisting individuals toward a deeper exploration of the evolving stages, providing hints for direction and offering guideposts that move the reader closer to penetrating the mysteries of creation. Each chapter ends with a section titled "Creative Practice," consisting of questions for self-examination along with explicit tools, exercises, and suggestions to help readers realize each step of the process. The second part elaborates on the creative impulse with a more in-depth look at three guiding principles of creativity.

The exercises have been tested through extensive classroom and workshop use. Throughout my teaching career, I have seen these tools prove their value to many individuals. Some have grown out of my own experience, some were given by my teachers, and some were offered by my students and peers. They are meant as suggestions and as guides for self-discovery—and to help shake loose the spontaneous, wild mind. Many of the questions and exercises are designed to help liberate the self from habit or formula, to open the door to fresh insight or unexpected discovery, and to encourage a connection with the largesse of one's deepest Self. My intent is to rouse your heart and mind toward authentic expression. If these exercises do not awaken your creative imagination, or burn as a homeward beacon, then please fashion your own tools out of your intuition, inclinations, and life experience. Experiment and explore—find the path to your center.

~

E.B. White, in his revision of William Strunk's marvelously lucid book on writing, *The Elements of Style*, comments on the creative impulse:

> *Who can confidently say what ignites a certain combination of words, causing them to explode in the mind? Who knows why certain notes in music are capable of stirring the listener deeply, though the same notes slightly rearranged are impotent? These are high mysteries...Writers will often find themselves steering by stars that are disturbingly in motion.*

This is all I ask: that you, the reader, may steer toward the constellations formed by the stages and principles outlined in this book, always keeping in mind that the guiding lights that illumine the creative process, helping us find our way home, are ever shifting—but only disturbingly so if we maintain a fixed standpoint or a formulaic approach. If we are fluid and open, inviting new experiences and challenges, we may discover the navigator within who is capable of sensing and knowing, in some primordial part of ourselves, the direction of land though still many miles beyond our current horizon.

While my own experiences and perspective grow from a sustained involvement with the visual arts, this book is for anyone wishing to examine and engage the creative process. To become an artist of life is an aim worthy of our humanity. Cooking, gardening, relating with others, addressing the challenges of our occupations, teaching, waiting tables, and advancing one's business can all be creative actions. The specific nature of one's activities is not nearly as important as how they are approached. Can we approach life itself as a creative challenge, through the medium of whatever it is that we do on a daily basis? This question forms the central inquiry of the book.

I did not plan the content of these pages, nor did I fully intend to write a book; it simply appeared. It began as a short series of working notes to my students, then became an urgent necessity as words and ideas flowed in rapid succession, often with startling organizational integrity. This process mirrored the twelve weeks of the class; one chapter for each session. Every week I committed to deliver a new section to my students. Without fail, the installments proceeded and grew in size and scope, until one day I realized that a book was forming. Much of the text revealed itself in my mind fully formed; there was little of the usual struggle of defining what to say, how to say it, and in what sequence. It seemed to emerge organically—as if I were giving birth to something that had been incubating for many years. Furthermore, my direct experience of the creative process as I endeavored to describe it in words made for an intensely interesting and enlivening inquiry.

I have tried to maintain the boldness, elegance, and energy of what Natalie Goldberg calls "first thoughts," discarding or expanding on the original material only where it seemed necessary for clarity's sake. It was a delicate balance: I questioned how to effectively edit the book while respecting the vitality of the original impulse. In addition, I needed to find a means of giving structure to the shades of variation in the progression of the process within each chapter. The metaphor of water presented in the title offered an evocative means of unifying the book's content, and was extended to subheadings throughout Part One.

When I was off track, or in search of additional clarification, my dreams often revealed inadequacies and how to resolve them. For example, when I felt as if the book was nearing completion, with nine sections behind me, I dreamt that I was the father of twelve children. How strange, I thought; having twelve children is almost unheard of today. However, in the dream, my family only felt whole with all twelve offspring. As soon as I willingly accepted the responsibility for that number of children, the chapter headings for the remaining three sections appeared. In retrospect, I see their necessity; the book would not have been complete without them.

The writing proceeded in its own time and place. Wherever I happened to be, or whatever I happened to be doing, phrases, thoughts, and insights would appear with great clarity and directness. Following the completion of this book, and much to my surprise, delight, *and* dismay—since I had hoped to put my pen aside for awhile—I received spontaneous insights in the form of concepts, titles, and chapter outlines for subsequent books in a series. The process seemed to have its own integrity and its own life; my only choice was to willingly submit to its organic development.

Thus, *The Widening Stream* was born as the first in a trilogy of books on the evolutionary unfolding of creativity and awareness in the individual. A profound sense of release accompanies the publication of these essays. I am touched and amazed by what I have been privileged to learn over the past three years of intense writing, in my search for lucidity of thought and clarity of expression. In the classroom, it has been frequently observed that teachers, through their inquiry and example, are those who learn the most. So too, I now believe, with writing. These thoughts and impressions have been gestating in the core of my being for some time—and their birth was imminent. I honor and acknowledge the many gifts from within, and feel humbled by the moments of grace that informed and guided me through this undertaking.

My wish for you, the reader, is that these insights may ignite your own creative gifts, fanning them into a blazing conflagration of authentic transformation; that there will be no turning back for you once you hear the thundering voices of spirit; that you will be shattered into fullness of being through your soul's longing; that you will discover with unshakable conviction that you have an indispensable thread of awareness to weave into the fabric of the world; and that your guiding lights will show you the way to grow gracefully into who you already are.

A PERSONAL ACCOUNT

Sometimes it feels as if all the elements of my life have lined up, conspiring to help me realize this endeavor of writing a comprehensive book on creativity. A lifelong passion for the arts, a propensity for teaching, a long-term investigation of the creative process as an artist and writer, and the resonating gifts offered by my own teachers have provided a solid, durable matrix for the unfolding of these ideas. Yet, by themselves, these ingredients form an incomplete picture, lacking the essential fusion, the one unexpected, stunning moment that brought my understanding sharply into focus, and that felt strangely at the time as if I were being given a keen lesson that would help others as well as myself. I wish, therefore, to share a deeply transformative experience that served to awaken a period of intense creativity—and provided me, once I could move beyond my paralyzing fear, with a powerful opportunity for growth and helped prompt me to write this book.

In 1983, at the age of thirty-three, I suffered an impact injury that could have cost me my life. While I was chopping wood, a small branch with a fractured tip flew up and struck me in the face, directly under the eye. Thankfully, I lived; tragically (especially for a photographer), I lost the vision of my right and dominant eye. It was the most traumatic and disabling event of my life—and by far the most enlightening and life-enhancing.

I did not realize the seriousness of the injury at the time of the accident. In the emergency room, the physician on duty urgently consulted an ophthalmologist. At that point, I understood that my eye had been seriously damaged, and I became terrified of the possible consequences. The doctor emphatically informed me that I needed surgery immediately to see if the eye could be repaired. I implored him to do his absolute best to save my vision—that I was a photographer and needed my eyes. Fears of a completely altered life entered my mind. Would I ever be able to drive again? To photograph? To live a normal life? Would I be disfigured? He then said something that has burned itself into my memory of that day. He said calmly and with great assurance: "You will be as good a photographer with one eye as you were with two."

After seven or eight hours of surgery—in which the surgeon removed the fragments of wood, repaired my crushed eyeball, tried to repair my massively torn retina, and performed cosmetic surgery to rebuild the lost tissue on the right side of my face—I was sent to the recovery room. Combinations of antibiotics were administered to prevent infection of my brain, which could have resulted from the foreign objects in my optic nerve. Mercifully, I never consciously knew that my life was in jeopardy, since the risk of infection had diminished substantially by the time I woke up.

The next week was pure hell. I underwent multiple tests and examinations to determine whether any useful vision could be returned to my eye. I had no light perception whatsoever due to the retinal damage, and was told that I would never see again with my right eye. Medical technology was many years away from transplanting a retina, and mine was far too damaged to repair. My doctor explained that the risk of sympathetic ophthalmia, in which the good eye follows suit with its injured neighbor and also loses the ability to see, was far greater than the chance of seeing out of that eye ever again—and that it should be removed.

My darkest hours of self-doubt followed upon receiving his diagnosis. Many questions arose for me about the role of fate, or accident, in our lives. Was this event fated? Or was it simply an accident? Could it have been avoided? I recalled an acute memory of a night when I was nineteen years old, contemplating my unknown future and feeling much hope and promise, in which an intuitive feeling persisted—one that I could not shake from my consciousness at the time—that I might someday lose an eye. When I reached my friend and longtime teacher, Nicholas Hlobeczy, to seek his advice on this momentous decision, he said, simply, "Thy will be done."

My mother, my girlfriend, and a select group of friends gathered at my home prior to the second surgery, with a bottle of excellent Armagnac, to drink a poignant toast to the thirty-three years of vision my eye had faithfully provided me. I did a small series of self portraits of my damaged face and eye, and went to bed wondering if I would—or could—ever again feel like a complete human being.

I dreamt that night of being inside a medieval castle, with two arched entrances, through which the light was streaming with a palpable force and energy such as one feels in the great cathedrals of Europe. Unexpectedly, one of the massive wood doors, the right one, began to close from the top down and to dim the light until it stopped on the floor, closing completely the arched entrance, reverberating with an echoing sound that spoke with authority and permanence. The sound was chilling. I went over to the door, and it was no longer a door or an opening; it had become simply a stone wall with no passage to the outer world.

The very next morning, I checked myself into the hospital to have my eye surgically removed. After settling into my room, several hours before surgery,

I was asked if I wanted a sedative. "Not yet," was my answer. It felt important to experience this moment as fully as possible. My anxiety was mounting. I didn't know what to do or where to turn. I decided to take a walk to the hospital chapel to try to digest the experience. I had never known such depression, fear, and despondency—it was completely paralyzing. I was scared to death of the future—and of the finality of the soon-to-be-performed surgery.

Then, in the chapel, came a moment of realization, in a burst of insight, that changed my attitude toward this event and gave me great strength and an unshakable sense of courage. A question unexpectedly arose in my mind: If I cannot let go of something as relatively insignificant as one eye, one small part of my body, what will happen when I have to completely let go of my entire body, when I die? If I cannot withstand *this* shock, I will never be able to gracefully and consciously withstand the moment of death. This experience was a kind of test—a foretaste of letting go. From that moment on, my experience of losing my eye changed—and the fear and depression never returned with anywhere near the same intensity.

Quite to the contrary, after the realization in the chapel, the entire experience of having the eye removed, of learning to see again, and going through the inevitable psychic transformation, became my personal creative quest. A quest that I more or less welcomed, and of which I tried to make the best possible use. Something had changed in me. I felt less under the dominion of my ego, and more open to life, to people, and to the changes inherent in our lives. I learned much about myself from questioning why such a massive injury had been the necessary catalyst to deliver me to the threshold of this new state of being.

A transformation had occurred on many different levels, physical, emotional, psychological, and spiritual, due to the ongoing effects of the injury. It served to break down many of the unquestioned and crystallized attitudes my psyche had developed as an armor; and provided an opportunity for renewal, for a regathering of my energies under different conditions.

First, I needed to relearn ordinary physical tasks: driving a car, pouring liquids *into* a glass, avoiding collisions with doorways or people on my right side, safely crossing streets, discovering where I needed to sit at a table or in a restaurant in order to see my companions and not just the wall, and acquiring a different sort of respect for my one and only good eye. It gave me the opportunity to prune my life down to the essentials, and to give up superficial interests and nonessential activities. One central goal was added to my life's purpose: to die seeing, on both a literal and a metaphorical level.

As I learned to face the challenges of living with one eye, I received help from an instructive guidebook: *A Singular View: The Art of Seeing with One Eye*. Written by Frank Brady, an airline pilot who lost an eye when a large mallard smashed into the windshield of his plane, the book is an important reference manual for the newly one-eyed, full of helpful hints and tricks for navigating through the process of learning to see with reduced capabilities. But for any interested reader, it returns the act of seeing to an art, to regarding human vision as an intentional activity, one full of potential and with perceptual possibilities we have long forgotten or glossed over. The imperative of learning to see again is an unusual opportunity for an adult; most of us, though genuinely appreciative of our vision, thoroughly take the act of seeing for granted and are mostly untrained in the banquet of gifts that seeing offers.

Observe carefully a young child in the act of seeing and note the sense of wonder, joy, and curiosity that accompanies this adventure. A child can become completely absorbed in examining the world through vision—or through any of the senses, for that matter. Seeing is truly a form of magic, a perceptual pleasure, a source of real learning and questioning, and a doorway to invisible worlds. As adults, we have much to relearn.

I offer here the initial realizations gleaned through the process of recovering my vision in the several years following my accident.

We do not see through our eyes alone.
Photographer Edward Weston described the process of his own creative work as "seeing through one's eyes, not with them." And Walt Whitman wrote in *Leaves of Grass*, "I am not contained between my hat and my boots." In other words, we see through our entire body. To focus only on the seeing of our eyes is misguided, and represents a common fallacy. Every cell, every part of our body is a sensitive receiving apparatus, and all are connected to the eyes. I remember sitting on a beach years after the surgery, on the island of Kaua'i, looking at the different colors in the world around me, and feeling each color, locating with precision where the particular hue resounded in my body. It was symphonic, the way in which colors touched different inner regions, and stimulated different thoughts, emotions, and sensations.

When I am attentive, I can sense, especially on my right side, when something or someone is there, and can sense the amount of space separating me from the object or person. I am surprised while driving to realize that I do not always need to look on my right side; I simply seem to know or feel when something is there. But this requires great care; it happens only when I am attentive. Otherwise, my lack of finely tuned depth perception causes clumsiness and errors of visual judgment. Attention is the key. I can sometimes sense the character or thoughts of another person by loosely resting my gaze on them, and staying within my own body, which provides insights and empathetic realizations.

I have consciously experimented with this phenomenon in order to understand it. Probably the most vivid impressions came on a number of occasions while riding the subway in Manhattan. I discovered that by empathetically looking at individuals on the train, I could place my attention inside their body, so to speak; to feel and sense their posture and weight with my own body, and understand what that posture felt like, from the inside out. From feeling the weight and shape of their posture, other realizations about what they may have been experiencing in that moment presented themselves. This division of attention, where we maintain a measure of our awareness within ourselves while simultaneously directing some toward and into the object of our perception, stimulated many key experiences for me. It was a remarkable discovery. My understanding was no longer limited to looking at the outsides of things. The inner world is within the capabilities of our seeing.

It is the brain that sees, simply making use of the eyes.
The brain, as I have learned, is a remarkably adaptive instrument. Over the course of six or eight months after losing binocular vision, the brain learns to adapt to the monocular cues of perspective, such as the way objects appear to change size in relation to distance, and the way motion is perceived relative to space (for example, bushes in the foreground appear to be passing by faster than mountains in the background as we walk or drive), and depth perception is slowly regained.

I also discovered that other senses—especially hearing—become sharper and more acute when I need to locate objects or persons on my right side. Although I suspect that my physical capacity to hear has not increased at all, sounds are now more within my field of awareness, as I must depend on them to drive, walk, and navigate through space. I now have difficulty getting around adroitly and being attentive in noisy environments, or having background music or the television on while engaged in activities that require judgments of depth and spatial relationships.

Listening and seeing are interrelated, as are all of our senses. Our physical vision perceives the light reflected from objects and our hearing perceives the vibrations of sound that emanate from, or are reflected by, objects or people. I believe there is a reciprocal relationship between all of our senses that can be encouraged and developed if we wish—and this is true for all sighted, partially sighted, or nonseeing individuals.

Seeing is a direct experience and represents a way of knowing.
This may be stating the obvious, but we do see what we want to see. What we call "seeing" is generally a reflection of our inner dialogue, which is constant and unceasing. Our inner dialogue tends to support our particular world view, our image of ourself, and our subjective beliefs. We know too much; we can name and provide a label for everything under the sun. We have our own agendas, our predisposed attitudes, and our own cultural biases. We rarely see the world in a fresh way or question the numerous and often unconscious filters that influence the nature of our perception.

Moments of real seeing are beyond the labeling propensity of the mind, beyond what we think we know. Seeing is a step into the unknown and requires some degree of intention and awakening. Real seeing—of ourselves, of others, and of the world—contains three defining characteristics: simultaneity, a direct perception in the present moment; objectivity, seeing things as they are, as best we can; and impartiality, freedom from judgment. For most of us, governed by our subjective attitudes and cherished opinions, such moments of direct perception are rare and depend entirely on our inner state of mind, feeling, and body. But they are possible. Most of us have experienced moments of inner accord in which, by chance or intentional effort, we are open, sensitive, and wholly present. The first step on the Buddhist eightfold path is "right seeing," which serves as a fitting foundation for our journey. In my mind, "right seeing" implies not only a positive, life-affirming attitude, but also a genuine effort toward direct, conscious perception.

The nature of our perceptions is relative and depends on our state of awareness and state of being. Suspending the internal dialogue, maintaining a dual attention that embraces both ourselves and the perceived object, and trying to be fully present to the moment in front of us are exercises that assist in the process of seeing.

Seeing is an exchange of energy that takes place between ourselves and the perceived objects of our attention. In losing the sight of my eye, I learned to depend to a greater extent on efforts toward self-awareness and connecting with my own body and feelings. I clearly observed how the objects of my perception registered their impressions on my being and stimulated widely varying inner sensations and feelings. Although I do not fully understand this process, perhaps the larger potential of seeing is found in these moments of self-awareness and the recognition that all impressions we receive register themselves within us. Seeing comes from within ourselves, not from the vague "out there" of the outer world.

To paraphrase D.M. Dooling, founding editor of *Parabola* magazine: Do we really wish to see? We associate the possibility of heightened awareness with renewal, a sense of joy and awakening, and the magical quality of direct perception. This Dooling claims is true: when awake, we see the world with infinite compassion and kindness, as a reflection of its inherent divinity. But, she goes on to explain, there are two ends to this stick. Seeing the world as it really is also brings us into contact with suffering, inequality, and the conditions inherent in our world, not all of which are life-enhancing and affirming. But can we afford not to see things in this fashion? Can our planet, and all of its residents, continue with the distorted perceptions of reality stemming from our lack of real seeing, and by extension, real caring?

Seeing can be cultivated, indeed must be, if we wish to live full and productive lives, sensitively receiving and richly giving to ourselves and others. It must always be borne in our hearts and minds that *we* are the primary medium of the creative act—not film or clay, paints or words. Learning to see, learning to be, and learning to come into accord with the deeper sources within and without—these are, undoubtedly, the greatest challenges given us, the most potent tests of our creative aspirations and capabilities.

~

After two years of diligently relearning to see, I felt the imperative to photograph again. I had done some casual picture-taking, but I hadn't worked on a sustained project for several years and was anxious to get back to work. I was considerably out of touch, however. I needed a challenging project and a kick in the pants to renew my once-passionate involvement with photography.

One morning I woke up and inexplicably knew that I must go to Hawai'i. I was drawn to the volcanoes of the Big Island—and sensed a potential for creative work in this location. As I experienced the land, culture, and traditions, I felt surprisingly enriched and nourished, well beyond any measure of my expectations. The ancient mythology, still vitally maintained by many contemporary Hawaiians, added a subtle yet potent depth and mystery to the culture. Most importantly, I felt that the transformative nature of the landscape, due to Kilauea Volcano, closely paralleled the major upheaval I had experienced in losing my eye. Thus, the project rapidly took on an urgency and intensity, drawing me back again and again, over a period of several years.

In my initial photographs of the landscape, particularly in Volcanoes National Park, I found myself making images that represented the process of death and rebirth. My camera continually led me to a place known as Devastation Trail, where the white skeletons of the top branches of dead ʻohiʻa trees are revealed—as the solitary, haunting remains of the Kilauea Iki eruption, which fountained nineteen hundred feet into the air, completely covering the floor of an ʻohiʻa and fern forest with molten ash. The white, bleached branches are everywhere, testaments to the destructive force of Madame Pele, the Hawaiian volcano goddess. Yet, in the midst of the ash-covered landscape, new growth of ʻamaʻu ferns, young ʻohiʻa trees, and ʻohelo berry bushes are breaking ground and creating the floor of what will someday be a new forest, built upon the ruins of the old.

Every image that I made bore witness to the phoenix-like nature of the Hawaiian landscape. It wasn't until printing many of the images that I recognized the obvious metaphor—that these white, bleached branches looked exactly like the stick that had extinguished my eye. What I was seeing reflected in this landscape of powerful destruction and new birth was my own fragile process of recovery and healing. The place and my self were one and the same. It was not merely metaphor, or autobiography, or geography; it was all of these at once. I was a part of the place and the place was a part of me. After this realization was firmly established, I was able to complete that project and begin work on my current interest: the cultural landscape.

In that initial body of work, titled *Hawaiʻi: Landscape of Transformation*, I tried to integrate two often-contradictory aims: the photograph as document, and as metaphor. I wanted to maintain the integrity of the landscape and convey a sense of place, and at the same time suggest symbolic content through the transformative nature of the volcano—seeing it as being deeply related to my own life experience. These photographs served as a profound form of release, offered a way of digesting my experience, and provided a way of working through my ongoing process of transformation and healing.

The inspiring presence of Hawai'i continued to beckon me. In January 1991, I took a leave of absence from my long-term position as Chair of the Photography Department at the Art Institute of Boston to serve as the first Executive Director of the Hui No'eau Visual Arts Center on Maui. In 1993, I was invited to become part of a team of four artists commissioned to photograph the island of Kaho'olawe—sacred to the Hawaiian people and used for ordnance training by the U.S. military since World War Two—for a book and traveling exhibition.

The island offers great contrasts, between the sacredness of the ancient cultural sites and the terrifying damage created by modern weapons. The photography proceeded slowly because of the unique conditions presented by the island's natural and man-altered features. I had never before seen or experienced a place that contained such subtlety of natural beauty and such powerful, seemingly untouched ancient shrines—nor one that had been so thoroughly devastated by military technology and modern attitudes.

The resonating challenge that was presented by turning my lens toward Kaho'olawe became a stringent, personal test of the many lessons I had learned through losing an eye. I needed once again to find the right balance between active intent and surrender, between self-confidence and humility, governed by a deep trust in the integrity of the creative process. Simply stated, my hard work created the conditions for the process to unfold, and helped open me to the guiding visions and synchronous moments that arose from a deeper place than my ego's desire or its habitual nature.

The underlying question that informed a new way of working was how to allow meaning to emerge out of my direct experience of the island—to listen and see, to stay in the moment, and not to rely on my past accomplishments, preconceived attitudes, or photographic formulas. In a very real sense, I felt that we as artists were merely the lenses through which the island could speak. I sensed the possibility of making images that integrated in a single gesture the massive destruction with the underlying sacredness, a subtle and pervasive energy that I couldn't quite grasp, that remained elusive to my understanding. These images found their way through my lens only after I ceased grasping and relinquished my desire to use the island as a means toward furthering my own strictly personal ends. Due to the continuing importance of Kaho'olawe to the people of Hawai'i, it was clear that something much larger was at stake.

Kaho'olawe taught me a great deal about "right seeing" and the necessity of staying open to the process itself, rather than seeking results. The dark sacredness of the land challenged us to go beyond our artistic intent and individual styles as photographers. In respect for the power of the island, I learned finally that higher energies should not, cannot, be called upon merely to serve our own creative, personal needs. Rather, we stand humbly in service of a larger purpose. Though creativity may nourish us profoundly as it makes its way *through* us, we are the vehicle, not the destination.

~

More than fifteen years have elapsed since that moment of impact, which seized me with an abrupt intensity and force; a seemingly purposeful blow, it was a literal whack to the side of the head that took from me part of my sight. The reverberations of that event continue to this day. A tidal change has taken place in me from deep within; I feel it has affected me on even a cellular level. I am attracted now to the deep, volcanic contrasts of life, death, and rebirth, and the possibilities inherent in destruction for renewal and regeneration. The wounding of the land, its sacredness, and its need to heal constitute more than a metaphor for me. This is true on the level of our planet, and it is true within my own experience. The earth is no differ-ent, in this respect, than you and I.

We are as we respond. Like is attracted to like, as metal filings to a magnet. We see what we are. Vision persists beneath our thinly disguised masks. We resonate with that which corresponds to our being. It can be no coincidence that I wish to photograph conditions of strife and contradiction, as well as those places on earth of sacredness and transformation (either due to natural forces or to the influence of humanity). I am surprised and not surprised that this interest persists. Our linkages arise from within. The implications of losing an eye, the transforming energies of that event, are still vibrating in me—and perhaps they always will.

I would not wish to change the course that my life has taken.

PART ONE

Mounting the Dragons Toward Heaven:
Stages of the Creative Encounter

Bryce Canyon, Utah. David Ulrich, 1974

THE CREATIVE PROCESS

Everyone wants to be creative. And all people can learn to awaken their artistic capabilities. Pablo Picasso said: "Every child is an artist. The problem is how to remain an artist once he grows up."

Creativity is a way of life and is not the exclusive domain of artists, writers, and scientists. It is the birthright of every human being.

If we aspire to understand our most distinctively human capacity, the ability to create, we must first acknowledge that there are no universal formulas, certainly no quantifiable methods, and very few reliable road maps to assist us in our quest for authentic expression. The creative process draws on many different energies of the individual. It calls forth our deepest impulses, the full range of our life experiences, our most profound hopes and aspirations, and our most penetrating and insightful observations on society and ourselves, and awakens our search for something more in life than what is offered by the culture in which we live.

Creative work is nothing more—but nothing less—than a search to tap the deepest energies that make us human. To try to interpret the nature of these energies would be pure speculation. The question of the source and nature of creativity remains a mystery, but we have access to a considerable wealth of knowledge, derived from many sources, regarding its character and dynamics.

Contemporary science and psychology offer perhaps the beginnings of an understanding of the creative impulse, in the works of Sigmund Freud,

Alfred Adler, Abraham Maslow, Rollo May, and others. A broader and more inspirational guide can be found in the study of ancient ideas and traditional cultures, through their allegories and myths, interpreted by such scholars as Carl Jung and Joseph Campbell, both of whom brought the study of mythology and traditional beliefs out of the dusty corners of academia, giving us access to these truths and insights.

Arguably the most important source of understanding about creativity is the evidence presented by artists themselves in their notes, letters, and journals. The writings of Leonardo da Vinci, Paul Klee, Edward Weston, Georgia O'Keeffe, Theodore Roethke, Rainer Maria Rilke, Anais Nin, and many others provide intimations of a direct, personal experience—a view from within the creative process, with its trials and successes, and with its resulting agonies and joys.

These accounts represent a collective understanding, a combined wisdom. Beyond the requirements of a particular style or medium, and beyond the unique conditions of a particular time and place, there is much agreement among these artists. Each, in their own way, affirms the same truths about the *challenges* necessary to engage the creative process and the *conditions* that encourage its emergence.

As in the ancient Chinese divination tradition of the *I Ching*—in which the sage, "who sees with great clarity causes and effects, completes the six steps at the right time and mounts toward heaven on them . . . as though on six dragons"—we too aspire toward clear observation and understanding of this process. Through the writings and personal accounts of artists; through many of the works referred to in this book; through the perspectives found in psychology and philosophy; through the traditions, ideas, and rituals of ancient cultures; we find some consensus on the stages of development of the creative process. I have observed these "dragons" repeatedly in my own work, verified them through the experiences shared by many of my friends and students, and witnessed their disclosure through the challenges and questions posed by my teachers.

I do not mean these stages to be viewed as discrete and mutually exclusive. For some creative people, these stages may develop experientially in a different order than presented here, with certain steps breaking like large waves and others only causing a ripple. Indeed, depending on an individual's efforts, stages may interact with each other, bisect each other, happen concurrently or not at all—and deeply interpenetrate. Furthermore, these same steps of creation play out microcosmically *within* each of the seven stages, proceeding on many levels simultaneously. I mean them to be viewed merely as pointers toward the Way, and notes toward an ultimately unknowable process.

1

Discovery and Encounter

AT THE WATER'S EDGE

How do we begin? The writer faces the blank page, the painter the white canvas, the photographer an undifferentiated world, the scientist an obtuse and unproven premise, as all creative individuals face a bewildering array of choices and a multitude of possibilities. These challenges are legendary, and even cliché—but the struggle is very real.

Three central questions emerge almost immediately as we strive toward creative expression. How do we choose the medium suitable for our ideas, our temperament, our capacities? How do we discover what we really have to say; that which arises from our true nature? And, what is the structure and form that give shape to our concerns and discoveries—what is our style?

These questions present us with an elusive and rapidly moving target. They are not static and fixed; they do not assume the existence of a right answer, and they generally evade all of our attempts to find a formula or a crystallized solution. The key is in how we face these questions, and our ability to form an *evolving* relationship with them. For many of us, this is an uncomfortable and often fearful proposition. To live in the light of inquiry, not seeking immediate answers and simply allowing the process to unfold, is antithetical to our typical Western attitudes. Under the constructs of science and technology, and deeply ingrained within our educational system, we are taught to take a stand, believe in our own opinions, and have a definitive answer or point of view about everything under the sun. The ability to embrace mystery, to stand bravely in front of the unknown, and to encourage the *process* of discovery is the central need here, a key requirement of creativity and an element we observe in the lives of all highly creative individuals.

If we remain mindful of the dictum "the journey is the destination," then we embark on this path primarily to learn and explore life's many truths, not merely to accomplish something and produce objects. As the poet Rilke advises: "Try to love *the questions themselves*." The answers are never as important as the questions. What are the questions that grow out of the very core of our lives?

At the beginning, we need a direction, something that gets us out the door: an interest, a project, an aim, a burning necessity. Our natural enthusiasms and enduring inclinations can lead the way, if we let them. When we look within and seek a relationship with ourselves based on truth, instead of the multitude of siren calls that our desires and ego promote, we find core features that are immediately evident, that have been there all along, that await our attention and represent our chief strengths. What it is that we love to do, that brings *both* satisfaction and challenge? Where do we find our greatest enthusiasms *and* our deepest fears? Often, what we want the most is what we fear the most. The opposition between our greatest strengths, often perceived by both ourselves and others, and our deepest apprehensions is a vibrating region of authenticity. For every action, there is a reaction. Vital energy is found in the axis, the diameter between our bliss and our fears. When we discover where this region occurs, we are well on the way toward identifying what we may need to do, where we may gracefully unfold, and where we may make a difference.

Choosing a Medium

In finding a suitable medium—which may change and evolve throughout our lives—the most significant sense of discrimination that we may cultivate is what feels good to our bodies. The Yaqui teacher don Juan continually reminds his pupil Carlos Castaneda to use his body, to know when it is happy and inwardly at ease. The human body is a remarkably sensitive instrument. All of the tools that we develop serve to extend the capabilities of our organic nature. Some artists love the feel of clay and earth as it wends through their hands, others resonate with the timbre of the human voice or are enthralled by the power of words flowing from their minds and hearts across the page or screen. Our bodies long for certain styles or forms of movement, to be given a chance to help express our essential characteristics and inherent talents. When we discover these inner rhythms, our entire organism comes into sharp alignment; a focused channel thus opens for our creative energies.

This idea is marvelously illustrated in the film *Pollock*, which portrays the life of pioneer abstract expressionist painter Jackson Pollock. Portraying Pollock at the moment when he discovers the method of painting that later becomes his hallmark style and greatest contribution, actor Ed Harris's entire body is seized with energy, aligning with an internal force arising from deep within, as he drips and spatters and sprays the paint from a standing position across the canvas on the floor. Our body's extension, our medium, often lies dormant within us as an integral part of our organic nature, merely waiting to be activated. Deep satisfaction, an inner sense of aligning with something right and true, and genuine happiness follow the recontacting of the body's intelligence. The integration of mind and body brings vitality, energy, and a certain *joie de vivre*, and is one of the first steps on the creative journey.

The mind-body connection and its lucent expression through a medium grow through the climate created by the excitement of working, the ongoing search for the marriage of form and meaning, and the exhilaration of free play and experimentation. The greatest artists I know are the most humble; they do not rely on their own successes or egoistically revel in their gifts, but feel the need to explore anew every time they work. When the impetus is exhausted in one mode of expression, they often shift gears, changing media or voices, depending upon their passions and inner dictates.

As we slowly enter the creative stream, we may know, on the one hand, what we want to express. On the other hand, we stand reverently in the face of infinity, not knowing, questioning what may grow spontaneously out of the moment. The medium we choose is nothing more than an extension, a synthesis, of our greatest enthusiasms and resonating questions. In our quiet moments, we might ask ourselves to what are our bodies and minds magnetically attracted—fully; unreservedly; and sometimes secretly, because it is too precious to be intruded upon, too close to be impeded. To approach that simple question is enough.

Seeds of Meaning: Cultivating What We Have to Say

When we identify an initial interest, an enthusiasm for a medium, we naturally seek a way to engage the early steps of the journey, to study the language and learn the necessary tools and techniques. Most individuals choose some type of structured approach, such as taking a class, researching a craft or an activity, or enlisting the help of a friend or colleague who knows something of where one wants to go. Excitement, confusion, and an overwhelming sense of not-knowing are often typical at this stage. Out of this chaos, an implicit order and shape will eventually emerge, as long as we persevere. The *I Ching* reminds us: "Times of growth are beset with difficulties. They resemble a first birth. But these difficulties arise from the very profusion of all that is struggling to attain form." The point is simply to begin with some degree of intent and focus.

All people are different. While some may need to slow down at this point and temper their enthusiasms with greater care, attention, and diligence, others may need to rev their engines and intentionally engage in free play in order to let go of the inner restrictions that bind their passions and joys. In either case, momentum and clarity build as we enter the stream. Even if false paths— usually fostered by the ego or an impatient desire for immediate success—present themselves at first, we should not be discouraged. We persist with courage and determination, and cultivate our innate sense that we have something to say, that we have our own clear voice and our own real direction.

We are often confident and floundering at the same time. It is important to remember that we all have our place of genius, where we have something to offer that can grow only from ourselves. We strive to discover the seeds of our true individuality. It is often subtle, a whisper from within that needs time, nurturing, and a degree of challenge for its inward potential to emerge. Faint as it may be, we listen for its distinctive, clear rhythm amidst the confusing cacophony of our illusions, stray desires, and wishful thinking. We search for what is genuinely our own and we work to uncover our latent talents and skills.

In these early stages of working on a project, we often must try many approaches, allowing them to grow and expand, without editing and without judgment. We simply see what arises in our search for meaning and direction by working, experimenting, and trying out new ideas or forms of expression. We try them on for size. This is the warming-up phase. In athletics, or dance and music, or any of the physical activities we engage in, we wouldn't consider running the race, or performing the concert, without this introductory phase. Now is the time to sketch and explore—and forms of sketching take place in all creative activities. Athletics teach us that in running, or swimming, or using our body in some way, there is resistance at the beginning. Our muscles are stiff, the movements are mechanical. But if we keep at it, something else kicks in . . . endorphins are released, an actual chemical change occurs that brings fluidity and clarity, and a heightened sense of being.

It is the same with creative work. We look for a place to immerse ourselves, a clear path from the shore into the flow of creativity. In the beginning—of a single project, a new direction, even of our life's work—we need a flexible working premise, a framework for our efforts. We experiment and explore until something does take root, and our ideas or evolving concerns cohere to a central rallying point. Our discriminative capacities recognize by "taste," by an unmistakable feeling, when our aim is true and we come close to the target. Rilke writes that "a work of art is good if it has arisen out of necessity." What is it that we need to do? We must look and listen inwardly for the answer. What are our deepest responses to the world around us and our most heartfelt questions? What is it that we care about, passionately and deeply?

For our work and our lives to be authentic, infused with our very being, it is essential that we address these questions. Although we must experiment and explore freely to find our own language and form of expression, we must also resist the approach by formula, the easily found and latched-onto solution, and those stray impulses that do not arise from our deepest nature. Otherwise, we can all too easily find ourselves displaced from our real mission, longing for something more real, more true to who we are.

An Approach to Style: Seeking Authentic Expression

What prevents us from discovering our true nature and authentic form of expression? Fears. Insecurities. Doubts. We all have them, often in abundance. Don Juan teaches Carlos Castaneda that challenging and overcoming fear is the first step toward becoming a "man of knowledge." In this spirit, we endeavor to live and work fully, in spite of our fears and self-limiting inner dialogues. Sometimes, it helps to search out of the corners of our eyes and look from an oblique angle. We can be sly and become the trickster. We often have great resistance to taking off our masks. What we fear the most is the very thing that we are called to confront and work with. Where we find fear, where we feel the most inadequate, is where the energy resides, where great potential hides, waiting to emerge into the full light of day. Once we begin, and move vigorously in the direction of our aims, a joyful moment comes when the fear and resistance move into the background and become part of our experience, but not the dominant feature. Our bliss then often emerges from behind this dark, smoky wall of fear.

There are excellent books on "creative recovery," on overcoming these obstacles, such as those by Julia Cameron, Bonnie Friedman, Ralph Keyes, and coauthors David Bayles and Ted Orland. The brief summary of their conclusions: There is no substitute for the simple act of entering the stream. Just begin—even if you are hesitant. It has been said that inspiration doesn't just arrive, it needs a branch to light on. How do creative individuals get down to work, slice through the sticky, milky mass of resistance, doubt, and fear, and find their unique voices?

Having a regular practice is a must; journal writing, sketching freely, taking photographs casually and spontaneously, or tilling our garden without an eye to the result are the means of proceeding at this stage. The energy is in the effort. Although this sounds difficult, the one sure touchstone that can tell us we are on the right path is what I call the "bliss factor." When we are having fun, when we wouldn't want to be doing anything else, when our actions are governed by an inherent joyousness in the process, we find a sense of "rightness." It is one of the many paradoxes of the creative process that it is both immensely challenging and demanding and, at the same time, the source of real joy and true satisfaction. When we come into accord with our deeper nature, we are participating in the larger movements of energy in our universe. Some call it "nature," some call it "god," and some simply acknowledge the profound sources of energy and inspiration that exist within and without.

~

These initial challenges of the creative process—of finding our medium, discovering meaningful content, and developing our style of expression—are, in reality, branching streams of the same river, and come together to form an integrated whole—a single, monumental and fundamental question in three parts: *Who am I really? What is my own? And what is my real direction?*

In *Toward Awakening*, Jean Vaysse recounts the ideas of Russian sage and teacher, G. I. Gurdjieff, who offers a highly illuminating view of the human being by making a distinction "between what belongs to us, comes from ourselves, is a part of our own nature, and what is foreign to us, comes from the environment and represents only a loan." Gurdjieff refers to this fundamental division in the human being as *essence* and *personality*.

Essence is defined as the truth of what we are, what is our own: our latent and innate tendencies, our inherent gifts, our sympathies and antipathies. Essence is what we are born with. There can be no question that small children have clearly defined traits not attributable to their environment, that appear almost at birth, and represent what they have an inclination toward and a "taste" for. This is seen quite clearly in the case of someone like Mozart, who was composing sophisticated music by the age of four.

I can speak here of my own experience and background. At age one, my favorite toy was my father's broken camera, which became my constant childhood companion. And at age eleven, I began to take pictures regularly and passionately, an activity that has persisted nearly my entire life. I don't feel that I ever really chose photography; rather, it chose me. I was simply inclined toward it from the very beginning.

Personality, on the other hand, is what is not our own: it comes from the outside, from our upbringing, from our education. Personality consists of our acquired characteristics. Culture is created by personality, and our personas are formed by the culture of which we are a part. Personality is necessary to navigate though the vicissitudes of life. It is our mask and the necessary intermediary between ourselves and the world we live in. Much contemporary theory in the arts has contributed to an understanding of how our attitudes, beliefs, and modes of expression are formed by the unconscious absorption of the cultural conditions that have influenced us, literally, from birth. We cannot deny these powerful and often subversive influences as we look outward and reflect on the attitudes, values, and priorities that govern Western civilization.

According to Gurdjieff, and now grudgingly acknowledged by the social sciences, human beings are a complex mixture of both essence and personality. Witness the "nature versus nurture" question debated within such disciplines as contemporary psychology, artistic theory, and gender and ethnicity studies. For most civilized people, the process of socialization focuses chiefly on the development of our personalities and our worldly skills. In the arts, however, we can seize the opportunity to discover and express something of our more essential nature. We cannot define it, but we can recognize essential expression by a subtle, yet undeniable "taste" that we sense in works of art in which something *rings true*—that is, they resonate with a sense of authenticity and a signatory imprint of the artist.

The process of working in an art form is a distillation, a clearing of the water, an alchemical refinement that reflects our deepest core. When Alfred Stieglitz initially encountered the drawings of Georgia O'Keeffe, he exclaimed: "Finally, a woman on paper!" And despite the stylistic evolution of O'Keeffe's work over sixty years, many of her enthusiasms persisted. Throughout her lifetime, she returned again and again to an underlying matrix of forms that gave a rich, essential consistency to her language of feeling.

> *I have things in my head that are not like what anyone has taught me—shapes and ideas so near to me—so natural to my way of being and thinking that it hasn't occurred to me to put them down. I decided to start anew—to strip away what I had been taught—to accept as true my own thinking. This was one of the best times of my life. There was no one around to look at what I was doing—no one interested—no one to say anything about it one way or another. I was alone and singularly free, working into my own, unknown—no one to satisfy but myself.*
> —Georgia O'Keeffe

Regardless of the content or medium of our creative efforts, don't we wish to be authentic—to strive to find what is our own—and to infuse our most deeply felt concerns, our very being, into the work itself? Many times, students have asked me: How do I find my unique vision or voice? What is my style? I do not know how to answer those questions, except to say: Become what you are. Our style is within us, waiting to be uncovered. Our vision or voice, or even our choice of a suitable medium, comes from the inside. It is organic. It grows out of our unique individuality and life experiences. It is our own. It comes from the whole of our character, our body, our feelings, our minds, our genetic code, and every detail of our existence. We have earned it by virtue of our identity and being.

Many times I have stood at the same scene with other photographers and wondered how each individual may see the same subject. And I am always pleasantly surprised at the uniqueness of each person's images, and reminded of how differently we each see, how different elements in the scene are emphasized by some and downplayed by others. It is a valuable lesson every time. In finding our own way, we strive toward a balance between a sense of confidence and an attitude of questioning. It is not as if we know who we are—that will take a lifetime—but we can find the courage to perpetually discover ourselves and our real concerns. We embrace both qualities: being and becoming.

Here too, the creative process contains deep paradox. Not only is it necessary to integrate being and becoming—seeing both who we are and what we can be—but we are asked to hold contradictory impulses in ourselves simultaneously. Creative individuals seek to find a balance between playfulness and discipline, initiative and receptivity, confidence and questioning, deep concentration and spontaneity. As navigators of our inner lives, in discovering our own "New World," we proceed by setting sail with a direction, yet leaving the destination unknown. In evolving toward genuine creativity, the artist must cultivate the ability to embrace contradiction and not-knowing, to stay with the resulting discomfort, and even learn to appreciate and enjoy the shifting tides of the process. Can we be large enough to contain both our complexity and our incompleteness?

Most creative people feel some measure of a gap, sometimes even a chasm between what we sense to be our potential and the actuality of our work. If we didn't feel this lack, we wouldn't have the drive, the necessary force, to continue. The impulse toward evolution is arguably a central feature of human nature. We often feel that something is missing, that we are incomplete—and we see this reflected in our creative efforts. The most important feature of this stage in our development is humility and acceptance; to fully embrace and even savor this state of incompleteness. To feel it and to know it intimately, and to allow it to act on us is the key requirement—rather than running away or hiding behind any of the things we use to fill the gap: false pride, self-delusion, alcohol, sex, or whatever our proclivity. To recognize this lack and to aspire toward a deeper participation in life; this impulse leads us toward the creative. The drive toward self-perfection, toward personal and social evolution, is reflected in our role as artists. Many of us aspire to the clean feeling of satisfaction that we experience when we produce something of *quality*, something that accurately and clearly reflects our enthusiasms, our values, our vision—something that has resulted from giving the work our best attention and deepest care.

I will always remember the impression made on me by the creative evolution of my friend and first photography teacher, Nicholas Hlobeczy. After many years of struggling with two mediums, photography and poetry, something opened up in him, a new vista of expression in which he at once became more himself and allowed something to simply pass through him, purely and elegantly. He writes of this condition:

> *At fifty-six I have reached an age when something at last begins to be possible. I do not see how it might have come earlier. There has never been satisfaction pure and clean for what I've done till now, but as these poems pass through my hands I feel a gratefulness to be a willing host of transmission. That once, bright ambition of mine, pales in the light of experiencing this.*

In *The Soul's Code: In Search of Character and Calling*, James Hillman proposes what he calls the "acorn theory," that every individual has within themselves the seed of a unique calling, a daimon which accompanies the soul and is the "carrier of your destiny." He believes that every person is born with this inner image of completeness, much like an acorn, which later manifests as a mature oak by following a vague, yet persistent, inner call. But our own inward calling only stays vague and unformed until we work to uncover the meaning found in these subtle intimations from within that mark our destiny and reveal our true selves.

We have within us an inner measure, capable of separating truth from falsehood. How can the acorn know that it will become an oak tree? It cannot; yet deeply imprinted in its genetic code is that potentiality—and no other. We must remain true to ourselves; we have no other choice. Yet we need to listen and to bring a rigorous sense of discrimination to our inner impulses. The voice of our true nature is unmistakable, though not immediately apparent. We must learn to distinguish this essential call from the many voices of our personality that clamor for attention. We cannot predict its sound, but we can know something of its quality. It has a different resonance, a different ring than all the other inward songs. Our true nature lies within us, waiting to be discovered, or more to the point, *uncovered* from the many years of conditioning that served to create a tough and inert outer crust over it.

Well prior to the advent of his mature work, Vincent Van Gogh wrote to his brother Theo: "How then can I be useful, how can I be of service? Something is alive in me: what can it be?" The path of greatness often lies in the early recognition of an unformed call and a life given to deep questioning. The call is there—for all of us. And so is the capacity for inwardly searching and enlarging one's experience through the quest for Self.

I don't know of more useful advice for recognizing the true form of our creative impulses than is found in Wassily Kandinsky's *Concerning the Spiritual in Art*, published in 1912, in which he describes the principle of "inner necessity." What is it within us that continually demands expression? In striving to identify what it is we must do or try, which our life wouldn't be the same without, which grows out of a sense of inner necessity, we come home to ourselves.

Everything in us has a place, and we discover through our work, our explorations, and by listening for the still, small voice within, what it is we are called to be and to accomplish. We endeavor to hear the rumblings from deep within and follow the path, wherever it may lead. For this effort, we need courage and discrimination.

~

Why do we feel such a need, such an imperative to be creative? And why does our creative work generally require a *physical* involvement, of forming something out of raw materials? Isn't this a strange phenomenon? It should be enough to strive toward understanding and insight, to bring a quality of attention and care to our lives, to genuinely communicate and to learn to be with others, and to transform ourselves into something more whole. As Gurdjieff once said, "the greatest art is that of making a complete human being out of oneself." While his powerful words offer a lifelong aim, most of us will also benefit from objectifying our insights and observations.

I would imagine that for a truly evolved human being, life itself is the great mirror and the great teacher. But then there are the rest of us; those of us still struggling to awaken from our sleep. To actually produce some *thing* that reflects our values, our viewpoint, our vision, and our very being is *to make manifest who we are*. The objects we create are our own reflections and an ongoing measure of our attention, of our growth, of where we are and what we care about.

If we sincerely begin work in any creative medium, we must confront and accept that we really don't know what it is we have to say, that we really don't know ourselves, that we are a wide mixture of contradictory impulses and mixed motivations, and our inner world is a constantly shifting amalgamation of states. The search for ourselves and what is our own must be the foremost aim of our initial involvement in any art medium.

Art is both a way of growth and a means of making manifest that very growth—to see it laid out in front of us in the form of images, or music, or carefully crafted words. It is an undeniable blessing and a real help to actually have a medium—represented by physical objects of our making—that can function, in photographer Minor White's words, as *mirrors* (of ourselves and our relationship to our world), *messages* (from the beyond; from the unconscious; from our collective conscience), and *manifestations* (of another world, another order of things; of our intuition and our higher impulses).

ENTERING THE STREAM

If our enthusiasms have informed us enough to get us started, and we have discovered an initial sense of direction, what then? Rollo May writes in *The Courage to Create*:

> *The first thing we notice in a creative act is that it is an* encounter. *Artists encounter the landscape they propose to paint—they look at it, observe it from this angle and that. They are, as we say, absorbed in it. Or, in the case of abstract painters, the encounter may be with an idea, an inner vision . . . Or scientists confront their experiment, their laboratory task, in a similar situation of encounter . . . the essential point is . . . the degree of absorption . . . there must be a specific quality of* engagement.

Now we are faced with the need to have an intention. This "degree of absorption" that May articulates is found primarily in the quality of attention that we bring to an activity. "Haste makes waste," "take care," "pay attention"; there are many admonitions in our vocabulary that pay tribute to this basic need. If the discovery phase of the creative process is essentially receptive and open to questioning, in this phase we become active, we must actually do something. The fundamental effort that allows us to fully engage in an activity is deceptively simple and extremely difficult—particularly since it is no longer held in high regard in the modern world. The relentless torrent of stimulation promulgated by media, technology, and entertainment, further compromised by our educational system, leaves us distracted and drained, in a state of fractured attention. At this stage, it is necessary to cultivate and maintain a primary feature of the creative act: *sustained concentration*.

In the insightful and elegant guide provided by Richard Boleslavsky, *Acting: The First Six Lessons*, a teacher of acting and dramatic arts (an elder statesman of the theatre) meets an inexperienced and shy eighteen-year-old student, known affectionately as "the creature," who implores the professor to teach the principles of acting. He begins with the first lesson:

Remember this word Concentrate. *It is important in every art and especially in the art of the theatre. Concentration is the quality which permits us to direct all our spiritual and intellectual forces toward one definite object and to continue as long as it pleases us to do so—sometimes for a time much longer than our physical strength can endure . . . This strength, this certainty of power over yourself, is the fundamental quality of every creative artist. You must find it within yourself, and develop it to the last degree.*

In spite of our conditioning to the contrary, we must try to give our full attention to the process. We strive to be present, to stay in touch with the relationship between our inner energies, those arising from our bodies, mind, and feelings, and the work itself. I have repeatedly seen a particular dynamic emerge in all forms of creative work. As we begin, it feels flat and lifeless. Something is missing. As we continue and try to bring a quality of attention to both ourselves and the activity at hand, something begins to open, a fluidity emerges, and a deepening connection to the process begins to take place. We enter the flow.

Like the moment in athletics when endorphins are released, entering the stream of creativity vitalizes us with a sharp inner clarity and buoyant feeling for ourselves and our activity. We feel a spacious inner joy, a vibrant inner stream, which as it begins to flow, attracts more of the same much like a river slowly widens its course. Yet, to avoid dispersal of these energies, we must contain them, nurture them, and focus them. Again, as in athletics, the great pay-off of entering "the zone," the flow, can only take place through energies that are concentrated in a desired direction.

Unfortunately, in our comfortable lives, we are given few opportunities to practice this quality and to flex our concentrative abilities. So much of contemporary life is antithetical and even opposed to this effort. We cannot engage in the clean, simple tasks of maintaining our life free from stimulation, from being plugged in, from seeking a multitude of distractions. In the average American household, the television is on for upwards of *six hours a day*. We have lost something very special, integral to our lives as creative individuals, if we cannot concentrate fully and intensely. The extreme reduction of our collective attention spans will, I believe, have serious consequences for our society over time if we do not move toward changing these conditions now.

Concentration is an intentional act—we must try, we must direct our attention; and it does not always come naturally. It begins in the mind as *purpose*, toward forming a closer relationship with our bodies, the organic sensation of the present, and as *mindfulness*, clearly observing our inner and outer conditions. Concentration is a unifying force that gathers our energies toward something, and invites a fuller participation of our feelings. We can take as an example of this state those moments when we are fully absorbed and more deeply connected; at such times we are present in equal measure to ourselves and what is in front of us. When working, the possibility exists to be here—in this moment. We savor this attentiveness. Our sense of time changes. It slows down as we enter the present, and reverts to a more organic pace and rhythm.

Artists and creative individuals frequently report the experience of losing themselves in the work at hand, being fully in tune with the process, with a heightened sense of being and focus, often emerging hours later as if from a trance. And we do speak of this quality of concentration as being "lost" in an activity; an artist is lost in his or her canvas, a writer lost in the unfolding words, often forgetting to eat or to attend to the daily tasks of life, like an absent-minded professor. However, I propose that using the word "lost" is misleading; rather, this single-pointed concentration is like an hourglass. As we focus deeply on a single task, something opens, deepens, and widens. We are fully absorbed and present to the activity and to the moment, to the exclusion of other elements in our lives. But we are also equally attentive to ourselves: our responses, our impulses, and our creative interaction with the medium.

In an insightful introduction to *The Decisive Moment*, Henri Cartier-Bresson questions how we might employ our attention to see with a camera. His question extends well beyond photography. Isn't it true that all of our responses to the world take place within us, in our bodies, minds, and feelings? Yet, when we look, we do not necessarily see; we generally focus all of our attention on the outer event, the scene in front of us. Seeing is not out there, it is *in here*, in the very core of our being. Cartier-Bresson has aptly described photographic seeing as having one eye turned outward and one eye turned inward; when the two images converge, a photograph results:

> I believe that, through the act of living, the discovery of oneself is made concurrently with the discovery of the world around us which can mold us, but which can also be affected by us. A balance must be established between these two worlds—the one inside us and the one outside us. As the result of a constant reciprocal process, both these worlds come to form a single one. And it is this world that we must communicate.

There is a directly proportional relationship between our ability to see and know ourselves, and our ability to see and know the world. The greater the attention we can bring to ourselves, to seeing and knowing, the greater the attention we can bring to outer life, to seeing the world and others.

Many spiritual disciplines address the need to have a dual attention, where half our attention is directed within ourselves, beginning with our bodies. Here we become aware of our sensations, emotional reactions, and constantly turning thoughts. As we stay within, we begin to find a connection to our deeper mind, the seat of intuition and insight. The other half of our attention is projected outward, toward the world, toward the other. In opening our eyes to the other, we become aware of its reality, its unique characteristics. We potentially see both what is in front of us, and what is within us—and the relatedness of the two, the nature of the interaction.

All creative endeavors call us to be aware of the dual nature of perception. Through our attention, we develop a full and enveloping relationship with the matter at hand and with ourselves. Our evolving point of view (the discrimination of what is our own, of what is our work to do) and the objects that we create depend upon the breadth and depth of our attention. And this awareness expands to include ourselves, our bodies and minds, our reactions and responses. This seminal discipline is known by many names: mindfulness, recollection, and self-remembering, among others. The key lies in forming an intentional relationship with our own energies and the object or task in front of us; to vibrantly enter the dance. Sometimes the effort required is simply sensing our bodies, becoming aware of our feet on the ground, or the sounds reaching our ears, or the weight of how we carry ourselves through space. Or we strive to be aligned with the movements between ourselves and the camera, the paintbrush, or the pen; to come in tune physically with the tool or the object of our attention.

Yet another paradox presents itself here. Although we try to bring an energized attention to our efforts, we must also remain loose and relaxed, rooted within our bodies and open to the flow of interactive energies. We endeavor to maintain a balance between our sharp, focused intensity and an open, sensitized awareness.

The fundamental task of creativity, therefore, is to be fully present—in this moment, and with all that it contains. In this way, work in any creative medium represents a practice, a discipline, for how we may live our lives, be with others, and bring a new quality of our innate being into our work and all of our interactions. As Picasso said, *I don't develop; I am.*

Attention is a gift that we are capable of giving at any moment. We know or strongly suspect that people (including ourselves), animals, plants, and all living things thrive when given our real attention. To bestow this care in our activities, whether it is cooking, artmaking, or being with another person, is the only sure means toward the richness of a true quality of relationship and engagement. It is a means of focusing and concentrating our energy on the task at hand; it is a means of including ourselves in the passage of energies; it is a means of caring about what we leave in our wake; and it is a means—perhaps the principal means—toward the growth and evolution of ourselves as well as our creative efforts.

Dorothea Dooling reminds us in *A Way of Working*:

> *So if we dare to use the word "creative," we must see that its possibility lies in that mysterious human property of attentiveness: not a merely mental attention, but an attention which relates and mobilizes the sensitive intelligence of the body, the affective intelligence of the feeling, and the ordering intelligence of the mind toward a more total openness to what is . . . and the real life, the living energy, which that contains.*

We begin.

CREATIVE PRACTICE

Questions

Look back to your childhood for keys of discovery and insight into who you are. What were you drawn to? What were you passionately absorbed with? Remember. Is this the same today? If not, why? What have you lost or given up in order to make a living or conform to the world around you? Explore the difference between the ideals of your youth and the reality of today.

Ask questions. Try to answer them only from your essence, in the still hours of the morning or evening after sitting quietly. Let the everyday rubbish of the mind dissolve; let the dust settle before answering:

What are your deepest interests?

What activities grow out of inner necessity?

What would your life be incomplete without?

What appears for you at every turn in the road, perhaps as a vague, unformed feeling?

Where does magic appear? Synchronicity? What is your "path with heart"?

What are you consistently called toward—from within and without?

What are you most afraid of? Where do you feel most at home?

What provides the greatest pleasure and the greatest challenge?

What would the world lack without your presence in it?

Tools and Exercises

Find time for a daily or weekly practice. Time for yourself is essential; make a contract with yourself. Just what you do is not so important; the very act of trying can give rise to revealing insights. Set aside your time, maybe just an hour a day, or an afternoon a week. Enough time should be given to allow the process to unfold, to encourage the process of discovery, and to help your activities gather momentum and eventually, in their own organic time, to bloom.

My experience is that as long as you do something consistently, even for a short time each day, then you will spontaneously begin to spend more time doing it, because you will naturally become more attentive to your inner calling. Be kind with yourself, but be disciplined. If you have a hard time getting started, or your practice slips, learn how to gently encourage your efforts. Maybe enlist the help and support of a friend, maybe replace one extraneous activity for a more affirming one (for example, turn the television off for an hour, or give up a magazine or two), or promise to treat yourself after a successful foray into your creative self.

Experiment, play, do what you enjoy. Sketch freely, write from the "wild mind" as Natalie Goldberg calls it, or take pictures of whatever captures your deepest interest and attention. Do not edit. Do not judge. Do not think about where it is going. Simply allow your impressions to emerge and take shape. Observe and take note of what arises.

Patterns will arise. Little gems will appear within the activity. Pieces of your deeper nature will appear within the random sketches, words, or pictures. Over time, you may feel called from a place within. Develop a capacity for listening to this inner whisper. A true foundation for creative work may be found and eventually developed, which will grow naturally out of your body, your feelings, your thoughts and impressions.

- Experiment with different media or forms of expression. Each medium has its own gifts to offer and its own particular challenges. Try them on as you would clothing in a store, just to see what fits your temperament and capacities. If you lack facilities and skills with an art form that interests you, visit the studio of a friend or of a local artist or craftsperson. Try your hand. See what fits; observe where you are drawn in and what inspires your excitement. Art schools, universities, and adult education centers offer introductory classes in a wide range of media and pursuits. Take advantage of them.

- Creativity is an encounter. Staying with the discomfort of not-knowing, and continuing in spite of one's fear and lack of knowledge or skill, is one of the keys toward innovative expression. Experiment with this. Cook a four-course meal without knowing what you will cook—an unplanned feast. Use only materials at hand, foods and utensils that are stocked in your kitchen. Let the process grow and expand. Stretch your boundaries. Be open to each moment. What is needed now? What else can be brought to this meal? Do not stop adding to the meal until it feels complete, and nothing more suggests itself.

The first time around, do this alone—you are the principal cook. Then, try again; only this time as a collaborative venture. Share the process with another cook. Collaborate, experiment, and share ideas. Allow the meal to grow from your combined ideas and talents. See where the ideas of another may help, and what is added to the process. Notice your own skills and strengths, as well as your weaknesses. Observe the difference between a collaborative effort and your own individual expression. Remember, some arts are solitary activities, but many others (like theater, dance, and filmmaking) are often team endeavors. With which are you most comfortable?

• Be bold and confident. Do something you have always wanted to do, but have put off for one reason or another: not having the time, feeling fear or a sense of inadequacy, or simply procrastination. Perhaps you will take a class, begin a long-incubated creative project, start a garden, or buy a particular piece of equipment (like a camera) or painting supplies. Make no excuses this time. Do it. Try it. Exercise your intention. Let one simple step build on another, and on another . . . and so on.

• Sit with a pen in hand, or at your keyboard. Ask this question of yourself: What do I wish to accomplish, for the next year, for the next decade, or even for the rest of my life? What remains unfulfilled? What creative activities do I wish to engage in? Just write your answers. Allow any and all thoughts to find their way onto the page. Again, do not edit or analyze—yet. Do not even consider what is realistic or feasible. Simply write.

Review your list. What rises to the top? Can you proceed, one step following another, to realize your aims? Listen to your dreams. Visualize; use your creative imagination. Where do you wish to go? Where do you want to be? If you can wish it, or dream it, then it is already taking shape within you.

2

Passion and Commitment

RIDING THE RAPIDS

Passion and creative work are inseparable. Artists tend to be obsessed with their subjects and themes. They care deeply and passionately, beyond the dictates and limitations of reason; their interests or enthusiasms often burn with a focused intensity. In civilized society, obsession is generally viewed as highly suspect and downright dangerous—it can even imply violence. In the arts however, it can, if managed properly, translate into a highly positive and helpful characteristic: a sense of urgency about the work. Passion represents here a kind of controlled obsession, where we ride the wave—as Webster's puts it—of a "deep, overwhelming feeling or emotion."

To use a distinctly Hawaiian analogy, it's like surfing: we either ride the wave skillfully and gracefully, or wipe out in the face of the ocean's great and formidable force. As in creative work, a wave begins with a surge, gathers momentum and speed, takes shape and flows freely before it breaks, returning the surfer to the unformed mass of white water near the shore. The surfer then paddles back out to catch another, and then another wave, riding each of them until its energy subsides. The creative impulse builds momentum in the same way, with growing intensity, until energy flows freely and the artist is entirely absorbed in the work at hand.

Many artists gratefully acknowledge the unique role of creative work in unleashing the force of their passionate nature. Writer Edna O'Brien describes how she started writing literature: "When I say that I have written from the beginning, I mean that all real writers write from the beginning, that the vocation, the obsession is already there, and that obsession derives from an intensity of feeling which normal life cannot accommodate."

Paradoxically, this stage of the process asks for a balance of energies between skill and abandon, harnessing and letting go. We gently nurture the enthusiasms and passions that arise from our deepest selves while we carefully cultivate their expression. Our passionate inclinations are already there, an integral part of our being. We encourage their full emergence through our commitment to the process. The embers quietly glow within us; our work is the breath, the wind that ignites the flames. Ralph Waldo Emerson states uniquevocally: "If the man creates not, the pure eflux of the Deity is not his—cinders and smoke there may be, but not yet flame."

As we continue to work, the sense of inner necessity that prompted us into action becomes a burning necessity that can help our creative efforts gather momentum and force. It may initially feel that we are only going through the motions, until we warm up to the task and synchronize ourselves with the work. Gradually, something begins to activate. There is a moment of magic embedded in the process when we persist—a moment when a real connection arises. A new feeling for the activity emerges. We catch the wave. And from that moment on, we enter deeply into the flow. A reciprocal process between our initiative and our sensitivity begins to take hold, and we become increasingly receptive to the work itself. We work, play, guide, struggle, and take delight in the process, all at the same time.

At this stage, the gifts are many—we receive help, guidance, and energy from the process itself. Our hearts beat faster, our excitement grows, and we are encouraged to continue. A sense of freshness and joyous involvement permeates our activity. The work gains momentum and begins to find its own shape. We are willing to take risks, try new ideas, and freely experiment with form.

Many artists describe this condition as being "swept up" into the current or "seized" by an overwhelming passion for the process. New connections with ourselves and the work are being established, often for the first time, that call forth a deepened interest and a heightened awareness. The energy we derive from forming these early connections generously fuels our passage through the foothills and slopes of the ascent toward full creative expression. These moments of deeper participation with the work and ourselves can be best described as hints of awakening, a taste of greater consciousness. They momentarily stun the machinations of the wild, ordinary mind; awaken us to new and vast possibilities; bring in their wake an expanded sense of being and presence; take our breath away. We stand humbly in awe of the workings of a greater intelligence that permeates the moment. Growth and understanding come rapidly at this stage. We are filled with excitement and joy as we observe and engage the unfolding process.

I am once again indebted to *The Courage to Create* by Rollo May, who writes:

> *This leads us to the second element in the creative act—namely the* intensity *of the* encounter. *Absorption, being caught up in, wholly involved, and so on,* are used commonly to describe the state of the artist or scientist when creating or even

the child at play. By whatever name one calls it, genuine creativity is characterized by
an intensity of awareness, a heightened consciousness.

This is the stage in which many of the initial discoveries are made, in which the process of working leads to multiple "highs" and "peak" experiences. Though still in formation, the seminal features of the work begin to emerge. Unexpected revelations are in abundance; insights seem to arise from the atmosphere itself. It is crucial here that you keep your feet on the ground, even while your head is in the clouds. Like a meditative practice in which a finer quality of energy is directly experienced through attention, persistence, and commitment to the developing process, it must always be borne in mind that you are a participant in this unique dance, not the originator of it. The challenge is to stay grounded in your body, with the techniques and movements required by the task at hand. At this point, the artist opens to a deeper relationship with the work, with energies that arise from a deeper source, but must stay vigilant and neither allow the ego to assume ownership of the experience nor allow the mind's endless commentary to impede this sensitive connection.

A dual role is asked of the artist at this point: to become the master and the servant concurrently. Although we initiate and continue to guide the work—infusing fresh ideas or new techniques, and providing our best efforts—another need arises, that of serving, or midwifing, the process. In crafting a novel, writers observe how the characters take on a life of their own and the story unfolds before their very eyes, without their knowing how it might turn out. Painters apply paint to the canvas in ways surprising even to themselves. Photographers discover unexpected elements and a deepening connection to the content of their pictures, and actors take on the coloration of their characters. The original intent is modified by the work itself. We begin to serve the process. If we are able to listen and pay close attention, with sensitivity and awareness, the work itself will suggest the next step . . . and the next . . . and the next. Many artists and creative individuals have rightly observed what we need here: to get out of the way, to become transparent.

This is the condition of creative work that many artists aspire to experience—and once experienced, strive to return to, again and again. At this point we feel compelled to continue, often in the face of difficulty, economic hardship, lack of public acknowledgment of our work, or pressure from our friends and loved ones to get out of the studio and "get a life." Despite these obstacles, we proceed, fueled by the discovery of the place in which great energy resides, where we feel we have transcended our limited natures and are participants in a greater whole, where we are truly cocreators with a deeper order of things.

I believe that most people, if they carefully examine their experiences, can find moments when they have genuinely touched the flow of creation. The distinguishing mark of great artists, however, is in their enduring efforts, the level of their commitment, their ability to ride the wave to completion. In studying the lives of highly creative individuals, several key requirements of staying with the current may be observed and emulated.

First and foremost, they are engaged with something that they care about, passionately and deeply. Change is inherent in our lives; the location of our passion may be a shifting point, an elusive moving target. We constantly search our experiences and discriminate, asking the question: Where is the juice for us now, where can we fully engage our energies without reservation or hesitation? Students frequently ask: Why will this moment and not that one make an interesting and compelling photograph? The only answer that I can honestly provide is simple: Why do you fall in love with this person and not that one? It grows naturally out of our being. Or, as Alfred Stieglitz observed: "If what one makes is not created with a sense of sacredness, a sense of wonder; if it is not a form of love-making; if it is not created with the same passion as the first kiss, it has no right to be called a work of art."

The second requirement of sustaining the flow is related to the *quality* of our work and efforts. We once again find the need to be truly present in the moment of interaction with the materials; to be more deeply connected with our bodies, experiencing the demands of the task in front of us. Our feelings are engaged, responsive to the growing relationship we have with the painting, the writing, the photograph, or the meal being cooked. And our minds are active, focused, and alert, constantly scrutinizing, questioning, and searching. Is this the right word, the right spice, or the right color to apply? It is often said that the primary difference between the creative efforts of children, with their innocent spontaneity, and those of adults lies in the power of the mature mind, which brings a depth and woven complexity to the work, often with many layers of meaning.

Finally, creative individuals recognize that to stay in the flow, they must remain open and receptive. The boundaries between the self and the work dissolve and become seamless. We listen—to the work, to our intuition, to the guiding voices within. We look around for signs and messages from within and without. When we are working rightly, confirmations often come from unexpected sources. After making a particularly salient point and witnessing a crow flying over at that very moment, don Juan said to Carlos Castaneda: "See, the world agrees with me."

One of the defining characteristics of this stage of the process is a proliferation of moments of synchronicity, when it seems that all elements are conspiring to help us; unforeseen discoveries are made, and unexpected gifts revealed. We feel that we are in the right place, at the right time, and doing what we need to be doing. Our work seems right and true. We remain highly engaged, yet detached from the final result. We realize that a primary identification with the product at this phase can only impede the integrity of the process—a difficult point for many young artists to accept.

Identification with the work is a subtle and insidious phenomenon, one that we all are prone to experience to some degree. We view the work—rightly—as an extension of ourselves. Yet we cannot become the work. We must maintain a critical distance, and be capable of a more objective relationship with the content of our efforts. This detachment is a form of freedom: we enter into a real dialogue with our materials and ideas, rather than a fragile and trembling codependency with the natural results of our efforts. The work comes *from* us, or *through* us; it is not *of* us. This is an important distinction to recognize if we hope to continue on the creative path. We wish to attune ourselves to the process, engage our energies as deeply as possible, and allow the work to emerge as the by-product, the child, of a mature relationship between ourselves and our materials.

A consistent factor found in moments of genuine creativity is a kind of "tuning in," in which we come simultaneously into accord with three participating elements: ourselves, the work, and our relationship to the process. Similarly to tuning the dial on a radio for better reception, attunement begins with ourselves; with turning toward the energies of our bodies, using our feelings as an instrument of discovery of what rings true, and engaging the mind toward the task at hand, reflecting on implications of content and meaning. In these moments of greater awareness, when our component parts are working in unison, we have—at least temporarily—the potential to be whole. We are awake and alive. Like an animal sensing, sniffing the air, feeling for changed conditions or danger, we are fully present in the moment.

As we make discoveries and test new forms and ideas, in sensitive accord with what the process requires and with what we want, a heightened sense of being is invoked and nourished. The work calls forth our best efforts. We care deeply. Invisible tentacles of energy link the artist with their creation; the artworks ripen and unfold with the juice of passion, enlivening the senses, emboldening the heart, and exhilarating the mind.

Gertrude Stein believed that "there can be no truly great creation without passion." According to Stein, an artist must embody passion, not merely describe it, and the best artists transfer their passion to the work through their very being. Passion, she explained in an interview with John Hyde Preston, is "the whole force of man" and is not to be confused with our mere *passions*.

THE BROAD CURRENT

Can passion be created? Is it something that we can call forth in ourselves? In trying to understand the nature of passion, I have come to the conclusion that passion cannot be simply willed into being. It grows out of our compelling interests, our most vital responses, and our unique experiences. It grows out of interaction, and in this sense can be *encouraged*. Thriving in a climate of deep relatedness, passion is realized and furthered through an abiding commitment to our chosen path and a heightened awareness of ourselves and the surrounding world.

Conventional wisdom generally treats passion as something given; we either feel it for something or someone, or not. A similar dictum is often stated about talent: that we either have it or we don't. There may be a certain element of truth to this. We all have inborn talents that must be respected, honored, and continually nurtured. Great talent must be accompanied by disciplined and sustained work, if it is to be realized. The potential of some form of genius is undoubtedly present in everyone, but the fulfillment of it depends upon the full employment of our talents, the intensity of our encounter with the process—and perhaps just a little luck. And it is within our power to strive toward this—toward all of it, including the combined graces of luck and supportive circumstances.

Passion is synonymous with our capacity to deeply commit our interests and energies in a desired direction. When we bring attention toward ourselves and our world, we marvel at the shifting tides of life's energies and we embark on the path of learning. How can we not be interested in this, the life that we are privileged to experience? Boredom cannot exist in this environment; to be bored is to be without attention, without the capacity for observation.

To find passion, all we really need to do is observe. The world is interesting and becomes far more so as we closely observe things, people (including ourselves), and events, and contemplate their significance. Once again, heightened awareness becomes a transforming agent for ourselves and our work. Through the action of directing our attention, we revel in the commonplace; the ordinary becomes extraordinary. A green pepper, as photographed by Edward Weston, contains worlds within worlds. A simple dinner conversation between two playwrights, as featured in the film *My Dinner with Andre*, reveals a rich dialogue on life and art. There is no plot, no action, no scenery except a restaurant interior, only one supporting actor; yet the film provides material to contemplate for years to come. Look around. Take the time to see and feel. Go beneath the surface. Everything has meaning. Everything is a reflection of the ultimate cause, an unseen esoteric reality that is the source of creation itself.

Recently, with photographer Elaine Mayes, I cotaught a five-week summer session in photography and digital imaging on Maui. It was an intense program that included field trips, classroom explorations and critiques, interpersonal and intercultural exchanges, and the prospect of a substantial development of creative work.

The environment was unfamiliar to most of the students, city kids who came directly from New York. The prevailing view of Hawai'i as a laid-back beach paradise was quickly replaced in most of the students; within days they encountered cultural standards, languages, and lifestyles radically different from those they were accustomed to on the Mainland. Most valued the opportunity to witness an extraordinarily beautiful and diverse natural environment, coupled with a highly complex social structure. And all of the students were faced with the very real demand to respect, honor, and acknowledge the differing traditions and beliefs of the many artists and cultural leaders who patiently guided them, explaining much about the nature of this mysterious place. These factors combined to present a formidable challenge to their ability to see and understand—and of course, to make images.

Many of the students literally worked to the point of exhaustion—in the field, in the darkroom, in the digital lab, in their journals, and in their minds and hearts. They saw, they questioned, they took interest, they paid attention, they interacted with many new people and places. More times than I would have preferred, someone knocked on my door at one or two in the morning with questions and requests for assistance. Needless to say, the resulting creative work was vibrant, thoughtful, and penetrating. An undeniable passion for their chosen themes and subjects was immediately evident.

Inspiration may come, at this stage, in small doses. Its source is a mystery: given by the proverbial muses, our intuition, the energies passing between us and through us, energies descending from a higher source, or all of these. Though there are notable exceptions, the muses visit most of us sparingly at first. A stream often meanders and tarries, gaining force as it makes its way toward merging with the river. It is our hard work, our unflagging efforts toward clarity and fullness of expression that will bring the work eventually, in its own time, to fruition.

Passion, I believe, evolves naturally from commitment. No matter what we want, or what we strive toward, it will only grow out of a sustained and committed interaction. There is no other way. Commitment, in this context, means not holding back, doing what is necessary vigorously and unreservedly—to have a "no-holds-barred" relationship with our creative work.

It is in the nature of the creative process that we strive to nurture and support our own efforts toward creative expression with kindness, compassion, and the proper inner and outer conditions. Yet that is not enough. For our creative energies to fully emerge, we must continually challenge our ego and false personalities. Ken Wilber makes a qualitative distinction between real compassion and "idiot" compassion when he states: "What most people mean by 'compassion' is: please be nice to my ego. Well, your ego is your own worst enemy, and anybody being nice to it is not being compassionate to you." We need to be ruthless and push beyond our own perceived boundaries of our limited understandings, abilities, and tendencies—not to indulge our sly personal demons. Genuine creativity unambiguously asks that we staunchly resist the ego's insistent voices, which manifest as influences that are self-calming ("this is good enough"), self-adulating ("what a great artist I am"), or self-loathing ("this is no good"). We must embrace hard work, cultivate discipline, and joyfully accept the value of creative frustration—discovering the ability to work things through, no matter what the level of difficulty. In the words of Alfred Stieglitz: *to grow more tolerant toward others, stricter with oneself.*

There is no mystery to this. Persistent efforts, day in and day out, are the means by we which we grow and evolve. Incremental progress, barely observable, and measured in months, years, and even decades, may not be exciting or instantly gratifying, but will give rise to verifiable results. It is an organic process. Through a commitment to the authentic parts of ourselves and through a long-term involvement with our chosen work, we find the force to simply become who we are. And isn't this what we really want, the ultimate aim of our creative journey?

Making the commitment is the key. The flow of the creative process is a reciprocal exchange. Though it seems contradictory, through firmly standing behind our intent, and passionately, diligently approaching our creative aims, we can let go into the broad current of creativity. Here we are swept along by forces, both inner and outer, that give our work and our lives meaning and direction. This dynamic reminds me of the folk wisdom my grandmother imparted to help meet any challenge, any sorrow: "God helps those who help themselves." The fact is, as we near our authenticity and begin to discover our original face, our unique source of passion, our creative work opens into a joyful engagement. Our work with materials and our cultivation of the seeds of meaning in our expression evolve into a highly satisfying quest for both understanding and excellence. Commitment, then, compels us forward into the uncharted realms of realization and mastery.

Nourished by caring attention, tempered through challenge, and fueled by passionate striving, an inner change occurs. We ripen and unfold, become open and permeable. With practice and discipline, experimentation and play, our work is refined to a distilled essence, a blend of inborn talent and sustained effort. We can view the life's work of many artists and find the threshold, the place where something really begins, where their work assumes its own authority and confident presence. Their vision or voice becomes truly their own, and at the same time, a receptive vessel for the myriad energies of life.

Constance Hale, in *Sin and Syntax*, encourages writers to "be simple, but go deep." She explains: "The exquisite 'cutouts' of Matisse and elegant line drawings of Picasso came late in long careers of painstaking work and wild experimentation. In writing as in painting, simplicity often follows considerable torment."

Creativity is a transformative discipline. The refinement that many artists seek takes place within the context of a contributory life's work, not through the romantic, self-destructive, and highly illusionary attitude that one must suffer in order to create art. It is another one of creativity's many paradoxes: a subtle, but *joyful* torment naturally arises as we perceive the truth, the magnificent pathos and possibility inherent in the human condition. The recognition of our ignorance, the awe-inspiring glimpses of our potential, our place on the path of learning, and a broad acceptance of the reality of our current condition is enlivening and disconcerting in equal measures. *This* is the path of the artist that leads to illuminating breakthroughs and deep inner growth.

A thorough study of art and creative endeavor reveals that the mature expression of most artists, writers, musicians, or scientists develops gradually over a lifetime, after many years of working with intensity and passion. Most of the paintings by Van Gogh that we know and cherish, for example, were made in an extraordinary period of creativity during the last year of his life. My students often look at me with expressions of doubt, surprise, and questioning when I describe artists in their thirties or forties as generally "young" artists. As Saint Catherine of Siena so beautifully stated: "All the way to heaven is heaven for He said I AM the Way." If we embark on the path of growth, the destination will always be one step ahead. We can enjoy the journey, embrace the process, and enter the moment fully and unreservedly.

In his novel, *The Notebooks of Malte Laurids Brigge*, Rilke writes:

> *Ah, poems amount to so little when you write them too early in your life. You ought to wait and gather sense and sweetness for a whole lifetime, and a long one if possible, and then, at the very end, you might perhaps be able to write ten good lines. For poems are not, as people think, simply emotions (one has emotions early enough)— they are experiences.*

If we see and feel deeply, in time our experiences will inform our efforts, and our creative expression will arise with a collected force, where something comes forth and is born through the very core of our being.

The heroic quest and the lifelong commitment to an ideal are central to the creative process, yet seem antithetical to the conditions of our times, in which instant enlightenment is bombastically sought and efforts are expected to mature and bear fruit immediately. In our society, we have unfortunately come to expect rapid results. Even more distressing, we actually believe that creativity is something that we "do," that we are capable of through our ordinary efforts alone, without the illuminating guidance that stems from the deeper sources within.

Yet the nature of the human organism suggests that creativity *appears* through a certain kind of inward turning, that it is not merely a task accomplished by the ordinary mind. The body, the mind, the feelings—each requires its own form of nourishment and each offers its own kind of intelligence. The creative act arises from an intentional relationship with this triad. When we bring attention from the mind into the body, and locate ourselves in our physical being, in our center, then we are here in this moment. From this intentional action, a new quality of feeling arises; not the emotional distraction that dominates our everyday lives, but a subtle taste of understanding, of the feelings as a doorway to new worlds and as a sensitive instrument of discovery. We feel our way. All of this seems true. Yet as we are, we are not enough. It is only in opening to another influence, by which something is born into this world through us, not from us, that we are truly creative participants in the evolutionary movement of life.

When we realize the role of creative individuals as conduits for life itself, it cannot help but engender deep humility. We are nothing, a grain of sand; yet we are everything, the spark of divinity lives within us. The cultivation of an enlightened humility, honoring those forces passing through and between us, follows the recognition that on our own we are limited and incomplete, that we need the help of deeper impulses, intuitions, and flashes of inspirational insight in order to proceed and work creatively. It is often the case that many false paths, usually presented by the ego, must be tried and put aside before our real work, our real mission, may be discovered.

What we need to do at this stage is to ask, sincerely and honestly: Where can we truly make a sustained commitment? Where is it possible for us to contribute our finest and best energies—not for all time, but for now. It is simple, really. Our commitments arise naturally from within—if we let them.

> *If one believes in something sufficiently, one will find a form through which to create what one must, even if to do so involves death itself . . . The subconscious, pushing through the conscious, driven by an urge coming from beyond its own knowing, its own control, trying to live in the light, like the seed pushing up through the earth, will alone have roots, can alone be fertile. . . It is not the spasmodic burst of activity based on 'ideas,' but the sustained growth and devotion to a dominating force—a force upon which one's very life depends—that moves me.*
>
> —Alfred Stieglitz

To explore, to challenge, to take risks, to try in spite of our limitations, to embrace the evolving process, to bear the glorious discomfort of not-knowing, to knowingly step into the unknown—these are the things a body likes, a soul strives for, and an artist or creative individual joyfully requires.

When I was quite young, perhaps eight or ten years old, I remember complaining to my mother that my toys *were not challenging enough*. My poor mother—she had no idea whatsoever how to respond to that plaintive and unusual statement. Nor did I. I didn't know what I wanted. My brothers and I seemingly had everything that any child might need or want, including some of the latest gizmos, gadgets, games, contraptions, play weapons of both personal and mass destruction—all the toys available to the children of American postwar culture. To this day, I remember my acute dissatisfaction and my profound yearning for something different, something more than these objects could inspire or provide.

From the words of a child, a good challenge *is* hard to find. And isn't this precisely what we need to grow and expand, and to push beyond our real or imagined boundaries?

CREATIVE PRACTICE

Questions

Make a list—a top-ten list—of your passions, obsessions, and deep interests. What abiding passion (in contrast to mere passing desires) do you embody, which you can transfer to your work? Is there a thread, a connecting factor among your top ten interests? What gives your life richness and dimension? What could you not live without?

• Stop, look, and listen. Take nothing for granted, make no assumptions: look at everything as if for the first time. Explore the material of your own life. Discriminate. What do you keep returning to? What do you want? What nourishes you? Where are you capable of making a real commitment? What would you edit from your life if given the chance? What role is expected of you by others, representing a duty, an obligation, that does not arise from the core of your being? What infuses your life with meaning, joy, direction, and the feeling of making a real contribution? What are you most proud of amongst your accomplishments? What do you *really* love to do?

Tools and Exercises

Your response to the works of another represents a key, a clue, to your own passions and commitments. What do you admire and emulate in the work of others? What influences you? Very often, by examining the creative efforts of others, we discover something of our own path. Keep a collection of quotes, images, and objects that inspire, incite, bring "fire" to your belly. From time to time, examine them and search for unifying threads and connections. Continue this as an ongoing activity. Keep it private, for yourself alone, your own treasure chest of impressions and ideas.

View your treasures with an eye toward stimulating your own creativity. Most artwork represents an ongoing dialogue with the accomplishments of others in the field. Do not hesitate to use another's work as a means of awakening your own originality. You are different, unique. Use the elements in your collection as a springboard to launch yourself on a trajectory toward realizing your own aims. Let ideas flow and meander through your mind and being. See how they feel. Smell them. Taste them. Cultivate them. Let them expand and naturally translate into action.

• Some artists have a passion for words, others for colors and shapes, and yet others for sound and musical expression. Some artists reflect in their works the intensity of their interest in the outer world: people, events, history, culture, social conditions, nature, or politics. Others are intensely absorbed by the inner world: feelings, abstract mental constructs, psychology and philosophy, autobiography, or the universal questions found in the search for meaning. Where are you in this spectrum? Do you love well-crafted words on a page? Do you gravitate to poetry or prose? Or do colors, sounds, or dance move you?

Your deepest interests and passions are the foundations of your creative work. What do you pay attention to—social dynamics or autobiography? Nature or politics? Discover your own point of intersection with the world. In your creative expression, begin with what captures your mind and heart.

• Observe. Take an hour on a day when you are relatively free of responsibilities and of the "tyranny of the urgent." Simply look. See what is around you and within you. Do not let anything escape your attention. Contemplate things, the actions of people, the flow of life itself, and your own responses to the objects of your attention. As Bonnie Friedman writes: "Things are saturated with significance. . . . Things themselves are translucent with meaning." What happens within your body, emotions, and mind as you observe life? What are you curious about, what interests you, what grows within you from this observation?

In my early photography classes with Nicholas Hlobeczy, when responding to the content of our work, or exploring a theoretical concern, he would consistently raise the question: *And what else?* Our understanding of our work or of life itself is always incomplete. One of the conditions of human nature is that we are subjective and limited; we seek to know and understand with greater clarity. With this simple, unassuming, yet elegant question, Nicholas reminded us that greater depths of understanding and creative response are always possible. To answer a question with finality is stagnation—to keep it open to further exploration is life itself. There is always more around the next corner.

So, as you observe, try to look deeper into the moment. Empathize with what is in front of you—put your attention within the object or event. Sense its energies, its rhythms and its inner shape. Ask questions of your observation. Try asking: *And what else?* What are you missing or not seeing? What could you see with greater clarity and directness? What is your connection to this person, place or event? What are its own inherent characteristics? What *really* interests you?

When you are attentive to what is in front of you, real interests will emerge. New directions may be found for your creative work. Certainly, real feeling for the world and people will arise that will deepen and inform your creative efforts.

• Examine your responses to the world around you. Discriminate. What really attracts your attention? Where do you feel moved to interact—with your whole being? Why, for example, would you marry this person and not that one? What belongs to you by virtue of your identity and being? When photographer Joel Meyerowitz was asked why he lingers at this scene and not another, he proclaimed: "Aha! I'll tell you what it is. It's like falling in love." And Frederick Sommer describes the activity of a photographer as: "walking about the world searching for something we carry within ourselves. Consequently, we would never photograph anything unless we have become attentive to it because we carry a great chunk of it within ourselves."

What are you in love with? What do you carry great chunks of within yourself?

3

Crisis and Creative Frustration

BOULDERS IN THE STREAM

There can come a moment in any project or ongoing activity—even in our life's work—when we "hit the wall," we reach a plateau, and further progress is painfully difficult, laborious, and *feels* impossible. We are stuck. You know how it feels. I know how it feels. We have all been there.

Some call it "writer's block"; others feel that their inspiration has left—for good. We become paralyzed, frozen in place and unable to move forward. We are full of self-doubt. A thousand reasons crop up to convince us that we cannot continue. It is an agonizing experience, particularly because it often comes on the heels of periods of intense creativity.

I remember when, midway through my first long-term photographic project, I suddenly came upon incredible resistance. I became extremely discouraged and announced to my friends I would never be a photographer again.

What is this crisis of creative expression, which seems an almost lawful, inevitable part of the creative process—and where does it come from?

The answers that I have found are not complete, but like a spiral circling in toward the center, they do seem to point toward a way of working and offer a means of proceeding.

1. The work has emerged; it has pushed through the earth and now reveals its particular shape. We begin to view it as an integral piece and see it as it actually is—not our original vision, our initiating intent, or our desired result—but the work itself. Like ourselves, it is incomplete, imperfect, and in need of refinement, reconsideration, and review. Here we must find the courage to willingly embrace the action of seeing; to see and feel what is needed, what is missing, and to allow the next step to emerge from this discomforting clarity.

    In *The Writing Life*, Annie Dillard elegantly writes of this condition: "You attend. In your humility, you lay down the words carefully . . . Now the earlier writing looks soft and careless . . . There is only one solution, which appalls you, but there it is. Knock it out . . . Courage utterly opposes the bold hope that this is such fine stuff the work needs it, or the world."

    We look for the questions being asked by the process itself. By stepping back, we often sense what is required to continue. We may simply need to review the work thus far and revise or refine our efforts—editing a manuscript, reprinting negatives in the darkroom, or reworking a canvas. As in any relationship, we want to get acquainted with the object of our attention, to get to know it better, with greater depth and clarity, to see what it needs.

    Creative practice evokes the sharp clarity of seeing things as they really are—if our pride is willing to accept the consequences. Our work is the measure of ourselves. It reveals the true nature of our passions, interests, and experiences, as well as reflecting the unique shape of our obstacles and limitations. The challenge is to risk seeing our work and ourselves, in the moment, without fear or judgment, and with as much impartiality as we can bear.

2. The process itself has reached a natural plateau, a resting place, or an interval. This is a kind way of putting it. Many of us experience this as an irresolvable block, a place of great frustration where our progress is impeded. The flow of the original intent has been realized and spent— and is now stopped dead in its tracks. How we handle this moment is of vital importance to the continued growth of the work and, indeed, to our entire future as artists and creative individuals. How many people, of great talent and potential, have allowed this condition of frustration to stop them cold, often for months, sometimes for years, or even for the rest of a lifetime?

At this stage, if we listen and look, the work itself contains the solution. It is telling us that it needs something: a change of direction, an influx of new ideas or methods, a fresh point of view, an expanded understanding, an infusion of energy, or simply greater care and attention. One of my students perceptively observed that in coming up against the wall, attempting to force our way through is futile. But to climb the wall, look around, examine the sights from a new and heightened perspective—herein lies a way of intelligence, with potential to move gracefully to the other side.

Sometimes we need to simply search within and question: What is needed . . . now? Somewhere within, we know. The solution may be as simple as gentle persistence, or falling back on the sheer joy of one's craft while waiting and listening for new insights to appear. By staying with it, you will discover new conditions that bring fresh energy to the process. Zen philosophy teaches that we cannot force anything—but we cannot afford not to try.

3. The stakes have now become higher. We are coming closer to home, nearer to ourselves. As the work proceeds and grows naturally from our being, we encounter our own negative attitudes and inner blockages. Our deeply ingrained habits, our comfortable well-rehearsed roles, and our relentless automatic reactions are thrown into relief by the demands of creative work. We are impeded by ourselves, which leads to mounting levels of frustration. The developing work bids us to continually question ourselves and attempt to move beyond our habitual repertoire of well-tried formulas and familiar reactions. As painter Ad Reinhardt observes: "art cannot exist without permanent condition of being put into question." We must risk the known for the sake of the unknown, for new discovery. We are, in fact, being asked to grow, by the requirements of the work itself and through our quest for authentic expression. For many of us, this presents a great challenge, and we stand in front of the abyss, overwhelmed and temporarily unable to proceed.

As a teacher of art, I can often recognize where my students will get hung-up and bogged-down, where their habitual tendencies lie, and where they need greater freedom and flexibility. It is far more difficult to observe these same limitations in myself. We need mirrors. Other people, trusted friends and advisors, can be invaluable at this stage, helping us to move beyond our own self-limiting tendencies and inner dialogue.

Creativity and innovation arise from stepping off the bridge of what we know, where we are comfortable, into unsettled lands and untested territory, taking calculated risks for the sake of discovery. We challenge our obstacles and habits, one small step at a time. When I write, for example, I try to resist my inherently restless nature, always wishing to get up from the chair and wanting to be anywhere else but there, facing the computer and the words on the page. When I make the persistent effort to relax my body and bring attention to the task at hand, something deepens and activates, helping the words to flow more freely through my mind and across the screen.

4. Resistance is natural. It is part of life and a necessary part of the process of growth. The Grand Canyon was formed by millions of years of water and wind working against the firmness of rocks. A plant pushes up within and against the earth. The very substance that provides resistance is also one of the primary sources of nourishment and life. Often the projects and pursuits that interest me the most, that I feel the most committed to, contain within them the greatest obstacles. Although it has taken some time, I am now comfortable enough with the process that I actually become excited when resistance arises, as it signifies that something is really going on. It is a measure of the value of a project or a direction.

One of the fundamental tasks of creativity is learning to embrace the challenge of facing obstacles and resistance. How do we proceed? Do we run away in fear or indulge in self-pity? Or do we work toward surmounting the obstacles with grace and courage? Do we recognize—and truly know, from a deep place within—that difficult or trying conditions are often the key ingredients of inner growth, giving us the strength and fortitude that we need to approach the varied demands of our lives and creative work? Fire is created by friction; mastery of ourselves and our medium will only come through meeting resistance honorably and willingly. We try to live, in don Juan's words, the warrior's path. Remember his quiet admonition, reported by Carlos Castaneda: "You indulge too much."

Another of creativity's many paradoxes is found here. We must strive to overcome resistance with energy and determination, yet we also need acceptance and forbearance. Violence, in any form, will not help us transcend obstacles; a polarization of energies will result in increased anguish and frustration, creating a vicious cycle that most of us know all too well. Can we bring both passion and compassion to bear? To maintain a wide and deep attention to ourselves and the process, to center our energies and aspire toward growth and evolution, to seek clarity and recognition of the truth of what is: these contain the greatest possibilities and offer the only sensible means of proceeding.

One evening, while working on the manuscript for this book, I witnessed the results of a real breakthrough by a photography student who had "hit the wall" and successfully worked through to the other side. She brought to class several of the finest photographs she had ever made, reflecting a quantum leap from those of the past. The nature of her project had required her to battle against numerous obstacles over the previous several weeks: pouring rain, many solitary hikes from dawn to dusk in a thick tropical jungle, subject matter that was difficult to locate, and the responses of classmates who found her work uninteresting and unreflective of the strength of her subject. Through it all, she had maintained her perspective: her belief in herself, her commitment to the value of the project, and her clear vision of the potential of the work. Her persistence prevailed, and a new, fresh energy in her images became visible to all. She taught the entire class a lesson about getting beyond impediments with acceptance, determination, and a highly positive attitude.

A former teacher whose thought and example continues to have an enduring influence on me, the late Dorothea M. Dooling, once observed His Holiness the Dalai Lama at a press conference in New York. She recalled his extraordinary presence as he stood calmly and with great attention, drinking his tea. Asked about the difficulty of leading his people, and of working in forced exile from his native Tibet following the violent Chinese occupation of the country, he paused, and finally commented: "I consider it a great honor and a privilege to be working in these conditions." Though in exile for most of his life, the Dalai Lama radiates joy, kindness, and great compassion, which he directly attributes to the Buddhist teachings on training the mind "to transform adverse circumstances into favorable ones."

～

One of my greatest lessons in the art of photography—and in seeing—came from the words of a blind man (though he was not without "sight"). Jacques Lusseyran, French writer and teacher, lost the use of both eyes in a school-yard accident at the age of eight. In his autobiography, *Let There Be Light*, he relates the experience of overcoming the obstacles of his blindness and learning to see again, through the act of being attentive to inner and outer conditions.

Lusseyran describes a momentous discovery made shortly after the injury. Though he had lost the sight of his eyes, he could still experience the pervasive illumination of light. "I found it *in myself* and what a miracle!—it was intact." He realized that it was contingent upon his inner condition—his attention—and his emotional state. "There was only one way to see the inner light, and that was to love."

When he experienced negativity—sorrow, anger, fear, or envy—he lost his connection to the inner light. His world darkened and became smaller. It became harder to navigate through space without colliding into objects, doorways, or anything in his path. When he embraced his inner world with awareness, when he felt courage and joy, his world opened, the space and light inside increased and he could "see." His physical coordination would immediately improve. "The necessary condition is . . . one has to be attentive."

Lusseyran describes the great efforts he was compelled to make as being much more than simply efforts: they were also discoveries. When he was attentive to his inner condition—to himself—he could see and describe people, objects, colors, and shapes. He could directly perceive the tangible traits and intangible "presence" of the object of his attention. He felt an "effluvium" emanating from all things, a pressure, a field of vibration. He could hear the sounds emitted by objects or people, which likewise revealed their essential characteristics. "Finally," he said, "even thoughts take on weight and direction." During World War II, as part of the French Resistance, he was responsible for interviewing prospective members because of his remarkable ability to see and sense motives and character.

He portrays his blindness as his greatest happiness and as a gift of great opportunity. He gratefully acknowledges the "order" his blindness created. "We constantly accuse the conditions of our lives. We call them incidents, accidents, illnesses, duties, infirmities. We wish to force our own conditions on life: this is our real weakness. We forget that God never creates new conditions for us without giving us the strength to meet them. I am grateful that blindness has not allowed me to forget this."

Lusseyran's story teaches that adversity can be seen as a barrier, or as the greatest gift. By struggling through difficulty, we grow and move beyond our limitations and perceived inadequacies—and we probably wouldn't find the force to do so without the obstacle. Our true measure can emerge. We produce some of our most significant works and find many innovative solutions when a clear demand is made and our "back is against the wall." Learning to value and welcome the potential found in these trying circumstances will call forth our best efforts and lead to some of our most insightful and hard-won discoveries.

A force arises within us in proportional measure to how we approach obstacles. Are they a hindrance to our passage, or an opportunity for growth? We gather force and strength as we make our way through the fertile ground of resistance. Using resistance as a tool, embracing the difficult as well as the easy, learning to navigate skillfully through rapidly changing conditions: these constitute the path of the artist.

While teaching a fall semester at the Art Institute of Boston, I saw this principle clearly demonstrated. The facility was undergoing a complete renovation while classes were in session, and the students were challenged with extremely trying conditions. The darkroom complex was located in the basement of the building, and by late November the heating system had not yet been finished. Dust and construction workers were everpresent. And it was *cold*. You could see your breath. Students were working in down jackets, wool hats, and gloves. Coffee had a twofold purpose: to provide sustenance and for handwarming to make it even possible to work. However—and this came as a surprise to everyone in the department—many of the photography students did, by far, their best work that semester.

Hexagram 39 in the *I Ching* succinctly illustrates the path through adverse circumstances: "Water on the mountain: the image of obstruction. . . . Water on the top of the mountain cannot flow down in accordance with its nature, because rocks hinder it. It must stand still. This causes it to increase, and the inner accumulation finally becomes so great that it overflows the barriers.

The way of overcoming obstacles lies in turning inward and raising one's own being to a higher level."

We are given poignant examples of this dynamic when we examine the biographies of artists. Many great works of art and literature have arisen directly from tragic or extremely trying conditions in the lives of their creators. Some of this is the stuff of legend: Beethoven's Ninth Symphony was written when he was nearly deaf; Edward Weston's later photographs from Point Lobos, presenting metaphors of death and rebirth, were created after the onset of Parkinson's disease; and some of Maya Angelou's prose and poetry derives from her direct experience with racial discrimination and sexual abuse.

As an artist friend once told me, "Our real gold as artists comes from our wounds." The work of healing necessitates reaching deep within ourselves, reordering our inner world, and seeking the intense clarity of genuine, impartial insight. Paradoxically, our wounds become a rich opportunity for gaining self-knowledge, cultivating authentic expression, and lending grace and power to our creative efforts. And—in true bodhisattva fashion—we cannot ignore the far-reaching value of our experiences in helping others. Artists often use their own wounds to create inspiring and challenging works that serve to assist the reader or viewer in overcoming their own similar challenges.

Much art throughout the ages addresses universal aspects of the human condition: our mortality, our battle with the ego, our efforts toward growth of being and consciousness, and our attempts to genuinely relate with others. Rainer Maria Rilke's poem "Requiem for a Friend" was written in response to the tragic death of his friend and confidante, painter Paula Modersohn-Becker. Several poignant lines toward the end of the poem reflect the perennial struggle experienced by artists attempting to move beyond their own limitations and obstacles, toward awakening, freedom of expression, and a heightened sense of being:

> *We can so easily*
> *slip back from what we have struggled to attain,*
> *abruptly, into a life we never wanted;*
> *can find that we are trapped, as in a dream,*
> *and die there, without ever waking up.*
> *This can occur. Anyone who has lifted*
> *his blood into a years-long work may find*
> *that he can't sustain it, the force of gravity*
> *is irresistible, and it falls back, worthless.*
> *For somewhere there is an ancient enmity*
> *between our daily life and the great work.*
> *Help me, in saying it, to understand it.*

To be creative, we need to be open—to ourselves and to the world, fully and deeply. Just as the first step toward awakening is the recognition of our ignorance, so the first step toward an open awareness is the development of the capacity for self-observation, through which we recognize our rigidity and mechanical habits. We begin to understand what prevents us from truly being open, from being touched by joy and sadness, from having a fresh and spontaneous response to life. Most of us will soon recognize that the chief culprit is ourselves: our ego, our petty preoccupations, our pride and our distorted view of who we are. Genuine creativity throws the ego into relief, places it at risk, presents grave peril to its false authority. The ego resists relinquishing control and assuming its rightful place—that of serving our real selves and our real impulses. There is no question that this is often the heart of the crisis.

Real freedom grows in a climate of surrender and letting go. The creative spontaneity that we seek implies a simultaneous liberation from ourselves, from our ego and mundane attachments, with a growing receptivity to the deeper, more essential parts of our nature. We learn to place our trust in our integrity, our genuine impulses. This may take place gradually or, for some, in one decisive, shining event. In my case, the loss of an eye served as a moment of deep liberation. I began to view life from an enlarged perspective that persisted for years after the event. It's a little like the old Zen practice in which the master whacks the student on the back of the head and, for a moment, the student transcends the ego and experiences something else. Something in me was shaken loose, and in that process, a new internal order emerged; a new order that was a little less dominated by petty concerns—and a little more influenced by a desire to simply be open.

~

I can't think of three words in the English language more potent than "in spite of." To be creative and to strive to live an authentic life, we work and we try:

> *in spite of* our fear and resistances
> *in spite of* our personal limitations and hardships, real or imagined
> *in spite of* our lack of clarity and limited understanding
> *in spite of* our clumsy efforts with vision and craft
> *in spite of* our difficulties in relating to the world and each other
> *in spite of* our lack of a durable connection to the deepest parts of ourselves
> *in spite of* our personal demons, our agonies and sorrows

in spite of the disharmony of the world we live in

in spite of our fragmented, busy lives

in spite of our brittle egos and false personas

in spite of ourselves . . .

. . . we continue. And from this simple effort, growth occurs and understanding comes. It happens gradually, in incremental steps, until one day we may awake to find that we are truly artists—that we too are a source; that we are on the road toward mastery of our medium and of ourselves; that the creative impulse lives within us; that we can navigate between our inner and outer worlds with bravery, confidence, and ability; and that we can embrace and live the role that we were destined for.

CREATIVE PRACTICE

Questions

Be true to yourself. Look at the challenges presented by your greatest obstacles and your deepest wounds. Ask yourself: What is your response to adversity? Could it be different? Could you be more courageous or accepting? How can you use your deepest fears, unhealed wounds, and persistent difficulties? What are they teaching you? Have you observed, over time, a transformative growth of being as you rise to their challenges? Have you helped—or can you help—others, through the value of your experience? Can the work of healing become source material for your creative expression? Conversely, can creativity assist your growth and healing? Are your experiences and their resulting expression a source of learning and inspiration for others?

Where can you be more persistent? Where do you have a tendency to retreat, to give up the battle? Can you believe in yourself and your ability to continue, in spite of fear or despair? Can you simply try, continue the effort, and gradually gain the confidence of knowing what is possible? Be brave. Be true to your deeper self. Can you honor its expression, no matter what it takes?

Tools and Exercises

Be courageous. Draw, write, paint, or take pictures of those elements that represent your greatest challenges and pertinacious obstacles. Work with them. Allow them their place in the sun. By communicating these elements through your work, you divest them of their power over you. They may become your allies, not your enemies.

Try to see and express the truth, however you genuinely experience it. Be careful not to get lost in wishful thinking or imaginary torment; both are equally dangerous. Learn, over time, to develop a new relationship with yourself, based on an attentive, impartial, and encompassing eye. The very act of seeing, of cultivating an inner witness, proceeds from a deeper level than ordinary, mind-based introspection, shedding light into dark places. From true self-observation, a new and heightened perspective may arise that in itself will be deeply transformative. Through seeing and feeling your contradictions, and not shirking the truth, a subtle, joyful taste of unitive consciousness may, over time, begin to emerge. Creative work can help immeasurably to liberate your vision, freeing the Seer from the seen, and help you to separate your essential being from an overly close, entangled identification with personal demons. In facing this perennial challenge, your inherent strengths and unique capabilities have a chance to emerge and make themselves known.

• Study the lives of artists, view their works, read their literature, and listen to music drawn from the well of their experiences. You will find much inspiration and realize that, no matter what your predicament, you are not alone.

In cultures both traditional and modern, in different ways, it is said that in healing ourselves, we heal the planet, and in healing the planet, we heal ourselves. In this respect, the world *needs* our inner work and creative efforts. We are, in fact, products of our own culture, our own era, and our own environment. The more deeply we delve into ourselves and our own unique circumstances in the creation of art, the stronger and more authentic our work becomes. Yet, the more deeply we penetrate through the masks that hide us from ourselves, the more universal the work becomes in its meaning. The implications of this are enormous in our postmodern civilization, which views the individual as primarily conditioned by his or her culture and circumstances. Beneath it all—black or white, man or woman, Asian or European, rich or poor—we are products of the human condition. Perhaps someday we will find that we are more alike in our humanness than we are different. The power of art and myth will not allow us to forget this.

• It will happen, if it hasn't already; you will reach a point in your creative pursuits at which you hit the wall, where the flow is impeded and you have exhausted your resources. You will be frustrated and stuck. What then?

Ask questions. Try different avenues of approach. Experiment with different strategies and find what works for you. Is it time to really push, accelerate the pace, and work through the obstacle? Is it time to step back, give some breathing room, and allow the next step to gestate from a deeper part of your being? Is it time for a new direction; is some new insight or research called for? Can you simply return to the love of your craft or chosen activity? Can you remember and renew the originating excitement that prompted your involvement in the first place? How have you dealt successfully with adversity in the past?

We often look at others who have experienced mind-bending obstacles and count our blessings. Talk to these individuals. Gain the value of their experience. Sources of inspiration are everywhere when we take the time to look.

4

Retreat and Withdrawal

ON THE SHORE: WATCHING THE RIVER FLOW

A time to be born, a time to die; a time to build up, a time to tear down; a time to advance, a time to retreat.

At regular intervals in the creative process, we need to disengage from the purposeful involvement with our project, place the working questions in the background of our consciousness, and move toward a state of active stillness. Although we may at times be blessed naturally with a state of inner clarity and quiet, the only reliable method of reaching it comes through our intent, making a conscious choice to step back from the work and our urgent concerns. Listening, waiting, ripening, and embracing "not-doing" engenders a fuller realization of our work at this stage. Returning to the banks of the river, moving out of the direct current, and resting or lying in the sun is not an idle activity. It is a highly necessary means of incubation, of reflection, of allowing the process to find its own shape and momentum, and of giving room for the unexpected insight and the on-the-edge-of-consciousness discovery.

Our culture unfortunately associates retreat with failure, withdrawal with weakness. Yet, in art and creative activities, isn't there a vital, even fundamental, rhythm of advance and retreat, activity and withdrawal? Music is created by sounds punctuated with silence, and visual images are formed through the combining of positive elements and negative space. Why is active doing seen as a more important gesture than allowing something to unfold? Why is one side of the coin so often considered better, or given greater weight, than the other? Aren't both sides necessary? Is winning better than losing? Don't we need the experience of both in order to gain understanding—and the beginning of wisdom and compassion? Can we stay at the center of the wheel—and hear the living silence beneath sound?

Many significant discoveries in art, science, and literature have emerged from what I would call the "space between worlds," where we run out of steam, and conscious inquiry and intentional work can go no further on their own. Our initiative is dwindling, yet nothing has risen to fill this gap. This is the moment of reckoning, where the future development of our work is at stake. Three options are available at this crucial moment: we can throw our hands up in frustration and passively wait for a change of conditions to occur, hoping that something or someone will come and rescue us; we can try to force our way through to the other side (the "bulldozer" approach); or, we can make an intentional effort to let go, and allow the process to organically unfold in the depths of our mind and being.

Entering the resonating field of silence seems antithetical to our times, to our action-oriented lives. Fax machines, pagers, e-mail, cellular telephones; we can be reached anywhere, anytime. No matter what else is taking place in our lives, we are expected to respond *now*. It is true that electronic communication does have its place, but is it making us forget how to digest and contemplate our impressions? Years ago, it would take several days for a letter to reach its addressee and several days to return a response. A leisurely interval existed in which to formulate an answer, integrate the information, or simply find the time to read and respond. Even in creative fields, the impatient quest for immediate gratification or the need to meet tight deadlines can overwhelm the natural rhythms of the mind and body.

We have all but forgotten the lost art of porch-sitting, the art of leisure—of leaving a wide margin in our lives. Clarity is restored through relaxation and quiet, by sensitively moving our attention into the body, letting the dust settle, becoming aware of the silence within—and leaving behind our tightly focused mind or urgent emotions. Some of us go for a walk; others may go for a drive; yet others may engage simple and enjoyable activities that renew and refresh. Leaving space within ourselves to allow for a regathering of energy and a gestation in the womb of our being is necessary to organically deepen creative growth.

Most artists feel that something is wrong when they are not working intensely on a highly regular basis, whether or not they are genuinely moved to do so. They judge themselves harshly when the well of inspiration has retreated from conscious view. Those involved in the arts will recognize this as a nearly universal condition. Furthermore, the institutions that support artists—publishers, galleries, and museums—actively promote this attitude by requiring a quota of new work on an annual or semiannual basis. For an artist to be worth their salt, a new portfolio, a current manuscript, or a recent film must be completed in a timely manner. To spend years of on-again, off-again work on a major project brands one as an unnecessarily slow worker, an underproducer.

In most art schools in this country, an unspoken and widely accepted expectation exists for students to be unfailingly productive at all times. Many faculty members resist having students' work shared by any class except their own. At the Art Institute of Boston, where I taught for many years, most photography students were expected and required to produce three to four *separate* portfolios of work every semester. Education thus becomes an endurance test. Is this appropriate or really helpful? Does it genuinely serve the student, or the real aims and ideals of education? While students clearly must cultivate discipline and learn to meet real-world expectations, shouldn't they also seek a natural integration of their talents, and strive to find the vital core of their own concerns and ideals?

Our culture values achievement over reflection, and production over incubation. Yet both are necessary and are integral to the creative process.

I remember meeting a colleague, a fellow photographer, at Walden Pond soon after my father died. He was taking pictures—I was just sitting in the sun. We greeted each other. I told him of my father and explained that I had been just sitting, trying to digest the experience and sort out the multitude of thoughts and feelings passing through me, and that this had been going on for weeks. He said something I found very strange. He said he never took time away from his work—no matter what. The work is too important to him. This sounded incredibly portentous to me, and filled with a false sense of self-importance. We all need time to digest our experiences, to settle the ordinary mind and percolate, giving room for the unconscious to operate and come through with new understandings and insights.

Our lives are governed by the tyranny of the urgent. We leave precious little space for reflection, for ripening and maturation. We are living in a "time famine," and it might do us well to slow things down—to give our creative work the broad canvas it needs to organically unfold and develop in accordance with its own kernel of potentiality.

Can we learn to balance the ingredients of focused initiative, sustained effort, and sharp intensity, with patience and active "waiting"?

Rilke reminds us:

Allow your judgments their own silent, undisturbed development, which, like all progress, must come from deep within and cannot be forced or hastened. Everything is gestation and then birthing. To let each impression and each embryo of a feeling come to completion, entirely in itself, in the dark, in the unsayable, the unconscious, beyond the reach of one's own understanding, and with deep humility and patience to wait for the hour when a new clarity is born: this alone is what it means to live as an artist: in understanding as in creating.

In this there is no measuring with time, a year doesn't matter, and ten years are nothing. Being an artist means: not numbering and counting, but ripening like a tree, which doesn't force its sap, and stands confidently in the storms of spring, not afraid that afterward summer may not come. It does come. But it comes only to those who are patient . . . I learn it every day of my life, learn it with pain I am grateful for: patience is everything!

The inner ripening of our creative juices comes perennially in its own season; yet, like a mother with a child growing in her womb, our role is to nourish and further this organic development. Many productive and useful activities take place at this stage of the process. The creative act builds to a release, an outer manifestation of our concerns and interactions. For these liberating moments of expression to occur, one essential prerequisite must be met: we must have something to say. Our work blooms from the digestion of our experiences and impressions. And very often, when we do not feel productive or capable of further efforts, we can still gather experiences and knowledge, preparing the ground. This kind of work is essential, and leads to the epiphanal moments in the flow. In the meantime, how do we till the soil and plant the seeds? What activities help?

1. Research and observation. We cannot force the expression of our growing interests. At times, we need to renew the process of discovery by reading, listening, looking, or otherwise seeking new information that will serve the development of our work. Staying open to chance experiences—the maverick variable—often holds the key to ongoing progress. When we are deeply engaged in a project and attuned to its needs and demands, new insights often come from unexpected sources. And when our mind is focused on a particular question or subject, it is akin to having an antenna in the air, drawing to us the impressions that we need for further growth. Or, we may seek inspiration more assertively by surrounding ourselves with books, objects, people, works of art, or anything that may deepen our knowledge and feeling about the content of our work. When I am photographing a place, for example, I immerse myself in the energy of that location and seek relevant literature, films, and advisors to assist my nourishment and education. While writing on creativity, I have books around me from my favorite writers on the topic, constantly within reach, and I frequently refer to their wealth of insights.

    The photographer Paul Strand was known to live in a place for up to a year before even unpacking his cameras to photograph it. He would look and learn, and become a part of the fabric of the place. From this intimate standpoint, he would then begin to work with devotion and passion.

When we have taken in enough nourishment, gathered enough material, when our impressions and experiences fill the well within, creative expression will come about naturally.

2. Put the work aside. Remember Rilke's advice: *Patience is everything*. Just let it be. After a period of days, weeks, months, or even years, we may return to it with fresh insights and a heightened perspective. Many artists and writers are just too close to the work at hand, and cannot see it clearly. If we can clear the current and perplexing issues out of the foreground of our consciousness, time and inner incubation will do the rest. It is often as simple as that. Sometimes even minutes or hours away from a problem or task will permit enough distance for seminal insights to emerge.

By the time we return to the work, even if we are not gifted with earth-shattering revelations, we have at least given some breathing room, a critical distance that is integral to our creative efforts. As in any relationship, when we are constantly in the interactive mode, we are often tangled in a web of ego desire and attachment. Taking a break helps us rediscover our genuine points of connection with what is in front of us—and serves to remind us of the initial impetus that brought us to it in the first place.

Two examples come to mind that illustrate the polarity between the enrichment of work over time and the honoring of the freshness, power, and grace of the initial impulse. The first was an exhibition of the work of photographer Ansel Adams at the Museum of Modern Art. This exhibit of his well-known images included a series of prints from the same negative that were made at different stages in his career, from early vintage prints to the virtuoso printings of his later years. In every instance, the later prints contained a boldness and vitality, combined with a sensuous subtlety, whereas the earlier prints looked vague and unresolved. We may surmise that, over time, the artist grew in under-standing and ability, and his later prints reflected this growth. With a background as a concert pianist, Ansel Adams viewed the negative as the score and the print as the performance. It took the better part of a life-time to acquaint himself fully with his most important negatives.

For a contrary example, read the original 1855 version of Walt Whitman's epic poem, "Song of Myself," comparing it with any of the multiple revisions Whitman made over thirty years. While moments of brilliance do arise in the later revisions, the original version remains the most forceful and astonishing, with the greatest clarity and breadth of vision. Several critics have referred to his incessant revisions, additions, and deletions as *tinkering*. Although we may seek refinement of our work, we must deeply respect the originating impulse and be careful not to revise the life out of it. In our true moments of accord with the deeper sources within—when bathed in the light of inspiration—often the best thing that we can do is simply leave it alone.

3. Return to your body. Bring attention to it and stay within. Exercise. Release some energy and get the blood moving. Go for a walk, a swim, or any of the physical pursuits your body enjoys. The natural intelligence and sensitivity of the body plays a far more important role in the creative process than most of us realize or acknowledge. Along with my experience of sitting meditation—or perhaps as a result of this quiet time spent early in the day—the vast majority of my insights and new understandings arise when I am engaged in simple, physical activities such as washing dishes, raking leaves, or gently playing in the ocean.

    Our clarity lies buried beneath the tangled morass of the ordinary mind and reactive emotions. Being attentive to the relative purity of the body brings a state of inner quiet and a liberation from the noisy, conflicting voices of our inner dialogue. One of the seminal means of gaining attention is coming into the body, bringing awareness and relaxation to the muscles and organs, centering oneself, and finding the field of silence within. From this groundedness, we may observe ourselves and the outer world with greater awareness, and our creative work—indeed, all of our activities—may arise naturally, seamlessly, from within. When centered, our senses, minds, and feelings are activated and enlivened. One of the most reliable criteria for gauging the quality of our attention, of how present we are in the moment, is the degree of participation of the body. Do we sense ourselves? Are we aware of our breathing and the blood moving through our veins? Are we aware of the silence within?

The body can also be viewed as a metaphor for the creative process. The human body takes in food, transforms it into energy, and excretes unused materials. The human psyche takes in impressions, transforms them through activities and work, and also needs to release, to let go of the waste. Otherwise, we become mentally and spiritually constipated, unable to proceed until we release some of the stray thoughts and feelings that are ricocheting through us. We seek clarity—not indigestion. And we seek insight—not a tangled mess of unresolved ideas, feelings, and background noise.

How may we begin to encourage a state of clarity, a clearing of the water? We must step back and allow room for a new perspective to emerge. Take a break. Go for a swim. Have a cup of coffee or a great meal. Read a novel. Play racquetball. Take a vacation. Do whatever you do—but get away. Give space. The work needs it. You need it.

Our conscious aims and direction must give way to something that arises from another source. Our role is to give the unconscious, with its widening breadth of insight, the room it needs to incubate. It functions in its own organic time, and not within the imposed deadlines of a project or in the fractured busyness of our lives. It stands apart from the daily fray and lies beneath the web of conscious thinking. We know that many of our dreams at night are no more than the integration of our daily activities and experiences; it seems that our mind requires this process. These should be distinguished, however, from the more vivid and strongly felt dreams that are harbingers from another world. These are highly instructive and revelatory, and contain in their symbolic language the keys to our actualization as creative individuals and contributing members of society.

Many artists have received clues and messages from dreams, waking visions, or images and words that arise from deep within and make their appearance in the conscious mind, often showing the way toward completion or indicating new, highly fruitful directions. These spontaneous moments of revelation are crucial to our personal evolution, integral to the development of our creative work, and offer hope and encouragement to others. Our conscious, purposeful efforts do not always reveal our larger mission, that which is ours to contribute. One of the principal maladies of modern Western life is that we do not easily find our place. Those of us with complex interests and talents often spend half a life merely in the discovery phase, seeking our calling, striving toward integration.

Awakening to other ways of knowing and connecting with our inner sources is vital to the process of creative growth and individuation. The vast recesses of the unconscious hold many secrets to our future development as artists and individuals. Active stillness is the means through which these mysteries are revealed.

In the introduction to *The Creative Process*, Brewster Ghiselin provides a succinct summary of the need for a "hidden organic development" at a certain stage of creative work, and states that this need appears to be universal. He says that many have likened this stage of the creative process to the growth of a child in the womb: "The comparison . . . nicely communicates the important fact that the process is an organic development, and it helps to dispel the notion that creation is simply an act of canny calculation governed by wish, will, and expediency." Ghiselin also describes some of the efforts that are required to nourish this gestation process: "Mastering accumulated knowledge, gathering new facts, observing, exploring, experimenting, developing technique and skill, sensibility, and discrimination, are all more or less conscious and voluntary activities." From these conditions, we invite spontaneous insights to appear.

One of the most perplexing aspects of the human condition lies in the dynamic between doing and not-doing, stillness and deeds. Not-doing, opening to the fecundity of a vibrating silence that carries on its wings fresh energy and new understandings, still requires some measure of intent and purposeful action. A regular transformative practice or discipline, whether or not it is directly related to our creative work, can help: meditation, slow walks, yoga, tai chi, or any of the contemplative activities available to us. The action-oriented parts of our constitution will often proclaim (and complain) that the discipline of seeking inner quiet runs counter to the freedom and effusive spontaneity of the creative process. These voices should not be heeded, though we give them room to have their say and blow off steam.

A meditative practice can be deeply transformative. It not only gives space in our minds and being for an inner gestation to occur, but it quiets our ordinary associative thinking and distances our awareness from an identification with our reactive emotions. It loosens the veils that hide our true estate. Active stillness refines our inner world, has a unifying affect on the body and mind, and opens to the finer vibratory rates of our higher centers or chakras. Through the cultivation of inner silence, we provide fertile conditions in the ground of our being for the creative impulse to grow and thrive.

~

Gurdjieff said that a measure of time should be spent daily "pondering," or in active contemplation. If we desire to contemplate, to actively think, we must release our attention from the stray thoughts and random associations that are constantly turning over in our minds, inciting our emotions, and distracting us from the moment. We talk to ourselves about everything under the sun, constantly and incessantly, without respite. How can a real thought or feeling emerge in the midst of this carnival of inner activity? We may not be able to stop the constantly ranging thoughts and emotional reactions. Can we simply allow them to proceed, not get stuck in them, and realize that they do not represent the whole of our existence? I like the advice of don Juan to Carlos Castaneda in the exercise of "stopping the internal dialogue." And the *Tao Te Ching* asks: "Can you remain unmoving till the right action arises by itself?"

How can we, living in the present time, truly become quiet? Through the field of silence, we invite the sensitivity of feeling, connect with the wisdom of the body, and open to the soaring thoughts of the mind, expressed through moments of intuitive insight. It can be quite challenging to relinquish the modern arrogance that believes the conscious mind alone—without the enlarging dimension of the deeper parts of our nature—can know everything and is our greatest tool.

Can we leave space for our potential wholeness to emerge? The key, once again, lies in our awareness, our mindfulness. We watch, witness, and observe the rapidly changing inner scenarios. We try not to get caught in the fray. Our attention can remain free, focusing instead on the body, sensing its energies and organic rhythms. From this action, a quieting naturally begins to occur. It is a form of retreat to an inner region, a place where we may simply *be*. The constant turning of the mind does not stop, we simply no longer need to give our full attention to these distracting elements. From this condition, a different form of thinking and new understandings can emerge.

Some of my best thoughts, most significant insights, and most vivid moments of understanding occur when I am engaged in simple physical activities and have put aside the burning question of the moment. I have let go of the problem and it is present only in the back of my mind. When writing, I carry a small notebook literally everywhere I go. And, without fail, while doing errands, grocery shopping, or even while watching television, fully formed thoughts arise suddenly, lines of words appear without conscious invitation, and a sharper understanding comes as a delightful gift when I least expect it.

"To every thing there is a season, and a time for every purpose under heaven." A time to assert and a time to allow. Creative work proceeds on its own—with our participation to be sure—if we can learn to stand out of the way. This is probably the most difficult lesson for most of us to learn, that we cannot "do" everything. The process has its own integrity and its own life, if we simply allow it to move forward.

CREATIVE PRACTICE

Questions

We need time. It is one of our most precious commodities. Ask these questions of your own life: What can wait? What really does demand your attention and response now—and what needs to be digested and integrated before responding? What does the "tyranny of the urgent" steal from our lives? What demands can we turn a blind eye toward, to allow room for creative projects and for the necessary unconscious insights to emerge? What can we edit from our lives, what activities are habit-driven and have outlived their usefulness? What anxieties must we let go of to realize our projects and creative interactions, allowing them to unfold organically, rather than trying to hasten their completion?

Photographer Paul Caponigro writes: "Who has the time today, really the time, to grow, to unfold, and develop in an activity or even to contemplate properly what others are doing? Life ought to be lived more like harmonious music. The pressure of hastening things, of skimming superficially, only destroys that sense of music in life."

What of future generations? Can we teach our children the value of living life harmoniously, slowing it down, giving real attention to a task or to another person? Can we resist the tendencies we have inherited from our media-driven culture that encourage the sound-bite mentality, the readily digestible concept, and the reductivist mentality, bringing everything down to the lowest common denominator? Can we slow things down enough to contemplate and digest our lives? Can we build toward the future with a responsible and humane use of these powerful technologies, which can overwhelm our lives if we are not careful?

Can we be still, and learn to cultivate the resonating potential of inner silence?

Tools and Exercises
Be still. Meditate. Make this your practice, maybe for only fifteen minutes a day to begin with. Then, over time, increase your commitment to half an

hour. Find your own method, that which suits your temperament and predilections. Sitting quietly in the morning, walking, having an afternoon tea or coffee, or finding time in quiet surroundings may help open the door to spontaneous insight and new discoveries. Try it, in spite of the crowded events of your life and the urgent demands of the day. You may uncover an integral tool for navigating through the creative process, or indeed, for approaching any of the questions that occupy your inner life. Pay attention to how and when your spontaneous insights arise. What are the conditions that seem to encourage their emergence?

• Be aware of the intimations from within, the subtle voices, the hazy, distant images, and the unexpected impulses. Allow them to form without editing and without judgment. Simply see and listen. Take notice. Sometimes it is the "whispers" that contain new understandings, reveal fertile directions, and provide insights and solutions to the question or problem of the moment.

Innovative problem-solving can only take place through looking outside of the conventional boundaries of ordinary thought and seeking these subtle whispers from within.

Carry a small notebook at all times to encourage the flow of images and insight. Write down the vague symbols, unformed thoughts, and words or images that appear on the threshold of consciousness. Simply allow them to arise, and see what develops.

• Allow the process to unfold instead of willfully asserting your conscious purpose and initiative. Just experiment, watch, and note what arises through interaction with your medium. Try simply to paint, sketch, write, or photograph without knowing what you will do or accomplish. Do what comes to mind freely, spontaneously. Let your hand guide your actions. Throw your plan out the window, at least for a short while.

Purpose and intent are of equal import to the process. However, in Western culture, we prioritize these elements at the expense of the organic development. Let go, allow the work to find its own shape, and simply get out of the way.

This may sound easy. But due to our conditioning, it may be the most difficult task of the creative process. There is a time for all things to proceed. Let it happen. Read the *Tao Te Ching* for inspiration and guidance. It will help.

5

Epiphany and Insight

FROM THE MOUNTAIN STREAM

Epiphany can be defined as a *massively liberating insight*. I love the sound of these words: massively liberating insight. What do they mean? Hearing the words themselves calls forth the hope and promise of radical realizations and moments of thundering wisdom. Roger Lipsey, who coined this expression in *An Art of Our Own*, claims that "some lives articulate around" these moments. Many artists, scientists, and thinkers provide us with accounts of a lighting flash of insight, a revelation that has changed their lives, or in some cases, changed the shape of the known world: Saint Paul's conversion on the road to Damascus, the creative efforts of Van Gogh in the last year of his life, Albert Einstein's discovery of the theory of relativity. In each instance, a vision appeared, whole and complete, suddenly, beyond the activity of the conscious mind, revealing ideas and insights whose power flowed into the world, influencing all of humanity.

These and other, similar experiences reveal the potential of a spontaneous burst of understanding, appearing through the cracks of the conscious mind with an inner certainty and authority. Such moments arise from a deeper source and illuminate the questions or the process of discovery active for each person at a given time.

To speak of Einstein and Van Gogh is to invoke the experience of unique and unusual individuals with extraordinary gifts. But what about the rest of us, with our more modest capacity and talent? Is this experience of insight, of epiphany, possible within the context of our everyday lives, our ordinary circumstances, and our youthful, wobbly efforts? Surely we can all point to moments of intense awareness, breaking through from the unconscious as a vision, an intuition, a foreknowledge of the future, or a sudden answer to a long-perplexing question. And these moments may have sufficient force to be characterized as life-altering or containing immense creative possibility.

Roger Lipsey cites the root meaning of the word *epiphany* as "a sudden disclosure of the sacred, as if it is shored up behind barriers and unexpectedly breaks into human awareness." Our mind, indeed our very being, contains hierarchical levels of awareness and understanding. Through the active stillness explored in the preceding chapter, we can relinquish some of our fixation on the wild, associative mind and reactive emotions, leaving the force of our attention free to circulate and infuse the inner pathways of the body and mind, opening to the deeper layers of consciousness. When we connect with the implicit order of what is, and surrender to the energy that organizes all things, a new channel for creative realizations is deeply activated.

Free will can be our greatest ally or most formidable obstacle. We choose our path. Although we accept all things, including the lesser gods of the ego and its myriad manifestations, we must also bring a rigorous discrimination and clear judgment to bear on ourselves and the world. What is worthy of our deepest attention and care? Do our creative aspirations grow from a search for wholeness and consciousness, or from the egoistic leanings we are all prone to indulge? Genuine creative growth often entails choosing the larger aim over lesser attachments, dismantling our egos, suspending the tight focus on our petty preoccupations, and opening to the mysterious fabric of an internal order. When we make that choice, that internal commitment, inwardly leaning toward our own integrity, the barriers dissolve and unexpected currents of epiphanal insight can make their welcome appearance.

If our creative efforts are to generate enough force and energy to make a difference in our lives and in those of others, such moments of illumination are often the key ingredient. They inform us, they guide our way, and they provide the necessary reinforcement—when we most need it—for bringing new understanding and fresh energy to the process. Often, such moments reveal the inherent shape or core feature of our works and assist us in bringing them to completion. The photographic images that I have made when I was led to a particular place at a particular time, without conscious intent on my part, have often been the seminal images of a project. They typically contain a depth of meaning and an elegance of expression that I could not have come to solely on my own initiative. In writing these essays, from time to time, paragraphs and phrases emerge from a deeper part of myself as gifts, harbingers of understanding from another source—and they have become a central component of the dialogue found in these pages.

What characterizes these moments of epiphany? What calls forth insight and the unique possibility in human beings to receive something from another order, to know more, to create more fully, and to see more deeply in a lightning-flash of consciousness? The accounts of creative individuals suggest that there are several common factors.

Preparing the Ground

Moments of vivid insight arise suddenly, and seemingly from nowhere. In reality, these moments occur as an outcome of intense conscious work on a project or a question, often after a long period of time during which the ground has been properly prepared. An artist will have been passionately engaged with a work, a mathematician with a particular formula or problem, or an individual may be in the process of closely questioning a relationship, a career choice, or a life direction. The insights come *as a result* of this past work. All the efforts that we make provide their reward, not always in the moment of making the effort, and maybe not in direct relationship to what we desire—but we are given help when we continue to strive forward sincerely, with energy and passion.

As Christopher Fremantle, in his book *On Attention*, states uniquevocally to a pupil: "People don't realize that when they work, conscious forces come to their aid . . . conscious forces are trying to help you. You are not alone."

In *The Power of Myth*, Bill Moyers interviews Joseph Campbell:

Moyers: Have you ever had sympathy for the man who has no invisible means of support?

[Joseph Campbell is momentarily taken aback by the question; then recognition dawns]

Campbell: Who has no invisible means? Yes, he is the one that evokes compassion, the poor chap. To see him stumbling around when all the waters of life are right there really evokes one's pity.

Moyers: The waters of eternal life are right there? Where?

Campbell: Wherever you are—if you are following your bliss, you are enjoying that refreshment, that life within you, all the time. . .

> *I say, follow your bliss and don't be afraid, and doors will open where you didn't know they were going to be.*

The doors to the unconscious and to our deeper nature open in direct measure to the efforts that we have made on the pathways of life and creative work. Our invisible means of support may come from an unknown source, but it is our work, our persistence, our conscious attempt to align with our "bliss," that unlock the power of these sudden bursts of realization. It is a lawful process. When we are deeply engaged in our work but unattached to the final result; when we open to our passion while maintaining a detached inner witness; when we balance vital action with not-doing and leaving space within; we create the conditions for guiding lights to appear on the horizon. And we must remember that their source is always present, at least in potential, but is veiled and hidden from conscious view until we are ready, until we have done the work and earned entrance to this mysterious world of greater knowledge and illuminating insight.

In the studio, when we are working and in the flow, fresh discoveries seem to arise out of the atmosphere itself. Words and phrases may appear with remarkable directness, new forms may be applied to the canvas with a certainty and authority not previously experienced, and fertile new directions may emerge that give the work greater dimension and meaning. It is a form of magic. It makes itself known in its own time—no matter how hard we strive for it—and usually not until we have exhausted all other possibilities.

Awakening to Sources
Among artists and psychologists who have studied this phenomenon, it is generally agreed that the central source of such illuminating moments is the unconscious mind, working in the background of our conscious efforts. In

this sense, however, I prefer the phrase "depth consciousness" to the term "unconscious." While we may not know precisely where this greater knowledge comes from, we do know with certainty that when something forcefully breaks through the crack between the worlds, we experience a moment of greater *consciousness*. Does it come strictly from the contents of our unconscious mind? Does it come from another, a higher source? Does it come from the energies and wisdom passing through and between our collective selves? Does it come, as the Hawaiians and other traditional cultures believe, from the generations of ancestors that live within us and permeate every cell in our bodies? Or are there higher centers awake in us that we are separated or exiled from as a result of our discordant existences? Many seekers and creative individuals believe that we live in a very small corner of ourselves, in touch with only a fraction of the entirety of our inner universe. I personally suspect that all of these beliefs contain some measure of truth, and that our moments of insight and revelation derive from a combination of factors stemming from these sources.

An essential element of creativity, then, is coming into accord with both the deeper energies within us and the subtle realms of greater intelligence surrounding us. Regardless of their origin, we contact these sources through our own inward being, by opening more fully into our Selves. We soon come to the conclusion that our everyday selves are not enough, that we are limited and incomplete when working solely from the self-will's tight determination. Without a connection to moments of guiding vision, the acute feeling persists that, in the words of Bonnie Friedman, "we are bereft of the experience that ravishes and transforms." Seeking a new balance of forces, the parts of us governed by our ego need to give way and become more passive, while our humility, our receptiveness moves to the forefront of our experience.

Examining the word "understanding," we see that it means "standing under," connecting to a larger order of knowledge. To understand something implies an opening to a broader awareness. A moment of understanding is a gift. It is a moment of insight, drawn from a larger perspective.

We tend to seek this capacity in distant lands—that is, outwardly. We read the latest book on self-improvement and spirituality. We take workshops on various forms of inner growth and development. We follow the newest trends or the wisdom of our favorite teacher. Yet the real treasure is within. It lies buried beneath our daily concerns, our ordinary mind and our opinions, our emotional reactions, and our fragmented energies. All we need do is unearth it.

The still, small voice that could put an end to our confusion and consternation is separated from us by the thinnest of veils. Yet, for most of us, it takes a massive effort, or a pilgrimage to a new country, or conditions of great beauty, or the experience of suffering to unlock the door and gain access to the guiding voices within. They are here, and they are so close. Right here. Right now.

When we write, or paint, or photograph, or approach any activity with a serious intent, we invite a pathway for these inner voices to emerge. Our creative work encourages the appearance of these moments of gemlike insight. We are stretched, pushed against our boundaries, and asked to transcend our perceived limitations. We know, from some inner measure, that the strength and elegance of expression that we visualize, that we intuit is possible, must come from a deeper, true place. We gently but relentlessly search within for an authentic rebirth of wonder.

We long to return home, to come closer to our real Selves, to recognize our original face, and to open into the depth consciousness that exists, at least in potential, in every human being. Contemporary psychology likens the mind to an iceberg; only a very small part of it lies above the surface. The world's wisdom traditions, each in their own way, offer means of penetrating the Great Chain of Being, going deeper into the successive, nested levels from the sensory to the divine. Yet our conditioning and education pay scant attention to the underlying sources beyond the conscious mind, even with the combined wisdom of the ages at our disposal. I find it sorrowful that so many people, myself included, live where we do: within our small selves, within our self-enclosed concerns, within our limited intellects, which are not even our real minds, and within our reactive emotions, which are not equivalent to real feeling. When we look within and face our own contradictions, and witness the effects our actions have on others, we eventually come to the inescapable conclusion that the world needs more from us than our mundane selves.

In the search for creativity and awareness, we know that the conditions of modern life do not readily support our efforts toward a deepening contact with the subtle, deeper realms. Western society is far from subtle. Media, advertising, entertainment, even much contemporary art and literature, certainly our educational system, our political system and national leaders, much of our collective interaction with each other, all primarily address our superficial, social selves—the tightly held images we have of ourselves—and our consumer desires and material needs. Something in us is crying out for more, in need of real contact, and searching for the guiding voices from within. In the words of the Lakota, we *are* crying for a vision.

The outer world and its conditions can, if approached properly, lead us inward toward our own personal vision quest. We may lament our disassociation with ourselves, and the kind of world our children will inherit. Environmental degradation, overpopulation, violence and terrorism, fear and greed, rear their ugly heads all too often. We may experience adversity and setbacks in our personal lives. However, these conditions can be embraced as an enriching catalyst, creating a hunger for inner change, for transformation and growth of consciousness. In other words, the trigger that helps open us to our inner sources of guidance can be found not only through the subtle work of attention, but it can also be distinctly modern and Western: large, loud, and external.

Awakening can be rude or gentle, through the Zen master's stick or through his patient wisdom and example. Behind the dam of our ignorance lies the everflowing river of knowledge and heightened awareness. Whether we are tempered by suffering or righteous outrage, wounded by the cruel radiance of what is, ignited by the search for truth, awestruck by the world's unfathomable order and transcendent beauty, graced by kindness and compassion, or quietly permeated by the soul's longing for itself, the potential for radical, genuine awakening is everpresent. The growing realization of our own profound depths often encompasses all of these catalytic experiences and more. If we allow it, all of our experiences, no matter how anguishing or astonishing, can penetrate our reluctance and loosen the boundaries that hide us from ourselves. I like the title of Rollo May's book, *The Courage to Create*, for it implies that courage, in bravely facing personal and cultural transformation, is an indispensable feature of the creative act.

As we know, there are many contradictions inherent in the human condition and, by extension, in the creative process. Through creativity we are called to be more, not less, of what we are; to embrace both our angels and our demons; and to arrive at a larger perspective, one that contains many contradictory impulses. F. Scott Fitzgerald once said that the sign of true intelligence is the ability to entertain opposing ideas in the mind simultaneously. If this is true, then perhaps the mark of the truly creative individual is the ability to embrace and integrate what are often opposing forces and influences. Perhaps it is in the reconciliation of opposites that creativity appears.

The practice of art can be approached as a genuine spiritual discipline, directed toward becoming whole and helping us open to the well of inspiration.

Artists are not alone. Much guidance is available through the teachings of the world's great wisdom traditions and through the advice of others farther along the way. Joseph Campbell has remarked repeatedly that any of the world's real teachings and traditional disciplines—if followed diligently—can deliver us to the sources of life with an awakening of consciousness and conscience. The artist's work, at its best, is alchemical, galvanizing the disparate parts of our being around a larger purpose and a broader goal: authentic transformation, personal or collective healing, social activism, or the poignant quest for harmony and beauty, the recognition of the radiant unity of existence. Toward this end, our creative efforts, if they are to be effective, must draw from more of the life around us and moving through us.

Isamu Noguchi, whose commissioned sculptures grace many works of architecture around the world, knew one of the greatest modern teachers of Zen Buddhism, D. T. Suzuki. In an interview, Noguchi was asked whether "art without the support of a spiritual teaching is an adequate means of refining the individual." He responded: "I don't think that art comes from art. A lot of artists apparently think so. I think it comes from the awakening person. Awakening is what you might call the spiritual. It is a linkage to something flowing very rapidly through the air, and I can put my finger on it [*he raises his finger as if to connect with something above him*] and plug in, so to speak. Do artists need a spiritual way or do they need art? You can say that one is the same as the other. Everything tends toward *awakening*, and I would rather use the word *awakening*, than a word derived from some system—because there are many systems."

This "something flowing very rapidly through the air" is always there, surrounding us, permeating us, moving within and around us. It is, as Joseph Campbell suggests, the waters of life. It is we who are not there—not open to it, and not fully present to it, most of the time.

The Crack Between Worlds

Sunrise and sunset. The alternation of rest and activity is a key component of the creative act. Don Juan speaks of the "crack between worlds" available at these special times of transition, when day and night coexist, when a sorcerer's seeing can peer into the subtle realms. The moment in-between. The silence beneath the audible. The experience of living stillness, radiance within phenomena.

Rollo May sees the appearance of sudden illumination as depending on certain practical conditions: "hard work on the topic *prior to the breakthrough . . . a rest*, in which the 'unconscious work' has been given a chance to proceed on its own and after which the breakthrough may occur . . . the necessity of *alternating work and relaxation*, with the insight often coming at the moment of the break between the two, or at least within the break." The essential balance that we must seek, then, is between initiative and receptivity. There is a time for hard and sustained work, and there is a time for letting go, for hanging out, for simply being quiet. While we want to be an active part of the world, and much of the material for our creative work derives from that involvement, there is another need, another order of experience that is absolutely essential for the creative process—time to be alone, time to be with oneself.

How difficult this is. The phone rings incessantly. The computer is turned on to voluminous e-mail from the preceding day. We are plugged in to portable CD players, have cell phones glued to our ears, commune with massive home entertainment systems, and can be paged at a moment's notice. In our homes, our vehicles, our businesses, a city street, even in the quiet of nature—we can be reached anywhere, anytime.

Not only do external stimuli exist in abundance within our lives, but there are a multitude of internal distractions as well. The mind never rests—

we are filled with thoughts and the internal dialogue that reinforces our self-importance and perceived realities. We talk to ourselves and to each other constantly and incessantly. We leave little space. We are addicted to activity and to constant entertainment. Our bodies are rarely still, our activity level is high, and our emotions are often caught up in some inner drama of great import. Drugs and alcohol, even sex, become means of escape—often from ourselves.

In the preceding chapter, we explored the need to let go and cultivate a state of inner quiet. At this stage, if we can stay with it, our attention broadens and deepens to incorporate the resonating visions and voices of the Muses. Between the known and the illuminating moments from the unknown exists a void, a place of nothingness, a region of active waiting—one that is extremely uncomfortable for most of us. Our attention is no longer holding on to the internal dialogue, but nothing has yet emerged to take its place. We sit, facing the abyss, waiting; in touch with the sensations of the body. They are a useful, necessary anchor. To enter the crack between worlds, we must make the great leap into the unknown—like Harrison Ford does as Indiana Jones, when he possesses the map to the cup of eternal life and must go through a series of trials and riddles to reach its sacred location. The final test of faith, the ultimate proof of his commitment, is to step into the chasm where certain death will result if something or someone does not appear to save him. He takes the step, and instantly help appears in the form of a tenuous bridge between the worlds. Of course, he reaches the inner sanctum, the location of the world's presumably greatest treasure.

Creativity requires that we enter the region of risk, not depending on what we know or leaning on our comforting habits or past formulas. Seeking a creative response, we sit quietly in front of ourselves and the task at hand, waiting but not-waiting… taking the risk of just being. Sometimes we experiment and play; sometimes we do nothing. Eventually, something wells up from within, a new impulse, a fresh response that can help and guide us. If we alternate doing with not-doing, activity with rest, insights will come in response to our deepest questions and most perplexing problems. And it does work. All we must do is try.

The Wings of Feeling

In our efforts toward awakening, the heart is both a reliable guide and a medium. Our moments of deeper awareness are carried on the wings of feeling. This is not to be confused with ordinary emotions, which are often mere reactions to the experiences of everyday life; or sentiment, a syrupy, greeting-card form of inauthenticity, or New Age idealism, where a cloying sweetness becomes a way of hiding from the truth. No, we seek real feeling, our true source of hope, faith, and love. A lawful, predictable process ensues as we attempt to contact the inner source of our creative impulses. When the mind and body are in accord, a new quality of feeling arises, one that is lighter, quicker, finer, and brings a subtle taste of joy.

In the Hindu system of kundalini yoga, seven centers, or chakras, run along an invisible channel allied with the spinal column. The three higher chakras, found in the throat and head, are the seat of our deeper potentials and vibrate at a finer frequency than our everyday selves. The three lower chakras, located in the gut region, govern our ordinary functions and serve to gather energy and send it upward. When the kundalini energy reaches the heart chakra, it is transformed and uplifted to a finer rate of vibration. We open to compassion and the wisdom of the heart. With the refined frequency of the heart, the higher centers are attracted and activated. And in this cosmology of growth, the higher chakras are the source of true creativity, intuition, and consciousness.

Through feeling, we unlock our most distinctive human characteristics.

At this level, creativity becomes a catalyst for our potential wholeness. Through the work of the mind and body coming together in the creative act, we attract a quality of feeling that is integral to our inner transformation. From the slow, incremental opening to the movement of energy through the invisible channel of the chakras, we are called toward awakening, to experiencing moments of intuition and consciousness, the guiding lights of our individuality.

And as we begin to discover our true impulses and authentic forms of expression, they may at first seem alien to us. But this is only because we have been exiled from our real self and real voice for so long, that upon its arising, it seems strange and unfamiliar, as if it were not a part of us. Over time, this condition changes, and we begin to feel that something is lacking without the assistance of our deeper nature. We know, by experience, that our work is flat and lifeless when approached only by our superficial selves.

The heart center is the source of our wish. Remember the old adage, "Be careful what you wish for." We feel our lack of a broad awareness, of a subtle, free attention and an open, receptive channel within. This creates a powerful impetus to connect, to awaken, and to reach the sources of life and creativity. What may help awaken the longing of the heart?

The grace of great things.

These words from a Rilke essay refer, I believe, to those impressions that have the capacity to nourish and invoke our deeper nature. The rhythms of the natural world, certain pieces of music, great art and literature, ideas of force and power found in the world's enduring teachings, extraordinary individuals, and the elegant achievements of science, technology, and medicine may all be characterized as "great things."

When I seek solace or inner quiet, I will often go into nature for a walk or a drive. The feeling of the immensity of the earth, sky, ocean, and stars liberates me from the mundane world and my small, preoccupied self. A new vista opens in which I can sense the grand scope and transcendent quality of existence, of which I am only a tiny part. Yet I *am* a part of this miracle and a participant in it. This recognition, when it appears, never fails to change my inner perspective to something more aligned with the truth of what is.

Similarly, contact with certain musical compositions, certain works of art, and certain extraordinary people helps immensely. We all relish the experience of being in contact with a great thing—or an inspiring person—that awakens something in us. One of the functions of art is to enlarge our perspective and deepen our consciousness. Time and time again, I return to specific works of art, books, and musical compositions that inspire me, stimulate my thought, or simply help me open more deeply into myself and enter more fully into the world around me.

What may we absorb by being in the presence of remarkable individuals—or even reading about their lives and experiences? By "remarkable," I mean those individuals of genuine accomplishment, or those who have traveled diligently on the path of awakening, or have successfully overcome great hardship or trauma, or simply those who strive to be in contact with their conscience and integrity. These people can be found in all walks of life. Clearly, we experience an exchange of energy. Something in us is brought to life through their very presence: by being in the same room, hearing their voices, or simply being within their energy field. We experience a resonance between their emanations and a special quality in ourselves. It is another form of awakening, in which we see what is possible for us through our own efforts. We receive their energy, take in something of their presence, and we experience, perhaps only for a moment, an expanded sense of being and consciousness, one that inspires and nourishes our creative spirit.

~

Carl Jung gave his philosophy and insights not as abstract beliefs, but through examples deeply rooted in his own personal experiences and those of his clinical patients. In his autobiography, *Memories, Dreams, Reflections*, he recounts being seized by an overwhelming vision that presented itself during a period of urgent creativity and intense dreamwork. He "saw" a gigantic flood covering all of Europe, except Switzerland whose high mountains provided protection. He "saw" civilization being destroyed and the "drowned bodies of uncounted thousands," while the sea turned to blood. This vision recurred with growing intensity and an inner voice spoke: "Look at it well; it is wholly real and it will be so. You cannot doubt it." Soon after this, World War I broke out and overwhelmed most of Europe.

Jung writes: "Now my task was clear: I had to try to understand what had happened and to what extent my own experience coincided with that of mankind in general. Therefore my first obligation was to probe the depths of my own psyche. . . . This work took precedence over everything else." Through his intensely personal work, Jung discovered and expressed transpersonal truths and collective conditions. His unconscious not only provided the material for his personal growth, but provided a foretaste of the world's future as well. His experiences further confirm my belief that the world needs its artists and creative individuals.

Many have said that intuition, when it makes its appearance, does so not for the individual alone. Carl Jung, Joseph Campbell, and Ken Wilber, among others, have all spoken about the collective good and collective meaning that can come through personal revelation and intuitive knowing; the fact that we are often the vehicle, not just the destination, for insight. Conversely, collective forces can be focused through personal revelation. These are moments of recognition that may have much deeper consequences than their effects on our own personal lives and individual evolution. It is the same with creative work. We all have something to give; we all see certain things more clearly than others. We all do have an indispensable place, a unique role to play, within the whole. And our genuine moments of insight may very well be what is needed here and now, in this time and place, for ourselves and others—and maybe for the world itself.

> *"The alarming fact is that any realization of depth carries a terrible burden: Those who are allowed to see are simultaneously saddled with the obligation to communicate that vision in no uncertain terms: that is the bargain. You were allowed to see the truth under the agreement that you would communicate it to others.... And therefore, if you have seen, you simply must speak out. Speak with compassion, or speak out with angry wisdom, or speak out with skillful means, but speak out you must.*
>
> —Ken Wilber, *One Taste*

As a means of illustrating the enriching potential found in sudden moments of creative insight, I would like to relate something of my own personal experiences. Having a ripple effect, these moments are never isolated experiences, but reverberate over the course of a lifetime, leading to successive insights and unanticipated outcomes.

In the late sixties and early seventies, I was a student at Kent State University in Ohio. For most men of my generation, the Vietnam War was a massively defining influence on our young lives. To think about whether or not we would go to the other side of the world to fight, and maybe die, in a dubious war for the possible freedom of a people we had never heard of was, needless to say, a huge and overwhelming question. We grappled with the practical and moral implications of the question as best we could. I was fortunate not to be called, but many of my friends were. Some did not return. Those that did return were forever changed—the fact is that none of us were ever the same after that ill-fated war.

As a photojournalism major, I photographed many newsworthy events both on and off campus. On May 3, 1970, the escalation of the war and the deployment of U.S. troops to Cambodia prompted a large student demonstration. On the following day, the demonstration heated up. Governor James Rhodes and President Nixon called in the National Guard to maintain the peace. The unarmed demonstrators, mostly young college students, hurled rocks at the guardsmen, who responded with tear gas to quell further violence. Then unbelievably, without much warning, someone gave the order to fire live rifle rounds into the crowd, at the students. Not above their heads, or with warning shots fired in advance: they fired real bullets directly and indiscriminately, taking aim at the large gathering of college students and demonstrators. Four students were killed, and others wounded. Even more incredibly, some of the dead and wounded were not even participating in the demonstration; they were just walking to class.

Prior to the shooting, I unknowingly made a photograph of a young woman who was to lose her life on that day. Her face radiated hope, youthful optimism, and a genuine sense of caring. Her image is indelibly etched into my mind and heart.

From the Vietnam War and the Kent State incident, I learned something about the frailty and the value of human life, and gained a sense of our mortality. And I understood something about the absolute stupidity and ineffectiveness of violence, and saw its effects demonstrated in these events and in the graphic television broadcasts of the war that came nightly into my home. In this context, I had the first of several revelations that were to forever alter the course of my life.

I don't know how or why—I had never before thought of myself as a potential artist—but, in a moment of revelation, I knew with inner certainty and utter conviction that I must become an artist. After Kent State I understood that, for me, social activism or photojournalism that focused on the social order was not the answer. I felt, in a moment, that no amount of demonstrating or reporting the news could truly bring about the fundamental changes our society so clearly needed. Such attempts came from the outside. And even worse, the inherent effect of the demonstrations and the prevailing feelings against those young men that did go to war, often against their own will, was one of polarization. The American people were polarized and there seemed to be no resolution and no healing of the wounds.

What I perceived was a need for change to come instead from the inside out. Some part of me knew and sensed that art had the capacity to nourish and heal people, and could assist in the process of expanding consciousness and awakening conscience. I simply knew this without any real study or preparation, but this knowledge resonated in every fiber of my being.

That very summer, I also sensed—and again the impulse arose from an unknown source with a surprising inner surety—that I *must* meet the photographer Minor White. I soon sought him out and, one summer's day, knocked on his door. He responded positively to my early pictures and to my youthful enthusiasm. We talked for hours, and he introduced me to one of his friends and colleagues, Nicholas Hlobeczy. They became my teachers, introducing me to the expressive possibilities of the photographic medium, and helping me to discover how to use creativity as a means of inner work.

Minor and Nick were accomplished artists and teachers, filled with passion and excitement about their work Most importantly, I saw that both men were striving toward deeper contact with themselves and the world surrounding them. They were attempting to open toward deeper layers of consciousness by working on themselves, such that they emanated an inner presence, a calm, and strength. As I witnessed their creative process, at times I felt something come through them: a teaching, a force that encouraged my own heightened awareness. And I felt some unknown process in me begin to open. It was highly infectious.

I left college and took a job delivering flowers, which allowed me much free time for photography, and began to study and read incessantly—sometimes several books *a day*. Hungering for knowledge and seeking inner growth, I read the writings of Zen teachers, the ideas of Gurdjieff and Ouspensky, contemporary psychology, philosophy, books on art and the spiritual search, traditional sacred texts from the East and West, Carlos Castaneda and other underground classics, poetry—everything under the sun.

I began to make photographs, regularly and passionately, and joined the small, intimate photographic community of the early 1970s. Searching for direction in my life and work, I started a daily practice of sitting quietly—I wouldn't even call it meditation—just sensing my body, watching my feelings, and trying to quiet the ordinary mind. I also began to study my dreams and the guidance they provided as I observed their patterns and contemplated the symbols that arose from my unconscious.

For a year and a half, I worked diligently as a photographer, learning something of the craft, attempting to deepen my responses to the world, and trying to understand what I might have to say. I attended workshops and took photographs of everything that incited my interest, worked daily in my small apartment darkroom, and hung out with other artists and musicians. It was a time of great ferment, filled with the gifts that only come to the young, and heartened by the magical rapid growth and understanding that comes only through our early efforts.

My first one-person show took place in the fall of 1971, at The Photography Place in Philadelphia, a newly opened gallery dedicated to photography. Ansel Adams was their premier exhibit, I was their second, Minor White was the third. I was in good company, and the exhibit actually garnered decent reviews. Definitely heady stuff for a twenty-one-year-old neophyte artist.

After the exhibit, I experienced a creative crisis. I felt spent. I felt I had expressed everything I could and there was nothing left to say. Though only twenty-one years old, I actually felt that I had exhausted my resources as a photographer, that I couldn't do it anymore. I no longer felt the burning impulse. So, I spent time thinking and reading, walking and driving around, working, and generally being depressed. And I relished my misery. It was a full-time job. As might be expected, and serving to further my pain, my girl-friend and I separated as well. I can see the humor in this now, but there was nothing funny about it then. I wallowed in this self-inflicted drama, without the understanding that incubation was a necessary stage in the creative process.

My one saving grace was that I continued my daily practice of sitting and gathering energy. Over time, this inner work gradually deepened.

One afternoon, several months later, I was resting on my couch, sensing my body, and observing the dream images arising from my relaxed state of near-sleep. Suddenly, a series of lucid visions, absolutely complete pictures, arose in my mind like a movie in living color, accompanied by an inner voice, which spoke with a force that physically reverberated in my head. I "saw" images, clear symbolic mirrors of my state of being, and was given deep insight into my present and future life.

This type of experience happened repeatedly over the next few months, usually as I sat quietly, or before going to sleep. Clear visions and distinct voices forcefully entered my consciousness, following a definite pro-gression of energy, arising from my sex center, into my navel, up my spine, and into the crown of my head. My entire life became motivated, driven by an inner necessity, captured by this compelling "daimon" of creativity, as Carl Jung would put it. I had no choice but to respond and follow its dictates.

I recorded these sometimes mysterious revelations and insights in a notebook. My daimon told me everything about my life, urging me into new creative directions and new relationships. Nothing was off-limits to this source of knowledge. It guided me cleanly and directly to a new body of photographic work and a new way of seeing.

The experience was always the same, beginning with the sensation of energy moving through my body, touching the different centers, and resulting in an increased sense of openness and transparency. My only real effort was to stay in touch with these organic energies in my body and to suspend my thoughts—not to discard them, but simply not to give them my attention, and to enter the void of not-thinking instead. Another consistent feature was the quality of feeling available in these moments. When the sensations in my body would reach the heart region, I would experience a subtle taste of radiant joy, an all-encompassing love. For moments, I was wholly present. I felt a greater sense of acceptance and forbearance toward myself and those around me. And I often observed that this higher quality of feeling seemed somehow to be the entryway to this new world of resonating insight.

It was as if an inner teacher or guide was present and available to me at those times. But I sensed that it did not come from outside myself. It was something in me that could be called forth through this type of inner work. Many things became known to me then that altered—and have continued to alter—the course of my life and work. Some of the images were highly symbolic and beyond my youthful understanding, and I have continued to draw from them as their meaning has become clear. Moving to the islands of

Hawai'i was partially the result of these insights from some twenty-five years ago, as was some of the material in these essays.

Carl Jung writes: "The man . . . driven by his daimon . . . truly enters the 'untrodden, untreadable regions,' where there are no charted ways . . . no precepts to guide him . . ." These powerful moments of insight, each leading to the next, have shaped the person that I've become, and it would be impossible for me to discuss the stages of creativity without both taking them into account *and* depending upon their continued appearance. Indeed, I could not have shaped this book without these inspired moments from my unconscious.

This experience felt like a youthful gift—in which one is shown the way, surely and unequivocally, then must do the work to gain entrance to new levels of being and understanding. These glimpses of truth created a hunger for transformation that might allow me someday to reach the source of this clear spring of wholeness and revelation. To this day, contact with my daimon of interior awareness remains within my reach—so close, yet so far—when I attempt to connect with the deeper sources of my being by staying on the razor's edge, the sensitive balance between effort and allowing.

> *Inspiration is a moment of contact with another reality, the moment when every-thing at once falls into its proper place, when as it were, the entire structure appears, and every part is seen to be related to the whole. So we cannot deny it exists, nor can we remain indifferent to the experience of this momentary, magi-cal change in our insight. Having had the taste of this other reality (for surely it is not our everyday fare), we yet wait passively for its unpredictable reappearance. We also know that without it we are cut off from the source of our true nourish-ment, and everything we make is empty, without life, belongs to no organic whole.*
>
> —Ilonka Karasz, *Design Forecast*, Vol. I

Questions

Observe. What obstructs the clear stream of your mind's awareness? What fills you? What kinds of automatic thoughts, emotions, and impulses impede your potential emptiness, your receptivity to moments of illumination? When spontaneous insights have occurred, what encouraged them to arise? Look and examine. What kind of activities were you engaged in? Very often, simple activities that engage the body and leave the mind free help open us to these moments of insight.

• Review. What nourishes you? What kinds of impressions awaken thought and open you to the deeper contents of your mind? Books? What kind? Films? What genre? Poetry, art, music, nature, ideas, wisdom teachings, and people—what in your life has the capacity to nourish and invoke your deeper nature? Conversely, what impedes your wakefulness? What kind of impressions are difficult for you, are poisonous, cause indigestion, or stimulate your fragmentation and lack of inner presence?

Tools and Exercises

Keep a journal. Record your dreams immediately upon awakening. The very exercise of writing them down will help you to remember their mysterious content. Be a scribe. Do not comment or embellish; simply record. Over time, certain patterns, scenes, and symbols will appear and reappear—and likely change and evolve. Observe the content, people, and events that emerge. Use your associations and experiences as a means of interpreting the hidden meaning of their symbolic language. It is your unconscious that has generated the messages; the keys to understanding your dreams lie within yourself.

Not all dreams are equal. Many are simply the mind digesting and integrating daily experiences. Others, often characterized by their vividness, can be carriers of important messages that have the potential to inform and guide us, help others, or make possible creative discoveries. My dreams, for example, have assisted in defining the content of these pages. Our dreams, waking visions, and moments of intuitive insight represent the language of our depth-consciousness—a language present in each of us, but all too often an unfamiliar, alien tongue. I believe that the potential for these moments of illumination is *always* present. Are we listening?

• Use your journal as a means of listening to yourself. Write. See what emerges. You may be surprised at what comes from the intersection of pen with paper. Write about anything you feel moved to express. I often use a similar technique while teaching visual art by walking up to a student's work on the wall without any advance idea of how I will respond. The exercise of simply experiencing the work, then opening my mouth to speak and observing what comes out, has been highly instructive and, at times, the source of personal revelation. Take the challenge of not-knowing. Take the challenge of listening to your thoughts, your feelings, and your body. Let your writing flow. Do not edit. Do not judge. Do not even worry about making sense. Words and insights may form from deep within and inform, delight, startle and astonish you.

Try the same with painting, drawing, photography, music, or dance. Notice if your creative work helps your unconscious material to emerge.

• Keep an idea notebook—not a journal, but a sketchbook to note your ideas, fragments of insights, stray observations, unformed impressions, and incomplete realizations. Let it evolve. Themes will emerge. Like building blocks, these fragments may begin to form a meaningful structure and sequence. Thoughts will find their way onto your pages at the oddest times, and may help to inform your ongoing struggle toward clarity. You can use words, visual sketches, musical or mathematical notations, pictures, or whatever form is required by your questions and interests of the moment. By keeping up this effort, you will encourage spontaneous insight; new words, phrases, and concepts may appear with remarkable directness and force. This is a process of distillation, of separating the fine from the coarse. It is true alchemy, and yet another path toward inspiration if approached with initiative, an attitude of questioning, and an open attention to the deeper contents of your mind.

• Give your attention to the outer world with a question in mind. The unconscious "sees" the world of outer events with an integrative, symbolic focus. Those observations, which are deeply felt and make a forceful entry into your inner world, usually mirror some part of yourself. What is being mirrored? Photographers Alfred Stieglitz and Minor White call these moments of recognition, of finding your inner landscape reflected in the outer world, *equivalence*. It is a language of symbol and metaphor, of the mind's ability to think in images, not concepts. For information vital to the creative individual, I recommend Carl Jung's *Man and His Symbols* as a means of connecting with the unconscious contents of your mind and gaining entry to this world of discovery and insight.

• Understand, through your experience, the role of inner silence in allowing your insights to emerge. Suspend the inner dialogue. Simply be—and listen.

Allow words and images to arise. Do not try to interpret them with your ordinary mind. Let them be. Let them act on you. Keep them in sight in the back of your mind. Over time, observe how they relate to your life or your creative work. Be childlike. Learn to think in images and with symbols or metaphors. Remember looking at cloud shapes as a child? Remember the rich content of your imagination when young? What have you lost in growing up? Can you reawaken this essential form of knowing?

6

Discipline and Completion

NAVIGATING THE CURRENTS

A river is formed as water flows in a consistent direction, wearing its pathway into the earth. Fire needs fuel to burn. The raw energy of our passion and the flame of our inspired insights need to be given shape, focused into earthly materials. Winged thoughts may fly free in the mind, but sensitive and skilled use of language provides the articulation of our ideas that allows them to go forth to others.

This is the work of craft, a dedication to the mastery of our medium, a quest for excellence, a living, growing translation of our realizations into physical form, and a disciplined approach to completion and follow-through.

The illuminating moments of understanding that we are privileged to receive require an appropriate form and structure for their expression; conversely, through attention to a sense of form, through careful yet expansive work with the materials of our medium, another fertile avenue presents itself for fresh discoveries to appear. Moments of inspiration have revealed the shape of the piece, the core of our ideas, and the general direction of the still-to-be-finished work. Now we must bring it to completion. We experiment with our materials and shape the work toward the desired end. We refine, revise, and review our efforts. We follow through with discipline and attention, and we take responsibility for our impassioned understanding by giving it structure, striving to cleanly embody our realizations in the work itself. We maintain a sharp inner balance, rigorously intent on fulfilling our objectives yet staying open, allowing for successive insights to appear and help guide the process. We move toward perfecting the work, and yet we accept the inevitable imperfections and the organic shape the work is gradually assuming.

It is important at this stage of the process to embrace the attitude that we will do whatever it takes to complete and manifest our developing work. Whether cooking a meal, writing a book, painting a canvas, or producing a play, we are committed, we have willingly yielded to the current. We have left the shore far behind and have no choice but to continue, in spite of not knowing exactly what challenges still lie ahead.

We feel our way toward completion. Something in us knows; we develop a taste, a subtle ability to sense when we are close to the target of our desired expression. We persistently hone the work, carefully monitoring evolution. The finish line is not yet within view, and we may begin to seriously question our talent, our sanity, and our capacity to sustain the endeavor. Hope and faith, though, appear on the horizon, like guiding stars that illuminate our destination. We balance our efforts with a deep trust in the process. Later, after once having the experience of seeing the entire process through to completion, faith can help prevail at this point. Then, we simply know that by working hard, attending carefully to the work, and maintaining a fresh relationship to each moment, a natural ripening will occur.

Fresh energy and new currents of understanding have infused our efforts through an inward leaning toward the depths of our own consciousness. This creates a momentum that compels us to continue; we feel honored to serve the forces interacting through us that now govern the growing work and its completion. Humility and right action are inseparable at this stage. The accumulated knowledge and skill obtained though the preceding stages can now be employed with clear focus, grace, and detachment. If we remain mired in the ego's persistent desire to dominate the process, the work will suffer—as will we—and it may not thrive to a natural fulfillment. Serving the process, obeying our higher impulses, is anathema to the ego, yet that is the very thing required. Tight determination and forced, self-willed efforts will exhaust us and our resources very quickly. Letting go into the mystery of the unfolding creation will, in its own time, bring the work organically to fruition. Although this is hard work, I agree with Noel Coward's pithy, insightful assertion: "Work is more fun than fun." For me, few areas of life are more satisfying than carefully midwifing, sifting through expressive options, and tirelessly refining my efforts to create objects that reflect the force of my true inner feelings.

Very often, spontaneous discovery offers enough material—just enough—to give our intent and conscious purpose a foothold, a means of proceeding. From this tenuous and fragile condition, we do what it takes to manifest the work with discipline and genuine confidence in our developing skills. When working rightly, our natural enthusiasm for the work and its developing content promotes and fosters the self-discipline necessary for follow-through. While discipline and enthusiastic spontaneity may seem contradictory to the mind, the body innately understands this balance of forces, and can spaciously contain and express them, skillfully dancing with the moment. Our physical energies come into alignment in response to the growing work, attracting the refined discrimination of feeling. We feel our way, staying sensitive and taking care not to over-revise to the point where the work starts to *feel* labored.

Here lies another of the central paradoxes of the creative process. We wish to be spontaneous; we wish to be free and even joyful in our creative expression. Yet, the greatest freedom comes through discipline, a rigorous approach to one's work. Only after learning the mechanics of the craft and fully engaging the process of our work with our bodies, hearts, and minds, can we hope to be truly creative.

Genuine creative freedom is developmental, not regressive—we cannot wholly and naively hearken back to the unmitigated joy of our innocent impulses. Examining the differences between the artwork of children and adults perfectly illustrates this point. Children are marvelously creative and imaginative, approaching their projects with an effusive, innocent, and highly spontaneous energy. However, their work lacks rigor, technical mastery, and conceptual strength. Experienced adults, on the other hand, cultivate critical discernment and a mastery of their medium, learning to appreciate the benefits of sustained effort over the long term. Ideally, when an adult can integrate the spontaneity and unselfconscious expression of the child's mind with the discipline, wisdom, and depth of the adult personality, a true fullness of expression may be achieved.

We seek to balance these opposing yet complementary energies. In Greek mythology, "Eros" and "Logos" represent the two poles of experience, both vital to the creative act. For our purposes, we may view eros as the raw energy of our enthusiasm and passion, and logos as the necessary structure and form, the rigor and discipline required to cleanly embody our insights. We need both. As artists, we stand between and mediate these reciprocal energies through the process of our creative work. As soon as our attention can expand to embrace these opposing, alternating forces—our passionate longing *and* our disciplined intent—we come into a greater alignment, activating our creative energies and attracting a new quality of heightened being.

We dedicate ourselves not only to a quest for excellence and quality in our chosen medium but to a cultivation of those same qualities in ourselves. For this lifelong effort, we seek a "path with heart." We need the motivating force and participation of what I call our "feeling nature." This is our emotional center, combining the breaking crest of the emotions with the wisdom of the heart, the gateway to higher centers. Without it, our work becomes drudgery and we may find it difficult to continue and complete the process.

A deep appreciation for the materials of one's craft is a real source of help in this regard. When we choose an activity that we thoroughly enjoy, that fits our temperament and capabilities, the entire process comes to life. It is the love of doing what we do that helps us continue through the difficult stages. When we are blocked, or facing the inevitable obstacles, we can fall back on the sheer joy of our craft. For example, I love the alternating cycle of photography. It gets me out into the world, exploring many things and places, followed by darkroom time that allows for solitude and the gestation of images into their mature expressive strength.

The root meaning of the word amateur is "lover." A true amateur participates in an activity for the sheer love of doing it. And this impulse shows in the completed works. As artists, we hope either to keep alive or to rekindle the fundamental passion that first led us to our chosen activity. We approach our medium with enthusiasm and care. Staying relaxed, being in the moment, is seminal work at this stage. Similar to an athlete stretching or shaking out their muscles before a race, we loosen up. To give in to the tension and pressure of the final stretch of the process, or to work in a hurried, urgent manner is deadening and counterproductive.

Although attention to craft is important at all stages of the process, it is at this point that we are moved to rigorously meet its demands. After the moments of clarity that reveal our work's true direction, after we discover what we have to say, then we are naturally and urgently motivated to learn the deeper requirements and the more subtle tools of our medium, so that we may express our concerns with grace, elegance, and the full force of our conviction. Up to this point, we have been learning techniques, now we begin to employ these tools toward our desired expression. At once, we work, play, struggle, and take delight in learning.

Dedication to mastery, of ourselves and our materials, is the aim of this stage. We kindle an authority with the language inherent in our medium—in paint, stone, sunlight and silver, graphite, clay, words on paper, film and video, musical instruments, or even found objects—and we try to develop solid working habits that can be depended on to complete our work and see us through our uninspired moments. We seek to hone our craft and to refine our skills.

It is much like gardening. In the preceding stages, we have nourished the soil and prepared the ground. We have planted seeds. We have watered, weeded, and cared for the growing plants and flowers. Our role has been that of midwifing, of seeing the growth through to ripeness, ready for completion. We cannot force organic growth, nor can we hasten or prevent it. However, now, a more precise, exacting effort is needed to reap a full harvest. Each developing plant, each fruit, each vegetable has its own individual requirements that must be identified and attended to, perhaps by trimming, spraying, fertilizing, or tying. The fruits of our labors will be directly commensurate with the attention and care we give the garden—they will be a natural by-product of the process.

How do we achieve mastery of what writer Katherine Mansfield called the "terrific hard gardening" that this stage requires? Our passionate involvement has carried us this far. Our work and projects have grown in the womb of our being. Now, the work of manifestation, the labor of birth begins.

The work is no longer just an extension of our being; it is a thing unto itself. A different kind of seeing is called for: less filtered and subjective, more objective and impartial. Up to this point, our tendency has been to focus on only that portion of the work at hand at a given moment. Now, we need to look at the work as a whole, as a nearly completed piece. Seeking a global vision, we look at the entire scope of the project in a single glance, with less of an attention to the parts. This is the time for revision and review, to see and feel with clarity what the work needs; not only to finish it, but to make certain that it communicates what we intend. What holes need to be filled? What is unclear? What areas are lacking in energy and elegance? In rewriting the essays for this book, for example, I am overwhelmed at the amount of material and the complexity of the task. How to organize my thoughts? How to express these concepts cleanly and directly, without unnecessary words? How to introduce the theme to readers in a cohesive and step-by-step manner, even though the topic defies logic and linear thinking?

Artists have devised many methods for applying the discipline necessary for vigorously proceeding toward completion. Perhaps the most significant source of help and assistance is that of external demand, when our backs are against the wall. We need to complete the project within a certain time frame, due to an exhibit, a publication deadline, or the ending of a class semester. Having a structure, a means of organizing one's time, makes a definite difference. Very often, when I am close to the finish line, and need that extra spurt of energy to finish a project, I will create an external deadline by scheduling an exhibition or promising a manuscript to my agent by a certain date. Since there is an organic process in working through a creative project, however, this doesn't always work. The muse does not necessarily visit upon demand, but this strategy certainly helps, and more often than not, does provide the necessary impetus to move forward with courage and conviction.

We also need perspective. This is a moment of reckoning in which we cultivate detachment and an enlarged view to impartially perceive what the work needs. Two sources of help are crucial at this stage: time away from the work and a trusted audience. When we need to pare down the material and uncover the essential components, time and distance are the best editors. We are often too close to the work to perceive its essential nature. We lack an objective, critical attitude. If someone criticizes our efforts, it is natural to take it personally. We see the work as an extension of ourself, rather than a thing apart, with its own life and its own requirements. When we can begin to view the work itself with a critical distance and a measure of objectivity, a new sense of clarity will emerge to help us understand how to revise and complete it.

It is precisely at this point that other people can be enormously helpful. There are times within the scope of a project when we need to keep our work close to the chest, when criticism that comes too early may be harmful to the process of gestation. Our relationship to the developing work may be too fragile to withstand the opinions of others. Insensitive and ill-considered responses might give rise to many doubts: of our intent, of our ability, or of the worth of the work itself. At this later stage, however, feedback is the very thing that will help us the most. Writer Anne Tyler offers wonderful advice: "I keep telling would-be writers to write their rough drafts as if no one else will ever see them—but then to read the final draft under the assumption that the pickiest person in the world is about to sit down with it."

So, show your work; gather responses; allow yourself to benefit from numerous hearts and minds. We need the responses of trusted friends, the wise counsel of teachers, and the input of trained eyes or ears. Through their perceptions, we can see more clearly what our work is communicating, whether our intent is carried through to an audience, or if we are viewing the work from an overly subjective and limited point of view. We should not fear exposing the work to others at this point. After all, close friends will be far more sympathetic than the marketplace. This is a time of testing our wings, seeing what is needed, and not being afraid to hear the truth. My experience has been that in spite of people's subjectivity, a pattern of similar responses will emerge when we show the work to enough people, and to the right people. And those comments from others often mirror what we already know about the work—its strengths and weaknesses—but may not want to admit. It seems to be part of human nature to want our own perceptions to be affirmed by others. It helps us see the truth, the reality of the evolving work, and it helps us continue with clarity and confidence.

Listen to others. Let everyone be your teacher. Even the most mundane responses might help. What is insignificant to you may not be to others. I have often received unexpected moments of understanding when particular elements of my work resonated with others in unanticipated ways.

Sometimes, paying attention to a simple and seemingly minor detail can bring the entire work to life. The addition or deletion of a word or paragraph, the subtle change of a color, or a slight shift of phrasing in a song may suddenly bring coherence to the piece, creating the sought-after elegance or clarity. Or a creative reorganization of the existing material may be all that is needed for our expression to soar above ordinary reality and reveal the evocative quality and mystery we desire.

The process of revision must also be a creative act. Nothing is more deadening than going into a final printing in the darkroom, or a book revision, or a dress rehearsal for a play or dance, believing that the creative work is already done. Ideally, the freshness of response is carried through the entire process. The mark of a great artist is the ability to edit and refine one's work, and the capacity to maintain excitement and interest in all stages of the process, bringing spontaneous, creative energy to bear during even the most mundane or mechanical phases.

No matter how inspired our insights, unless manifested in the physical world our ideas remain intangible, invisible. Our work must exist in physical form if it is to communicate with others and evoke what we intend. In addition to the overt content of our work, our experience, our attitudes, and our energy are infused into the plastic elements that constitute our expression, and are transferred directly to the viewer. We can, over time, examine this energetic form of communication, and take more responsibility for what is being evoked in the viewer by the inner qualities and attitudes that underlie our works. All art—indeed, all expression—contains a balance between the intent of the artist and the reception of meaning by the viewer. Art may not always be about making objects (witness performance art, theatre, dance, and so on), but it cannot be divorced from some form of physical expression.

Photographer Edward Weston writes in his *Daybooks*, with characteristic zeal and immodesty about his own experience of the realization, into concrete form, of the "flame of recognition," his definition of a moment of spontaneous insight and creative response:

The flame started first by amazement over subject matter, that flame which only a great artist can have—not the emotional pleasure of the layman—but the intuitive understanding and recognition relating obvious reality to the esoteric, must then be confined to a form *within which it can burn with a focussed intensity: otherwise, it flares, smokes and is lost like in an open bonfire.*

In its simplest form, art represents the use of our true talents and gifts, realized in material form. The idea of craft, of working means, has lost currency in our times, especially within the contemporary art community. We tend to equate craft with preciousness, or decorativeness, and an outdated mode of thinking and working. I would wish to return the idea of craft, and the implications of its primary message of transformation and exchange of energies between the artist and their materials, to its rightful place alongside the conceptual and feeling elements in a work of art.

∾

One of the most beautiful book titles that has ever crossed my path is Jean Giono's *The Joy of Man's Desiring*. Say these words out loud. Feel their clarity as they roll off your tongue, feel their sheer poetry, their resonant meaning, and what they evoke. The sharp poignancy of our passion and longing. The beauty of human striving. The impeccable ardor of knowing what we truly want, what we aim for, arising from deep within. The force of our wish.

Artists must carry their vision, allow it to swell and expand, let it rise from within, seed their materials, and nurture the growing results of their endeavors, their desiring. Works of art are born, not made. They grow from the living moment. We embrace the fullness of the process by deepening our relationship to the materials at hand as we keep alive our longing. We ask the materials to conform, and shape them according to our intent and desires. They respond with ease or resistance, at different times, depending on the relationship between our wishes and their inherent nature, their possibilities and limitations. We also listen to the materials. Where do they want to go, where do they want to take us? Each medium contains its own unique language. Our ideas, our themes can be influenced by the materials themselves and by the process. We listen to ourselves, to our evolving response to the work, and relate to the materials in a constant reciprocal unfolding. It goes on—it is, as we are, in ongoing movement and change. It is life itself.

Craft is a living exchange. We breathe a refined life into the materials of our medium, and the demands presented by the nature of the materials themselves call forth our genuine interest, a sharpened attentiveness to our movements and perceptions, and invite our most sensitized responses of feeling. This process of working with materials provides a means for our own growth and development and asks for our best energies.

The artist in the cluttered working studio, the carpenter in the well-equipped woodshop, the chef in the within-arms-reach-of-everything kitchen, the dancer in a mirrored hall with polished, spacious floors, the writer seated at his or her simple desk, or a writer like myself seated at a digital command module with a scanner, laser printer, full-page monitor, and several computers within easy reach; all these scenarios and many others invite a way of working for each individual that may encourage the muse to appear, invite inspiration and new understanding, and help incur fresh combinations of form and language. This is the work of craft: of paying attention to the materials of our work, the technical demands inherent in the process, and the search for the suitable—the right and true—sense of form to clothe our ideas. Craft, then, is a means and a process.

We should not equate craft solely with the technical requirements of a medium. Technique merely represents the tools, the study of the generating means of our work. Technique alone, without the guiding influence of the mind and heart, is sterile. While it is desirable and undeniably useful to maintain a respect and appreciation for the best tools or elegant solutions, it is important to avoid the common trap of mistaking technical excellence for the soul of creative expression. Picture the virtuoso in any medium, the great performer highly skilled in technical ability but without redeeming substance and true vitality.

Craft must be put into the service of our vision. I relate it to the use of our bodies, minds, and hearts, and extending them through our work with physical materials. It is self-evident: the camera is an extension of the eye, the paintbrush and pen an extension of the hand and arm, the potter's wheel an extension of the centered presence of the human body. And we should not ignore the digital tools that are revolutionizing art and science, commerce and communication. We can apply the same standards to technology. Although I initially resisted computers, as soon as I began to work on the keyboard I noticed that it was a very seductive activity, one that touched something in me I could not quite identify. It felt akin to my temperament and my organic energies. Then, in a moment, the realization came: the computer and the action of the silicon chip, with its billions of instructions per second, *is a metaphor for and an extension of the human nervous system, the human brain.*

It can rightly be said that we are the real medium of our work; we are the instruments of discovery in the creative act. The tools are just that: tools. The manner in which we approach our work is highly revealing and immediately evident to the sensitive viewer; our energies directly transfer into the work itself. When attentively viewing art, listening to music, or eating a meal, we feel a palpable vibration—we sense the care, passion, or attention in a work; or we perceive sloppiness, disregard, or arrogance. We respect the well-made object or well-performed work, and most of us yearn for a high order of integrity and caring from others in our lives. Do we not wish to embody this care, this quality, in ourselves and in our own way of working?

As we seek the perfection of a craft, or of any activity we engage in, we move closer to our own maturation and perfection. It is nothing other than a form of alchemy: to refine and transform materials is to refine and transform oneself. The process of creativity involves, as one of its highest and best purposes, an exchange and transformation of energies between oneself and an object, and addresses the circulation of energies and forces within ourselves. The work is the measure of the man or woman. We see our states of mind and feeling, our limitations and obstacles, and our potentials and gifts reflected in the work, whether we care to admit it or not.

To study a craft is to study ourselves. In desiring fullness of expression, we are, in reality, seeking inner wholeness. Artists seek to embody their concepts and concerns in their work, but know from experience that their state of being at the moment of creation is crucial to the process and is reflected in the final result. Our bodies, minds, and feelings have certain potentials but also have certain limitations and difficulties. We see these elements of ourselves reflected, moment to moment, in the process of creating.

Many artists deeply respect this alchemical process and prepare for visits to the studio with a ritual seriousness. Some prepare by quieting their mind and body, some have regular or highly idiosyncratic habits, and some prefer to structure their lives to allow their studio time to be spontaneous and governed by inner dictates. Some artists work best in the morning, some late at night. It is rumored that Georgia O'Keeffe liked to paint in the nude in her studio at Lake George during the summer. Natalie Goldberg likes to write in noisy cafes. And Frank Lloyd Wright was known to procrastinate on his drawings until hours before his client was scheduled to arrive. Each individual should find the working conditions and rhythms that suit their needs and temperament. Ideally these conditions allow for both poles of the spectrum: optimum discipline and good work habits and, at the same time, free experimentation and play. The ultimate aim is to create inner and outer conditions that allow for a free movement of attention; to transcend the ordinary mind and the reactive emotions. A student of mine, a former engineer, once referred to his own conditioning—which impeded his creativity—as "the subtle and pervasive tyranny of systematized thought."

Can we direct the process and shape our materials well, according to our intent, and stay open to evolving needs of the work itself? What do we want, for the work and for ourselves? The work of craft opens far more questions than it answers.

Photographer Paul Caponigro views the artistic process of creation as a means of "calling forth a higher consciousness. . . . Techniques are essential, but their use is in assisting to liberate an attention that is above the intellect. This attention can be kept alive during the entire process, enabling the photographer to make more pertinent decisions and discoveries . . . The total process involves both shaping of photo emulsions and the shaping of internal attitudes; and the goal is to keep the techniques in the service of that which is beyond the ego."

Isn't the real question posed by the creative process whether we can work toward liberating an attention that is *above* the intellect—a global awareness that embraces thought, feeling, and sensation, and that helps bring us into a deeper relationship with ourselves and the materials? This seems integral to our work. We wish to be present; we wish to call forth our higher nature; and we wish to place the artistic process of creation in the service of that which is *beyond the ego.*

Henri Tracol, journalist, photographer, and sculptor, formerly with the Musee de l'Homme in Paris, speaks about the relationship between self-knowledge and art:

To be precise, I believe the most important thing here is to enter into the experience, to feel that one is the material on which all sorts of relatively independent forces are acting . . .

Something in me is called on: as a human being, I am invited to take part in my own formation. And perhaps it is that which more and more strengthens my interest in self-knowledge through the experience of art—not an intellectual interest but one that is much more profound and comes from a deeper source. . . .

> *How can I be a conscious instrument of the forces which pass through me and define me? How can I be a workman in this work which . . . truly obliges me to try to see what corresponds best with what my real self calls me to be?*
>
> *There is a sentence from Elie Faure which has haunted me since my adolescence, that echoes what I have just tried to say: "The only man who adds to the spiritual wealth of humanity is the one who has the force to become what he is."*

STAYING THE COURSE

In discipline lies our real freedom.

In learning a craft, or in mastering any activity, only when we arrive at a certain degree of accomplishment, a knowledge of the necessary tools, techniques and movements, both inner and outer, can we freely express ourselves. We need to have learned something about the nature of the materials, of how to sensitively guide them and realize their potential, before we can communicate through them. The same dynamic holds true in the expressive use of our bodies. We must learn the necessary movements called forth in an activity; where to apply the vital tension, where to stay relaxed and loose, and what rhythms to employ. The creative process, quite simply, is a metaphor for life itself.

Some materials reveal their secrets quickly, others take a lifetime to master. Isn't this the same with ourselves? Certain paths and interests take only a short journey before we have spent their possibilities. Others can provide years of exploration and discovery. Everything visible in this world has a life span: our selves, our relationships, our interests and passions, our works, and our journeys. What form of creative endeavor can offer the longest, most joyous and challenging journey? Where do we feel compelled, from deep within, to find the force and discipline required for mastery of ourselves and our medium? We know that a durable, long-term interaction with our work, traversing both the peaks and the valleys, is the only reliable way to insure success in our creative efforts.

To maintain a sustained commitment, we need a larger vision, a broader purpose, an ideal—our own guiding light. When we have an abiding aim, one that can be counted on to offer both challenge and nourishment, we are already well on the way. Artists may be deeply committed to societal change or to environmental activism, or be deeply involved in spiritual teachings and traditional forms of knowledge; many are passionately interested in personal psychology and relationships, while others are concerned with healing the wounds of injustice. If our work derives strictly from the ego or our petty selves, the energy will eventually diminish and we will run out of steam. Ego cannot sustain the kind of energy and commitment that we need for our most significant work and contributions. What does it take to give something our best energies and efforts, often for years, without external rewards or public recognition?

Discipline is discipleship: the following of something—a teaching, a personal touchstone, what we aim for, an ideal, a form of approach toward manifesting our visions and insights. It represents a choice that we make, and as such, is a highly intentional activity. Many things are beyond our control, but one source of energy that is readily available to us lies with our psychic nourishment. We are what we eat. We choose what we follow. The first priority, then, for discipline and staying the course is finding something that can serve as a lifelong aim and ignite our interest. Once our deepest interest is activated, we simply will do what it takes to manifest our ideas and concerns. After establishing the foundation of honoring our deepest inclinations, we can then cultivate strategies for developing discipline and good work habits.

First things first. Therefore, what influences do we place ourselves under that can affirm, enrich, and inform our path? What do we allow ourselves to ingest? What do we interact with significantly, what kind of nutrients do we seek—in people, ideas, works of art, entertainment, and in all impressions that we receive? What will give us the energy to continue?

We can be justifiably concerned with our children's welfare when it comes to the quality and content of the media programming that they take in. The extreme violence, unquestioned materialism and greed, and overwhelming superficiality present in much contemporary media cannot under any circumstances be understood as healthy and life-affirming influences. As adults, we presumably understand the value of high-quality educational interactions with the world around us—those that feed us, that invite our highest and best potential, rather than bringing us down to the lowest common denominator. Do we, can we, must we, have the same concerns for ourselves that we do for our children? And what sort of influence do we wish, do we intend our work to have on others? Do we even consider these things? Or are we the cool, distant, artists-swathed-in-black, too jaded and cynical, too pridefully removed—with practiced and studied indifference—to think in such terms? To care in this way—about ourselves, others, and the effect that we have on society—has gone out of fashion, especially in the art school environment, the popular music, film, and entertainment communities, and the gallery or market world of the arts.

What do we follow?

The *I Ching* states: "Every man must have something he follows—something that serves him as a lodestar. He who follows with conviction the beautiful and the good may feel himself strengthened by this saying."

What is our aim, what is it that we search for, that gives us a sense of hope and promise? What is our guiding ideal, which can deepen and inform our efforts, provide us with the commitment and discipline that we need to continue, and offer us the energy and force that we need to approach our lifelong work?

Some of the most significant and powerful artistic projects are labors of love, growing out of a deep, personal commitment on the part of the artist, transcending all other considerations. Two examples spring immediately to mind. The first is *Schindler's List*, Steven Spielberg's film that portrays the courage and sacrifice of Oskar Schindler, a wealthy factory owner who exploited his friendship with the Nazis and risked his own life to save eleven hundred Polish Jews from the gas chambers. Spielberg knew, due to his own ethnic heritage, that he must produce this film—it was an obligation that he felt from the very core of his being. Deferring the project to midcareer, he waited until he had gained the artistic maturity and personal wisdom necessary to proceed. *Schindler's List* ignites outrage and revives an awareness of the most intolerable horror of the twentieth century, especially for the young, who may not have a prior awareness of the terrifying significance of the events depicted.

The second example, powerfully demonstrated in contemporary Hawaiian culture, is the rediscovery of wayfinding, or noninstrument navigation over thousands of miles of open ocean using only the constellations, winds, and ocean currents to guide canoes. Wayfinding and voyaging have become a touchstone, a rallying point for an extraordinarily creative effort undertaken by a small, passionately committed group of native Hawaiians who seek to find the meaning of their past, and to relearn the knowledge of their ancestors. In voyaging, we find a profound metaphor for the accumulated knowledge, discipline, and skill essential to the creative act—and for the beauty inherent in following the creative impulse.

Following much research, a double-hulled Polynesian voyaging canoe—named *Hokule'a* ("star of gladness") after the guiding light residing in the night sky directly above the islands of Hawai'i—was built using traditional design and construction. Spearheaded by a young navigator, Nainoa Thompson, who had apprenticed himself to one of the few elders left in the ancient tradition, in 1976 *Hokule'a* made the first of many voyages to the southern islands using strictly noninstrument navigation. Nainoa Thompson became the first Hawaiian in more than five hundred years to guide a canoe over these traditional routes. His accomplishments helped spark a Hawaiian cultural renaissance, increasing awareness and pride in an ancient seafaring heritage. The star of gladness, *Hokule'a*, came forth as the symbol for a journey home, of rediscovery—of a people's migratory roots, and the nearly forgotten art of Polynesian navigation.

Wayfinding is an esoteric discipline, requiring unusual powers of concentration and memory to know the location of hundreds of stars and constellations in the sky, to know by feel the ocean currents and winds far beyond any land mass, and to sense, to know in some unknown part of yourself, where land is—in what direction, specifically, and exactly. A tiny error of calculation made mid-journey, if you are traveling thousands of miles, will multiply with disastrous results.

While voyaging, you must be mindful, you must stay alert constantly—day and night. In the middle of the ocean there is no such thing as *I don't want to*. You are committed fully and completely. Your life, and that of your crew, depends on your discipline and hard-earned success.

In the creative act, we navigate between the inevitable voices of *yes* and *no*, affirmation and denial, moments of clear sailing and doldrums. Creativity often reminds me of wayfinding, in which we seek to define the most effective strategies, and find the clearest path for our passage through unknown waters. Artists—and navigators—consistently use the word "strategy" to refer to means and methods for cultivating discipline and good work habits. Several such strategies are listed below.

1. *Cultivating a sensitive awareness of one's "body clock" and discovering one's most effective working rhythms* can lead to fruitful work habits that enliven the flow of creativity. Some artists work best in the early morning, leaving the afternoon free for the mundane but enjoyable tasks of the day. Others prefer to work late at night, when the phone has stopped ringing, the children are asleep, and an exquisite sense of quiet prevails. Finding the schedule that best suits your temperament and lifestyle is a central component of fulfilling the creative process.

    Our body types and essential natures contain the keys to our most effective working patterns. When we learn to respect what really works for us, a momentum and force builds in our creative efforts. We simply allow ourselves to be who we are.

2. *The cultivation of discipline depends on the reconciliation of our conflicting impulses.* We must feed the beast: our desires, our cravings, our ego. We give these things the room to have their say; otherwise, they will get in the way and assume a dominant role. For most of us, forced discipline doesn't work. We cannot put an end to our restlessness and our desire to be doing something else. So, we might tell ourselves that if we write for several hours, or work in a concentrated manner in the studio each morning, we'll treat ourselves to lunch, or ice cream, or whatever it is that we desire. My own strategy is to work hard in the morning and allow myself a swim at lunch. I then work hard again for several hours, and with great regularity treat myself to a late-afternoon cappuccino. Whatever suits your individual temperament should be followed, no matter how silly or ludicrous it may seem. We are what we are, and we must acknowledge and tolerate with compassion our idiosyncrasies, and even reward them by giving them room to breathe.

In this respect, creativity can encourage a recognition and deep sense of acceptance of oneself. We may find a new quality of empathy and compassion that we bring to ourselves and our own particular brand of behavior. Real change and transformation will never come through violence—through forcing ourselves, and whipping the "beast" into submission. It is only through slow, patient work governed by taking care of ourselves that we may work toward the discovery and expression of our highest and best nature.

Natalie Goldberg reminds us of these internal battles in *Writing Down the Bones*:

Discipline *has always been a cruel word. I always think of it as beating my lazy part into submission, and that never works. The dictator and the resister continue to fight:*

"I don't want to write."

"You are going to write . . ."

All the while my notebook remains empty. It's another way that ego has to continue to struggle. . . .

If those characters in you want to fight, let them fight. Meanwhile, the sane part of you should quietly get up, go over to your notebook, and begin to write from a deeper, more peaceful place. Unfortunately, those two fighters often come with you to your notebook since they are inside your head . . . So you might have to give them five or ten minutes of voice in your notebook . . . It is amazing that when you give those voices writing space, their complaining quickly gets boring and you get sick of them.

It's just resistance. Ego can be very creative and make up remarkable resistive tactics . . .

> *It is important to have a way worked out to begin your writing . . . Finally, one just has to shut up, sit down, and write. . . . There is a Zen saying: "Talk when you talk, walk when you walk, and die when you die". . .*
>
> *When it is your time to write, write.*

3. *Effective working methods grow directly from the moment.* The sheer enjoyment of the process, a sense of satisfaction, and just plain having fun are important. Make changes in your habits to keep things fresh. Vary your activities when the routine becomes dull and begins to feel like drudgery. Doing what feels good sounds elementary, but is not always something we allow ourselves. I find that when I tire of sitting at my computer and writing, I will often switch to my notebook and go outside, or to a cafe or friend's house, to write. I enjoy nature and I enjoy the energy of people being around, even if only in the background. Other artists I know love the smell and touch of paint and take great pleasure in being in their paint-spattered studio. What is it that we feel? What gives us enjoyment and pleasure? What are our sensations and feelings telling us? What do we feel like writing about, or painting; which part of the garden do we wish to work on *today*? Listen within—search yourself for the answer. It's much like listening to your body to let it tell you what to eat. What does my being wish to engage itself in today? Not in a *self*-indulgent manner—but in a way that acknowledges one's *Self*.

4. *Discipline, in the highest sense of the word, means following a transformative practice.* What is a discipline, or practice—and how does it help? What can serve to bring us back to ourselves, toward our most essential energies and to a state of

inner attentiveness? Krishna teaches Arjuna in the *Bhavagad Gita*: "If you want to be truly free, perform all actions as worship . . . It is better to do your own duty badly, than to perfectly do another's; you are safe from harm when you do what you should be doing." Any activity that suits our inclinations, if we go deep enough, can open us to clarity, insight, and presence. A daily practice, a meditative discipline that we cultivate regularly, is highly transformative. It brings a deepening of attention, a ripening, and an opening to the sources of inward knowing. It develops our intent, nourishes the deeper parts of our nature, and brings an incremental but perceptible change in the nature of our energies over time.

Creative work itself can be a practice, in the truest sense of the word, if approached with discipline and regularity.

Ken Wilber writes in *One Taste*:

We need to be gentle with ourselves, it is true; but we also need to be firm. Treat yourself with real compassion, not idiot compassion, and therefore begin to challenge yourself, engage yourself, push yourself: begin to practice.

5. *Self-knowledge offers the deepest well of energy for disciplined follow-through and responsible completion.* Recognize the worth and importance of what you genuinely have to offer. So many books on art and creativity promote the development of a healthy sense of self-esteem; they are cheerleaders for the "can do" attitude: that we are good enough, that our efforts deserve their place in the sun, and that we should give ourselves the right and the privilege

to be creative. That is all well and good. We all have something to offer, something essential to bring into the world, that only we can give. When we recognize our true mission, our real place in this intricately inter-connected world, an energy for proceeding, for doing what we do, comes literally flooding in to inform and enliven our efforts. This realization goes far beyond the mere development of self-esteem. This source of energy comes from seeing the whole, and perceiving our place in it; it grows from the profound realization that the world might not be the same without the role that we are called to assume. This is not ego, or inflated self-importance, but the recognition of our essential nature and its great potential value to others.

When Paul Gauguin was dying of syphilis, he knew that his life's work was yet unfulfilled—that there was one last, great painting inside of him that demanded expression. He literally dragged himself, on his hands and knees, to the studio. Over several weeks of painful and laborious work, punctuated by much physical suffering, he completed what many consider to be his most important work—the mural set in Polynesia titled: *D'ou Venoms Nous... Que Sommes Nous... Ou Allons Nous?* (Where Do We Come from ... What Are We ... Where Are We Going?) now housed in the Boston Museum of Fine Arts. When I lived in Boston, and felt despon-dent or lacking in energy for my creative efforts, a visit to this painting never failed to put matters back into perspective for me.

~

If we have decided on taking the path of the artist, we have no choice but to fol-low the winding journey. We take the river, not knowing where it will go, or where the smooth stretches are and where the rapids will appear. Sometimes, yes, it is easy; at other times, we may wish to give up and run away. But all the while, we perfect our craft and ourselves in spite of all resistance or roadblocks. And we become the quintessential discoverer of our own New World; the navigator on the voyage of knowing the means of our craft, the shape of our inner energies and movements, the nature of our minds—and maybe even the meaning of no-mind, of a simple, direct, and true way of working.

> *"Do you understand," the Master asked me one day after a particularly good shot, "what I mean by 'It shoots,' 'It hits?'" "I'm afraid I don't understand anything more at all," I answered, "even the simplest things have got in a muddle. Is it 'I' who draws the bow, or is it the bow that draws me into the state of highest tension? Do 'I' hit the goal, or does the goal hit me? Is 'It' spiritual when seen by the eyes of the body, and corporeal when seen by the eyes of the spirit—or both or neither? Bow, arrow, goal and ego, all melt into one another, so that I can no longer separate them. And even the need to separate has gone. For as soon as I take the bow and shoot, everything becomes so clear and straight-forward and so ridiculously simple . . ."*
>
> *"Now at last," the Master broke in, "the bowstring has cut right through you."*
>
> —Eugen Herrigel, *Zen and the Art of Archery*

Bonnie Friedman observes: "To gain the book, one must give up all hope for the book. It is the only way the book can get written." Just do it. Work, word by word, brushstroke by brushstroke, step by step. Ignore the end result. Ignore the voices that say: *I am tired. I want to* _____ (fill in your own stray desire here). I can't really do this. What am I doing anyway? Ignore the ego's insistent assertions: this is good, this is no good. Melt into the process with as much care and attention as you can muster. Friedman continues: "Only then may the book, the real live flawed finite book, slowly, sentence by carnal sentence, appear." Work until "everything becomes so clear and straightforward and ridiculously simple."

A moment comes, usually at an unintended place and from beyond our conscious purpose, when we realize, sense, feel, with acute awareness, that to do more would be to subtract from, not to add to the work. We are stunned. Yet there it is—unmistakably complete; replete with beauty and flaws, but finished.

CREATIVE PRACTICE

Questions

Review. What are your working rhythms? Your body clock? When do you feel the most alert and the most energetic?

What is your particular predilection? Are you disciplined, comfortable with rigor and perseverance? Or are you more comfortable with spontaneity, responding freely to the moment? Which side of the axis must you work to develop, knowing that both qualities are essential to the creative act?

Do you have a guiding star? Something that functions as a larger goal or an abiding aim, that you can commit to, that can see you through your uninspired moments and assist in bringing your creative efforts to a natural completion?

Do you appreciate excellence in your chosen medium? Can you embody the search for it through your craft? Can you extend to meet your potential? Can you resist the cultural peer pressure that views *discipline* and *service* as four-letter words? Can you interrupt the impulse to say "that's good enough," "whatever," or any of the common expressions that encourage mediocrity?

How do you tame the beast, the ego and its insistent desires? Can you leave room for it, encourage its expression, yet not believe in it; find its place but not allow it to dominate?

Tools and Exercises

Develop your discipline. What is it that you really want? Choose an activity in your life that is unfulfilled, incomplete, and representative of your unrealized aims. It may be physical exercise, writing, painting, photography, or a long languishing project such as tending your garden or creating a workspace. You know what it is for you. Do what it takes to begin. Take a class, go to the library and undertake a process of self-education, or enlist the help of friends and colleagues. Make a commitment to the activity, to a regular engagement with it, and to seeing it through.

Once engaged in the activity, make it your lodestar. Make it your daily, or weekly, practice—whatever seems reasonable and necessary for a full involvement. This is your time, your special activity. Let nothing deter you. Yet be fluid and open to how the process may find its own shape and momentum. Bring your inner forces—your deepest attention—to bear on the quality of your involvement. Be present to it and to yourself in equal measure. This is your discipline and your practice. Be confident, yet humble. Allow the process to emerge with your full participation—and with an intensity of involvement. Use whatever strategies you need to see this through. Reward yourself in some way upon completion. Celebrate.

• Discover your true genius. Do you have an activity in which you truly excel, in which you might be considered a "master"? How did this mastery come about? It is likely that you have achieved this distinction through the combination of several conditions: an innate love and inborn capacity, years of practice, and the knowledge derived from an ongoing, intimate relationship with the activity. It is said that in order to do many things well, we must learn to do one thing well, to master it as fully as possible. Use your knowledge of the forces and energies required for the pursuit in which you genuinely excel, to learn something else, perhaps an art or a craft. You will be surprised how much you already know about how to proceed in any activity you set your mind to.

• Experiment. Explore your habits and daily rhythms. Try interrupting or changing your habitual patterns, simply to observe what happens within you. If you like to write in solitude, try writing in a noisy cafe. If you work best in the early morning, try working in the evening. Approach yourself as a question. What really helps you get to work? What conditions do you need, really, to pursue your aims with energy and vitality? You may not yet have discovered the strategies that will help you the most.

7

Responsibility and Release

INTERSECTING CURRENTS: THE ARTIST AND THE COMMUNITY

The work is now finished, but the process is not yet complete. The hard-won discoveries, significant observations, and physical objects resulting from our efforts cannot be for ourselves alone. Society needs our cultivated sensitivity, in the form of our creative works and our understanding. The living forces—cultural, collective, spiritual—that stand ready to be released into the world need us for their expression. Our knowledge, skill, and insights must be passed on—to others, and eventually to future generations—if we wish to assume our place in the ongoing flow of life. This is true of artists in any sphere of activity. Artists and creative individuals of all types reach beyond the natural limits of their bodies and mortality to bring new forms and new realities into existence for the benefit of the evolving culture.

We live in an increasingly interdependent world that compels each of us to take responsibility: for ourselves, each other, and the planet. Holding this larger view in mind, I am struck by the rich wisdom found in a Hawaiian word for which there is no exact equivalent in English. The word *kuleana* expresses "my privilege, my honor, my duty, my responsibility"—my place. In Western thinking, a responsibility or duty is often viewed as an obligation, which is quite opposed to a privilege and an honor. In Hawaiian sensitivity and thought, this concept represents a reconciliation of these opposites into a wholly unified function.

Beyond our individual creative efforts, there is the world with which we interact, which provides the material for our work, and with which we communicate through the results of our creative efforts. We should not ignore the communities of which we are a part and which support our very existence. We are in debt to the society and the people who have informed us, shaped us, given our lives meaning and direction, and provided us with conditions that we must stand *for* or struggle *against*. The model of the artist as solitary hero, living in romantic exile, is long obsolete.

The following paragraphs represent some of my thoughts and questions on the changing role of the artist, and speak to both our individual and collective selves.

There has been much dialogue about the role of visual communication in our culture. It is widely acknowledged that the images that surround and bombard us, and have entered our collective consciousness—through print and electronic media, advertising, the educational system, personal and family archives, and even through the viewing and production of works of art—shape our cultural attitudes in a highly subversive and unconscious manner. There can be no question of the pervasiveness of these images. They affect us, become part of us, and contribute greatly to the formation of our personal and social selves. These cultural representations and stereotypes color our attitudes about ourselves and the world, and influence how we relate to one another. In our roles as image-makers and image-receivers, do we wish to perpetuate and further the prevailing negative biases, brittle self-referential attitudes, and complacency and cynicism found in so many contemporary cultural references?

We must become more *responsible*, and we must become more *conscious*. These are essentially interrelated needs. Indeed, we cannot even consider the former without approaching and striving toward the latter. While we can easily see how our world shapes us and, in some ways, defines who we are, it is much more difficult to see our own contradictions, and to see that we in fact also shape our world. It is our attitudes, our biases, our greed, and our lack of awareness of ourselves, each other, and our environment that we see reflected in the world around us. Our culture is a product of what we ourselves are. Sadly, it is our own creation. If we wish to have a positive impact on others through our creative work, and through all of our activities and relationships, there is one fundamental necessity, the bedrock upon which all else rests: to see and know ourselves, to become more conscious and more aware of our deeper possibilities, as well as of our own contradictions, attitudes, hypocrisies, and inconsistencies. We can only understand the world and its people to the degree that we can understand ourselves.

To begin to see in this way is one of the great, humbling experiences of being human. It can be a source of real anguish, and the beginning of what we might call *productive* suffering, for it brings with it the possibility of real compassion and genuine empathy, toward ourselves and each other, toward our societal conditions, toward our upbringing, and toward the state of the planet.

Only under the light of this increased awareness can we move toward responsibility and caring in our creative efforts. Through the crucible of productive suffering—by beginning to see ourselves as we really are, and by looking at the world and our surroundings soberly, without hope or pity—we can aspire to become artists who may someday, in yet unknown ways, make a difference.

~

I have come to believe that there is a moral imperative to the artistic and educational process—that making and teaching art brings with it a measure of responsibility. The artist has a place, an evolving role to play in the life of the community by helping to shape and understand culture. The arts *do* bring something of real importance to the community: they offer knowledge, insight, beauty, and humor, and provide a means of understanding ourselves with greater clarity. They teach us about peoples of varying backgrounds and help us live together with greater understanding and compassion. They hold a mirror to and challenge the society from which they arise, and offer a means of questioning the world around us. Finally, they hold the potential to provide hope and inspiration in an unsettled world and deeply enrich the lives of people. Anyone who lives as an artist may bestow these gifts. The creative impulse, as we have seen, is available to everyone. Mothers, teachers, students, executives, business owners, and workers of all types can be artists in their own sphere. Through our creative efforts, we can deeply give to each other and the culture at large.

Many traditional societies believe that an artist's work is but a vehicle for the transmission of knowledge, insight, and revelation. The Lascaux cave paintings, the Sistine Chapel, the voices in stone, petroglyphs and pictographs of native cultures, the Japanese pottery traditions, the medieval craft guilds; these and many other examples reveal a purpose, whether earthly or divine, for the creation of art and the making of objects that serve a collective need.

It is not so different today. We ritualize our lives in creative acts, such as the photographic documentation of events, celebrations, and family. Song and music still play an integral role in both our everyday lives and our special moments. Visual design, architecture, and images, both still and moving, are potent forms of personal and cultural communication. And artists still serve to reflect the society back to itself, tending our values, nourishing our aspirations, and expressing our insights into the many levels of physical, psychological, and spiritual realities.

Artists offer their gifts to the world in many ways; the following archetypal roles can shed light on finding our place in society and assuming responsibility for what we impart to others.

1. The Visionary

As Kandinsky observed in *Concerning the Spiritual in Art*, the artist can be likened to a ship, pushing back new layers of experience and insight as the bow cuts through the sea, in advance of the culture at large. Artists, intellectuals, and creative individuals of all types often function as the avant-garde of a society, leading the way toward new understandings and revelations. Artists are typically among those attuned to the more subtle energies, who carry a vision for their world, and who bring an intuitive perception to the awareness of their culture. Artists reveal the culture to itself, release insights necessary for their times, and see more, with greater clarity and with occasional glimpses of prophetic awareness. A world without art could be likened to a world without mirrors: without the capacity to see our own reflection, both metaphorically and literally, and lacking in the subtle foretaste of the future.

2. The Midwife

Artists may function as midwives for what is born through them into the world. Artist have their antennae up and are sensitive to the new dimensions of experience and insight that the culture fundamentally needs. They may act as a conduit for forces to pass through, stemming from a source beyond their knowing. The artist's role as a shamanistic figure, as an intermediary between worlds, holds true in our times as it has throughout the history of human endeavor. Often art produced on this basis has the capacity to truly nourish, teach, and inspire; to touch people to their very core. Some of the most enduring art arises from the culture and its conditions (as Kandinsky reminds us, an artist is the child of his or her times), but the paradox is that it goes beyond the culture into the universal. Many artists, musicians, scientists, and creative individuals speak of their revelatory insights and understandings with great humility, sensing a grace and blessing in the knowledge that their work has contributed something of substance and value to the world.

In his *Daybooks*, Edward Weston observes:

To really blossom, one must feel wanted, loved: must feel a place is open for one's especial capacity—not just any job. One's work must have social significance, be needed,—to be vital. Art for art's sake is a failure: the musician cannot play forever to an empty house. There must be balance—giving and receiving—of equal import whether in sex or art. The creative mind demands an audience, must have one for fulfillment, to give reason for existence. I am not trying to turn the artist into a propagandist, a social reformer, but I say that art must have a living quality which relates it to present needs, or to future hopes,

> *opens new roads for those ready to travel, those who were ripe but needed an awakening shock,—impregnation . . .*
>
> *My work has vitality because I have helped, done my part, in revealing to others the living world about them, showing to them what their own unseeing eyes had missed . . .*
>
> *Most certainly I have not done this consciously,—tried to put a message into my work. But my own desire for identification and its realization has placed me in the van as a pioneer, focussing a universal need.*

3. *The Wounded Healer*

The personal experiences of the artist—the particular nature of their joys or struggles, their unhealed wounds, their search for inner completeness and a more comprehensive relatedness with life, their spiritual strivings, their deeply felt contact with nature and with others, their agonies and ecstasies—all of these become grist for the mill. It could be said that one of the primary roles of the artist is to universalize their personal experiences, to place them in a language and form that communicates these intimate, private stories in a way that is meaningful to others.

Countless times in my own life I have been helped immeasurably by reading literature, viewing works of art, and hearing songs or musical compositions that serve to expand my experience and affirm my own processes of growth and discovery. When we see our joys, our challenges, our strivings, or our suffering reflected in the work of another, we feel a sense of release and a profound kinship with others, an affirmation of our shared humanity. We need each other. None of us can do this alone. We need to exchange and share our discoveries and insights. Regardless of the nature of the activity, whether it is learning a trade, approaching our own psychological evolution, relating with others, engaging the spiritual in ourselves, or simply living a life directly and honestly, we depend upon other seekers and those that have gone before us. In this sense, art represents the potential of a profound healing force, an impetus toward true awakening of our highest and best natures, and a means toward genuine self-knowledge and insight.

4. *The Magician*

We take delight in discovery. The unexpected juxtapositions of form and language, the startling quality of new observations, and the uniquely individual solution found or created can be a shock to our senses, an awakening. *Samvega* is a Sanskrit word that refers to this aesthetic shock of awakening, which we may encounter in a work of art when a heightened sense of being is invoked and nourished. Alexey Brodovitch, art director of *Harper's Bazaar*, who became a functional guide and teacher to such notable photographers as Richard Avedon, Diane Arbus, and Irving Penn, had one primary dictum in sending his protégés off into the field or on assignment: *Astonish me!*

All fresh discoveries engender astonishment, surprise, and an element of aesthetic shock. We are arrested into the present when an elegant, graceful solution surfaces. Most personal or social domains—business meetings, family councils, classroom dialogue, decision-making, the creative arts—can provide the impetus that opens the door to heightened awareness and spontaneous revelation. Above all else, throughout this book, I am promoting an attitude, a way of life; that each and every moment, lived fully, offers a chance for stunning innovation and radical insight.

All knowledge must be perpetually renewed and reinterpreted for each age, each epoch. The language of the past, of other cultures and eras, may contain the seeds of truth, but it becomes increasingly remote unless it directly relates to the experience of our own lives, translated into our generation's tongue, and using art forms relevant to the present.

5. *The Seeker*

Art is an expression of the consciousness of its makers. As they have through the ages, artists continue to occupy the integral roles of seeker, mountain-climber, and high-altitude guide. Artists reach deeply into themselves to find a connectedness to the entire range of human experience. Many seek a relationship with the subtle energies that underlie all phenomena—the sacred dimension of life. And artists strive to express, or actually embody, their understandings and experiences in works of art.

Works of art created through an artist's search for the meaning of life often contain the embodiment of higher states of consciousness. Even though the artist may only temporarily experience these states, their taste is strong and lingering. The hints of profundity and radiance of being that we perceive in certain works—the music of Bach, the poetry of Rumi, the paintings of Van Gogh, and many more examples—are reflections of the artist's direct experience of unity and deeply felt connection to the cosmos.

This form of art stirs something deep within the viewer: the longing for consciousness. It awakens subtle intimations from within, a once-known but forgotten sense of being beyond our mundane selves and preoccupations. These can be deeply nourishing, healing, and uplifting—mirroring our higher natures. Art can reflect the world that our souls fervently ache for—one of inner unity and expanded awareness. In this sense, art reveals what can be, our future and our highest potential, not only what is, in our current condition of fragmentation and disassociation. The universal creative forces that interweave existence and permeate all living things can find subtle expression on our level and be hinted at through works of art.

~

One of the perennial challenges that artists face is the apparent contradiction between the need to work primarily for themselves, and (at the least) to maintain an awareness of their potential audience, or (at best) engage in actual dialogue with them. As with many elements of the creative process, we are called to embrace a larger view that transcends duality-based thinking.

Rainer Maria Rilke writes in *Letters to a Young Poet* about the seeking of confirmation of one's creative work through external means:

> *Now (since you have said you want my advice), I beg you to stop doing that sort of thing. You are looking outside, and that is what you should most avoid right now.... There is only one thing you should do. Go into yourself. Find out the reason that commands you to write; see whether it has spread its roots into the very depths of your heart . . . This most of all: ask yourself in the most silent hour of your night: must I write? Dig into yourself for a deep answer. And if this answer rings out in assent, if you meet this solemn question with a strong, simple "I must," then build your life in accordance with this necessity; your whole life, even into its humblest and most indifferent hour, must become a sign and witness to this impulse.*

Surely this means that we should not approach our creative work with the goal of pleasing others, or for recognition or approval. Rilke's profound and eloquent statement speaks to the need for authenticity; that our efforts must arise from an inner necessity. But does this imply that we must remain aloof from our community, our potential audience, or our peers with whom we share our work? Does this mean that our work does not, or will not, have the capacity to communicate our deepest concerns to others? If our work is to be authentic, it must arise from our deepest impulses; it must come solely from our own initiative. Yet, in some way, it must include an awareness of our audience, those with whom we are impelled to interact.

In reviewing the history of art and culture, we quickly realize that the mature artist and creative individual often becomes a living force for the advancement of culture and the nourishment of others. On the heels of this awareness comes a deep sense of responsibility, and we cannot discuss this responsibility without addressing two arenas of accountability: upholding high ethical standards, and offering high-quality impressions to others. The impressions that we provide through our work can be nourishing or depleting, depending on the work's inherent substance and the nature of our audience.

Sincere artists, when moved to convey their insights to others, continually question and explore whether their work communicates what they intend. They endeavor to learn how their work may nourish, enrich, or challenge their audience. And they ask the question (as I feel we must): Does my work, or the process of making it, exploit another human being, violate deeply held cultural beliefs or *legitimate* community standards (we are not talking about censorship), or provide poisonous impressions (as much contemporary media does)? We must balance personal initiative with responsibility.

Although an advocate of free expression, I was shocked, for example, when I heard of an artist who kills living creatures in a form of performance art. And I was saddened by the antics of a Photoshop artist who manipulated a portrait of O. J. Simpson to make his face look darker and somewhat blurred for the cover of a major news magazine *before* Simpson went to trial. And by hearing of a woman photographer who photographed several other women, pushing them down onto the bed or floor, then bending over them to take a picture in a form of symbolic rape. Censorship aside, it seems to me that these actions violate legitimate community standards and compromise the principles that our freedoms are based on, even if they are within the scope of the law.

We see much self-indulgence and egoistic grasping in the art world today—more than most people care to admit. And isn't this just another form of masturbation, of foisting one's private soap opera on the unsuspecting public? Many artists, regrettably, have distorted their role as society's watchdog, thinking that angst and shock value alone might make a difference or effect societal change, when all they really do is alienate and polarize others. Artists should vigilantly avoid exploiting others merely to advance their own careers. But neither should we betray our authenticity out of false modesty or fear of controversy, if our insights demand that we shout from the heart with angry wisdom or vigorously advance polemic dialogue. Genuine responsibility means seeking the incisive expression of our most relevant and sincere observations, which evolve over years of questioning and working—not the artistic quip of the moment, or the desire to be rich and famous.

Perhaps the day will come, if it hasn't already, when we have a real audience for our work, and our work will be meaningful to our community due to the potential for insight or nourishment that it provides. Seeking relatedness has been, and will always be, one of the primary aims of the artistic impulse. I believe that most artists, as they undergo their creative development, reach a stage in which they feel compelled to extend beyond their strictly personal domains.

John Updike describes his inner state while writing short stories: *The material me, the social me, and the spiritual me are all lined up when I write, with a beauty and directness that obtains in few other areas of my life*. Many artists use their highly personal experiences as the principal motive, the primary basis for their creative expression. Yet, most also sense that their lives have meaning beyond themselves. Without the feeling that our experiences are meaningful to others, that we are speaking on behalf of the human condition, we may not find the energy to transform our impressions and insights into works of art. Though many theorists believe that all experience is relative and culturally determined, certain shared conditions among human beings are indisputable. We all breathe, hunger, sleep, and grow old. We are all mortal. Our need for, and striving toward, relatedness and connection with others seems universal. I believe that we all wish to experience and express love, kindness, and compassion. We all want to find our place, be part of the whole, assume our essential and genuine role, make our unique contribution, and feel some measure of acknowledgment from other members of our society. This shared sense of humanity is beautifully articulated in Walt Whitman's *Song of Myself*:

> *I celebrate myself and sing myself.*
> *And what I assume, you shall assume,*
> *For every atom belonging to me as good belongs to you.*

∾

Some psychologists, including Mihaly Csikszentmihalyi, author of *Creativity: Flow and the Psychology of Discovery and Invention*, assert the controversial belief that creativity must have an object, that it must contribute to one's domain or field and "leave a trace in the cultural matrix." He refers to the subjective illumination that may enhance one's life as *personally creative*, but ultimately limited. Csikszentmihalyi believes that without an interaction with a sociocultural context, the creative act is incomplete. He describes the way in which many innovative contributions arise from a synergy derived from many sources, not only from the mind of an individual, and explains that our environment and culture contribute substantially to the creative act, providing the fertile ground for new understandings and unexpected, elegant solutions.

While I do not wholly subscribe to his view—rather, I believe that subjective illumination is the source of many great discoveries, that what we discover of ourselves is ultimately meaningful to others, and that much great art arises through the grist of the artist's mill—his point is well taken. Csikszentmihalyi's perspective articulates a highly positive trend that I see beginning to gain a foothold in the art world today. The era of the artist as an individual, solitary figure seems to be drawing to a close. A new and emerging paradigm of a sense of community—both regional and global—is rapidly becoming part of our reality. Media and technology can now deliver information simultaneously to all corners of the globe. Some artists are feeling the limitations of their isolation and are seeking a greater connection to their community, neighborhood, or culture. They are looking to establish a new relatedness between their work and their audience, those who will be affected by their efforts.

Despite these widening currents, many artists and educators, and much of the general public still hold tightly to the view that art is principally about self-expression and is a mere enrichment of our lives, rather than an essential component of an evolving society. As a result, many members of our communities do not have access to the arts and unfortunately believe that creative expression is not for them. This attitude is regrettably perpetuated by artists who think of themselves as a special breed, that they alone hold the key, that they somehow guard the entrance to the mysteries of the creative process. Artists have largely not been educated to think about their position in society—or their responsibility to a larger context beyond their own self-directed expression. Suzi Gablik points out: "Students need to think about their work . . . not in isolation, but in relationship with an audience and a larger societal context. The artist's relationship to the public and to an audience has not been addressed in art-school pedagogical situations. . . . The mutual alienation between artists and audience is a matter with serious consequences for society."

We live in troubled times. The long-standing romantic, modernist ideal of the aloof and alienated artist no longer serves as a suitable model for the needs of our society and our planet. This ideal has shifted: first to a model defined by identity politics, whereby the artist views life through the lens of their unique circumstances; and now slowly, ever so slowly, to a recognition of our shared humanity and interdependence. We are all in this together. Alienation and separateness will not help solve the massive problems of the modern world—with the environment at risk, with so many human beings living in conditions of oppression and violence, and with the rampant materialism and greed of Western culture. It seems self-evident that artists must begin to address the conditions of our interconnectedness and help to provide models for healing and positive change in our psychic, physical, and societal existence.

Significant changes must occur in the way that art and creativity are perceived by the general public if they are to regain their rightful places as primary touchstones of our culture and vital components in the educational process. Efforts to invite the general community to participate in the arts should be convincing and encompassing. And if these outreach activities are to be effective, we must all lend our help and support—for the sake of our society's future and the welfare of our children.

Suzi Gablik writes in *The Reenchantment of Art*:

> *Exalted individualism . . . is hardly a creative response to the needs of the*
> *planet at this time, which demand complex and sensitive forms of interaction*
> *and linking. Individualism, freedom and self-expression are the great modernist*
> *buzz words. To highly individualistic artists, trained to think in this way, the idea*
> *that creative activity might be directed toward answering a collective cultural*
> *need rather than a personal desire for self-expression is likely to appear irrele-*
> *vant, or even presumptuous. But I believe there is a new, evolving relationship*
> *between personal creativity and social responsibility, as old modernist patterns*
> *of alienation and confrontation give way to new ones of mutualism and the*
> *development of an active and practical dialogue with the environment.*

As artists, educators, or creative individuals, we must honor, acknowledge, and perpetuate the many cultural and ethnic traditions that enrich and diversify our communities. We have the skills to provide meaningful creative experiences to many members of our communities, including school children and the underserved segments of the population. We can participate in our communities through educational and volunteer activities, sponsoring and participating in artistic projects that benefit our friends and neighbors, and lending our expertise where needed.

We must breathe the world through our art, offering radiant hope and promise, and reflecting life's unity through the smooth mirror of our being. And, of course, we must continue to develop one of our most indispensable roles, that of providing passionate and critical commentary on the ills, injustices, and disparities of our society—and we must learn to do so with compassion and caring.

THE RIVER'S MOUTH: RETURNING TO THE SOURCE

Photographer Minor White likened the process of artistic production to the phases of the moon. In the waxing phase, we are building, creating, forming, and shaping the work toward its completion. The full moon represents the completion phase. And the waning moon symbolizes a new phase of the cycle: the need for release, to cut the umbilical cord and give the work its own life. For some of us, until we send our offspring into the world, we are not ready for a new phase of work. I find it difficult to begin another major project until the previous one is out the door, or somewhere in the finishing stages.

A new cycle presents itself. We must let go. The work may or may not find a large public audience. Maybe its place is in the classroom, or within a small circle of friends—or maybe it truly does belong in the Museum of Modern Art's permanent collection. But without a doubt, it does have a place, and that place is probably not in storage under our beds. Cutting the umbilical cord to our work fulfills the final step in our engagement with the creative process, and *commences* the process for those who will interact creatively with our works.

When your works, founded on inner necessity, are complete, release them. Take responsibility for their passage into the world. Put them out there in whatever manner is possible, reasonable, and realistic. This stage is important in order to move on. We must prepare the ground for new actions and fresh insights.

Through our work and our creative efforts, we participate in the ongoing exchange of energies that is life. We give to others. We receive what we need. The *I Ching* again teaches us the proper attitude toward our work through the metaphor of water: "It flows on and on, and merely fills up all the places through which it flows; it does not shrink from any dangerous spot nor from any plunge, and nothing can make it lose its own essential nature. It remains true to itself under all conditions. . . . Water reaches its goal by flowing continually."

Regrettably, many professional artists and creative individuals focus too much on the external conditions of working, on career moves and the seeking of recognition and confirmation. Will my book get published? Will I be offered an exhibit at a major gallery or museum? Will my performance be well attended and reviewed by the *New York Times*?

Leave it alone. Do the best work you can—from your heart and mind. Intelligently seek appropriate opportunities for your skills and talents, to give of the fruits of your labors. Approach the external web of professional opportunities and their pitfalls with confidence and assurance, and with an attitude of humility and sincerity. Be what you are. Stay true to yourself. Seek the finest and most authentic expression you are capable of, and refine your work continually, until you know from deep within that it is ready, poised to make its offering. Give to your work your best efforts, your intensity, and your caring. Ask the questions: What am I communicating? Where does my work belong? Let the rest take care of itself.

The world often appears uncaring and seemingly hostile to the emerging artist. The commodification of art has resulted in intense pressures and many distractions for sincere artists intent on maintaining the integrity or relevance of their observations. Learn to be an artist of your life. Navigate through the obstacles, white-water rapids, and smoothly flowing currents with grace, skill, and compassion. Do not become discouraged. The work will find an audience—through your own efforts, to be sure. The size and shape of the audience is likely to derive from the content and the quality of the work itself. There is no other way, no quick fix. Like water, everything finds its own level and its own pathway. Grow from there.

Do your work steadily, with discipline, commitment, and passion, in spite of the fears and inner voices that would deter you from your aim. Learn to see yourself and your work as objectively as possible. Do not fool yourself, one way or the other. We are prone to extremes: to believing that we are nothing short of god's gift to the art world, or thinking that our work and efforts are insufficient, not good enough, and not deserving of attention. Find the proper balance, the moderate and true perception. We need the courage to see things as they are, in their beauty and complexity, with a realistic appraisal of ourselves and our efforts; and to seek opportunities accordingly. This is true self-esteem. The root of the word esteem, from the Latin, is "to estimate"—to see clearly, to weigh and evaluate without the veil of illusion or self-deception.

Study, work, look, and listen—in order to find your place. Examining contemporary practitioners, reviewing art history, and studying the peoples and art of different cultures and epochs, is not a shallow academic exercise. It provides essential information that we need in order to locate ourselves in space and time, to know ourselves. Like society itself, we need mirrors and contrasting elements to see ourselves with clarity. If we are only ensconced in our own milieu, we are too close to our own cultural conditioning to see clearly its pervasive influence. We cannot deny that our culture is unique; it is our own creation, born of our time. And no matter how fractured and dysfunctional our civilization has become, it is our background, our field of discovery, the raw material for our work. Picasso, O'Keeffe, or even the Beatles could not have existed centuries ago, anymore than Beethoven or Bach could exist today. As Minor White once said: "Grow gracefully out of the background that has always been, and will always be, yours." In its time, the acorn will grow into an oak tree, above ground, visible to others, exchanging energies with the atmosphere. It stands firm in its place, yet influences all that is around it.

If you achieve a measure of recognition, do not become complacent. One of the greatest dangers of success lies in imitating and repeating ourselves.

When the public desires our work, it is all too easy to fall into a formula, a recipe that has worked in the past. A patent formula is a lifeless thing, useful for assembly lines, but withering and deadening for human beings. To continue to grow artistically, risk taking and innovation must be perpetually renewed. A fresh and spontaneous connection to each moment—a creative response—demands a sacrifice of the known and familiar, a step into the unknown. What is needed is a willingness to explore, to free-play, and to move into new directions reflecting our personal growth and embodying our deepest responses.

If you lack external success, do not become despondent. Stay unattached. Both success and failure are likely to be part of your experience. Both are relative and are learning experiences. Many great artists, scientists, or writers have at times felt like anachronisms, out of place, such that their guiding visions and voices were not heard, seen, or appreciated—often for many years. Be patient. Be true. The world's embrace of your efforts is not entirely up to you, and is not why you do the work (at least, it shouldn't be). Flow like water. Find your own level. We can never quite know how, where, when, or even *if* our work will inspire, nourish, and move others, how it will find its place. There are no assurances or guarantees—as with life itself.

Do not resign yourself to lack of response and marginality. If the Museum of Modern Art does not want your exhibit, or Random House will not publish your book, there are many alternatives spaces and presses that will give a fair and honest consideration of your work. You never know from whence success will come. Make no assumptions. And do not ignore your own community, your peers, your neighbors, classmates, or coworkers. Your world is the place to begin. All else derives from what is nearest. Like a pebble thrown into a pond, the expanding ripples begin from the center, from what is closest, and move outward from there.

Take what you need from life. No more, no less. Both fear and greed are equally dangerous and are prime motivating forces in the modern world. They can and must be overcome and transformed if we wish to become what we are and move sensitively through the paths of life. We must approach life with respect, with care for ourselves and others, and with an attitude of acceptance; not complacency, but a deep recognition of who we are and where we belong. The lifelong quest for self-knowledge is one of the greatest aims we can have. We must learn to see ourselves as impartially as possible and broadly accept what we find. Seeing the truth of what is helps us gracefully proceed. From the search for self and self-knowing, we may find our role, our calling, our place of intersection with the world—the place of our greatest nourishment and greatest contribution.

In our quest for what is real, when we are doing what we need to be doing, synchronicity can function as a measure of our success. When we are getting warm, closer to ourselves and our true estate, our genuine mission, our place where we can make a difference; this is when unexpected gifts, unforeseen opportunities, and surprising assistance arise from chance circumstances. Take a step forward and, in the words of Joseph Campbell, doors will open where you didn't know they existed, where a "thousand unseen helping hands" issue to help and assist the process.

As creative individuals, we depend on these unseen forces and energies, which pass through the world and through us, informing and enlivening our efforts. Release becomes the ultimate creative act. Leaping into the great void, surrendering to a larger order, to the creative process of the world itself, is an act of supreme intent that will reveal to us the true measure of ourselves and our work. For the sake of self-knowledge, and to come into accord with the collective forces that need us for their expression, we take the leap.

Seeing our work amidst its kind—in our writing group, in the marketplace, the classroom, the museum, or the local eatery—brings home who we are and exactly what we have expressed. Finally, we can view our work in a larger context, taste its flavor, sense its particular vibration, listen to the resonance of its sound, smell its subtle scent, and witness its unique texture. To see our work in this fashion is another form of revelation. And here, in viewing our own work and that of others, another form of vigilance is necessary.

If we recognize art as an essential form of communication and transmission, we might take a critical view of such common assertions as "It's all subjective" or "I don't know much about art, but I know what I like." These and similar comments reveal a state of ignorance, prevalent in our culture, about the role and uses of art. How does liking or not liking something have anything to do with our response to the insights contained in a work of art? We cannot dismiss our own or someone else's significant expression based on whether it corresponds to our shallow subjectivity and limited personal experience at a particular stage of our development. How many times have I not "liked" one of my own works, casting it aside, only to discover years later that it played a seminal role in my ongoing life's work!

Rather than reducing the world of art to the common denominator of our particular personality, wouldn't it be more fruitful to use our senses, feelings, minds, and intuitive capacity to uncover what a work is communicating or evoking within us? Can we search our responses for the answer to the question posed by a work of art? After all, some art (even our own) may precede our understanding, and we need to reach out and grow toward that knowing. In other cases, the purpose of a work may be to challenge, to provide disharmony, and to stir things up. Real response or critical commentary should reflect more than idiosyncratic likes and dislikes.

Indulgent subjectivity and reductivism are the great enemies of art, for they trivialize experience, reduce it to a surface level of meaning, and strip it of complexity and life. Instead of reaching up toward an idea or experience that lies beyond our comprehension, we often try to bring it down to our level, to the sound-bite or the readily digestible commodity. We need to rediscover the practice of contemplation, turning something that we don't understand over and over in our minds, living the experience, until eventually, maybe years later, we suddenly have a flash of insight and say, ahah, now I understand! The great Platonic ideal of personal and collaborative inquiry found in the classroom, the art studio, the coffee shop, or the reading group offers a seminal means of gaining perspective.

Sharing our observations, giving of ourselves, and receiving feedback is a necessary part of the artistic process. We value well-considered responses to our completed works. Art is, after all, an exchange of energy and insight. And others also benefit from the opportunity to share in our process and provide input. Now is the time to bask in the light of our accomplishment. Now is the time to acknowledge the whole truth, to witness the consequences of our actions. And now is the time for gathering impressions for future works. Let others speak their mind freely, and listen and learn—with detachment. We never know when the results of our efforts may move, influence, or positively change the lives of our contemporaries, or of future generations. I have occasionally received letters from former students or collectors, years after my last contact with them, conveying gratitude for some form of delayed insight that they received from my words or my work. It helps me to realize the responsibility that we all have toward our work and our contact with others. Everything that we put out into the world, that flows from us, ultimately has some effect.

Confucius states (in reference to a line in the *I Ching*):

The superior man abides in his room. If his words are well spoken, he meets with assent at a distance of more than a thousand miles. How much more then from near by! If. . . his words are not well spoken, he meets with contradiction at a distance of more than a thousand miles. How much more then from near by! Words go forth from one's own person and exert their influence on men. Deeds are born close at hand and become visible far away. Words and deeds are the hinge and bowspring of the superior man. As hinge and bowspring move, they bring honor or disgrace. Through words and deeds the superior man moves heaven and earth. Must one not, then, be cautious?

As in a jigsaw puzzle, we represent a part, an interlocking piece of the whole. We cannot determine our place if we examine only the individual piece. We must step back and observe the whole puzzle, which is life and our world, to see where we fit, where our particular shape can fill a gap, where we are needed, and where the fruits of our work may contribute.

Dag Hammarskjöld, a former Secretary-General of the United Nations, published a journal, a diary chronicling his thoughts and questions, poetry and observations. Entitled *Markings*, it is a remarkably insightful and inspirational gift of a book, in a time when the integrity of many world leaders is so highly suspect. Not so with Hammarskjöld. A man of high ideals and an unmistakably spiritual and artistic orientation toward his place in the world, he writes:

To be nothing in the self-effacement of humility, yet, for the sake of the task, to embody its whole weight and importance in your bearing, as the one who has been called to undertake it. To give to people works, poetry, art, what the self can contribute, and to take, simply and freely, what belongs to it by reason of its identity. . . Towards this, so help me, God.

Questions

Look beyond yourself to find a broader, more inclusive perspective. Ask yourself:

What would the world lack without your presence?

What can you contribute through your creative efforts, viewing your talents without false modesty or inflated self-importance?

Where does your work belong? Can you visualize a "right" place or venue?

What takes place in your heart and mind when you look around at others, at society, at the planet?

If given a magic wand, what would you change about the world?

Where may or does your creative work have an impact?

What are your strengths, as seen through the eyes of others?

What is the objective measure of your skills, talents, and achievements?

Where may or do you make a difference?

Where does your genius reside?

Where do you find hope—and passionate caring?

Tools and Exercises

Most creative activities eventually compel us to attempt some form of exchange with others. Whether cooking a meal, writing a book, painting on canvas, or strumming a guitar, our efforts can be shared and may nourish others. After completing your work, take the risk. Find a public audience for the fruits of your labors. It may be an exhibition in your local coffee house, a performance at a friend's birthday party, or showing your manuscript to a literary agent or editor—whatever it is, just do it. Do not hesitate. Embrace dialogue. Do not be afraid of criticism. More than fifty people read various stages of the manuscript for this book and contributed substantially to the finished product. Through their responses, I was better able to distinguish between my own idiosyncrasies and moments when my efforts were genuinely meaningful to others. These distinctions are crucial to the work and help us to refine our contributions.

• Pay attention to the world around you. See what is needed and where you can use your talents and skills to make a difference. Do not consider how it may benefit you personally. Remember, many great artists were not fully recognized or acknowledged during their lifetime. Some were not even dignified with a life beyond poverty. But each had an abiding vision, an innate belief in the worth of their insights, and understood the need for their efforts to be born into the world. The suffering of Vincent Van Gogh is legendary, yet the vision he brought us is unrivaled and irreplaceable. Despite the shortsightedness of his contemporaries, he persisted, knowing the ultimate worth—beyond price—of his efforts on behalf of humanity. Rainer Maria Rilke endured many difficulties during his lifetime, but emerged as one of the greatest poets of the twentieth century. His work has moved and inspired generations. Can you believe in yourself with this kind of commitment?

What in you calls to be expressed and deserves to be born into this world? Where is the point of balance between personal integrity and collective responsibility that allows you to discover and express your most significant insights, richly giving to others, and at the same time contributing to your own success and enrichment? What is your way of passion and caring, of giving and receiving? What may you give and what may I give, so that we can move toward the future together, taking the journey both as individuals and as one people, one mind?

PART TWO

Wayfinding:

Guiding Principles of the Creative Impulse

Makapu'u Point, Hawai'i. David Ulrich, 1990

8

The First Principle: Creative Courage

We must replace fear and chauvinism, hate, timidity and apathy, which flow in our national spinal column, with courage, sensitivity, perseverance and, I even dare say, "love." And by "love" I mean that condition in the human spirit so profound it encourages us to develop courage. It is said that courage is the most important of all the virtues, because without courage you can't practice any other virtue with consistency.

—Maya Angelou, *Even the Stars Look Lonesome*

With courage, we may realize our potential and touch the greatness of the human spirit. Courage is the trait that allows us to persevere in spite of fear and despair, to transcend our boundaries, and to travel the paths of life, in the words of the *I Ching*, "swiftly, honestly, and valiantly."

Psychologist Rollo May outlines four distinctive kinds of courage. The first three—physical, moral, and social courage—are fundamental to our lives, shaping our growth and development as human beings in a society. The fourth—and the most important for our self-actualization—is creative courage: the capacity to risk what is known or familiar for the sake of discovering innovative solutions and authentic expression. Through creative courage, we may become who we are.

The word courage has the same roots as the French *coeur*, meaning "heart," or the seat of feeling. To be courageous is an act that springs from the heart. Through genuine feeling, we are called to courage, and through courage we are called to create. And through the creative act, we are called toward being and becoming—fulfilling our growth and evolution, supporting the welfare of others, and making a contribution to the world that sustains our very existence. Creative courage begins the journey of discovering our most distinctively human characteristics.

MEETING THE CHALLENGE

To approach our own creativity unreservedly and passionately is an act of courage. We must overcome our resistances, do battle with our fears and self-limiting inner dialogue, and vigorously seek the discomforting clarity of seeing the truth.

What are the key elements of creative courage? How do we overcome the doubt and fear that seem to be everpresent conditions for those seeking authentic expression? How do we find support and encouragement for uncovering the innate capacity for creativity that lies within each of us? There is only one real answer: Just begin. Meet the challenge. Try—in spite of challenging obstacles and contradictory inner voices.

Human suffering is inevitable; it leaves no one untouched. If we can approach our challenges with humility and courage, suffering is a great teacher and often one of the chief motivating forces of the creative impulse. We are here to learn and grow. Creativity evinces the potential of alchemy, to transform adversity and setbacks into wisdom, compassion, and works of art. Can our attitude toward suffering become a practice, a means toward our growth and development? We needn't look any further than the current conditions of our lives to find the raw material for this inner, creative work. As Walt Whitman proclaims: "I exist as I am; that is enough."

As we view life and its conditions with a critical focus, a truth seems to emerge: never are we given difficulties beyond what we can bear. Our capacity is equal to the crosses we carry. Don't we see evidence of this all around us?

In *The Teachings of Don Juan: A Yacqui Way of Knowledge*, Carlos Castaneda recounts an exceedingly beautiful description by don Juan of the steps toward challenging and defeating the four natural enemies of becoming a man of knowledge: fear, clarity, power, and old age. I have read that passage countless times, and found repeated inspiration and truth in its words. (To preserve don Juan's language and particular style of expression, I will retain throughout my summary his use of the pronoun "he" and the word "man" to refer to all individuals who are striving to grow.)

Don Juan describes the first enemy as fear—the mind-numbing fear that prevents a man from moving in the direction of his aims. He is in conflict. He wants to learn, but finds himself venturing into new territory that is strange and unknown, not what he imagined or pictured. What he learns is not as he expected.

Don Juan then explains that the individual will never become a man of knowledge if he runs away and allows fear to put an end to his journey. He will become defeated and unable to proceed. To overcome fear, he must defy it and continue in spite of himself. "He must be fully afraid, and yet he must not stop. That is the rule!" Only then comes the shining moment when fear retreats. The man feels more sure of himself, his intent becomes stronger, and he is able to proceed courageously on the path of learning.

In every instance of challenging his natural enemies, don Juan asserts that a man must defy his fear, his incomplete clarity, and his misdirected power and proceed in spite of these obstacles. He must recognize that he is fully under the spell of his natural enemies and yet must stay on the path.

When Castaneda asks if defeat by any of these enemies is final, don Juan explains that it is only final when a man no longer tries, and abandons himself. If he continues to follow his aim while under the influence of his enemies, he will eventually conquer these obstacles because he has not given up, but has remained persistent and diligent on the path of learning.

Courage is paradoxical. It asks us to risk something; but what do we risk? Not our real selves. We cannot lose what truly belongs to us. Creative courage, then, implies only that we risk our easy answers and comfortable patterns for the sake of discovery. And the true purpose of this risk-taking is to separate the wheat from the chaff in our inner makeup. Within us lies an inner measure, the capacity to discriminate between integrity and falsehood. Through creative risk-taking, we are asked to place in question, to release, that which is merely our automatic or learned characteristics—for the sake of growth and discovering our essential nature. Though we may feel fear, we know from deep within that we must reorder our inner nature and loosen the dominance of our ego and false personality. We are only risking the outer layers of conditioning that serve to hide us from ourselves.

Clearly then, creativity requires courage. Not arrogance, or false bravado, or pretension of any kind, but genuine courage. The kind of courage that risks almost everything we know—in order to grow and expand and become what we are. What are the chief characteristics of this creative courage?

1. *Belief in Oneself*

   We must believe in ourselves, yet which of the many roles in our inner cast of characters can we truly stand behind? The work of uncovering our true voice demands a lead actor or actress, one with purpose and intent, who can galvanize and help direct the supporting players. We allow our different selves their place in the sun; we observe them, know them intimately;

yet we must discriminate and create order within our inner universe. Contrary to the cloying idealism of those who think that everything in us is equal and divinely perfect, we need to be vigilant and discern what is real in us and what constitutes the many tricks of the ego. The gradual cultivation of the Seer brings us closer to our genuine individuality than does our identification with what is seen. The witness resides in the stream of awareness, bathed in the light of the Real.

Belief in oneself is not a personality trait, which some people have and others don't. It lies beneath our differences—and it resides in each one of us. Belief in ourselves is not found where we expect to find it: in an assumed self-confidence, a cheery "can do" demeanor, or through our ego. In fact, a predominance of these traits often masks a deep-seated insecurity and a lack of true self-esteem. The capacity to believe in ourselves is found within our humility, within the search for Self and self-knowledge; it is found through taking off the masks that hide us from ourselves, and through an attitude of acceptance. It is often said of real knowing that it begins with the recognition of our ignorance, with an acknowledgment of how little we really understand about life and ourselves—and proceeds from there. Photographer Alfred Stieglitz proclaims: "To see, means to know that one does not know, yet not to be ignorant. And then to act in the light of one's knowledge." Belief in oneself implies a capacity to be open to discovery, to find the deeper sources of knowing within, and to maintain an unquenchable desire for learning.

Risking external criticism is one of the many courageous acts needed for a full engagement with the creative process. Greater perspective lies within our grasp as soon as we take the step to share and exchange with others. We need to know who we are, and fearful as it may be, the mirrors offered by others help uncover the seeds of our unique range of variation, where we distinguish what is uniquely ours, and what belongs to our shared humanity.

True self-esteem is intelligence, and requires a deep recognition of what we are and what we are not. We cannot do or be everything; we have limits. We are enclosed within bodies, we have specific genetic codes and deep-seated conditioning. We have real talents, unique challenges, and obstacles to overcome. Belief in oneself means, at times, proceeding along the line of least resistance, and when needed, meeting the resistance head-on. But we do so with an attitude of intelligence—knowing where we may find smooth sailing and where we may run into gale-force winds. We measure our energies accordingly, and give ourselves over to the process.

The willingness to try, to extend beyond our boundaries, to meet resistance with an attitude of humility—like the T'ai Chi master warding off blows with a relaxed and loose presence of mind and body—is one of the key requirements of this form of courage.

Belief in oneself does not mean putting oneself in harm's way. Nor does it mean running away from difficult conditions or cowering in fear and anxiety in the face of obstacles. It means understanding that adversity may call forth our best energies and most innovative solutions. It means, as don Juan said, being afraid and proceeding in spite of one's fear. It embraces a deep acceptance of not-knowing, yet knowing that we can learn. It gives the fortitude and resilience to stay with the questions, proceed on the path, and aspire toward becoming a "man of knowledge."

2. *Unbending Intent*

Intent follows our attitude. Intent is a directing, generating force that is the seed of genuine will and differs from the more general state of "having an intention," which can come from any number of places, including the ego. Intent first cultivates, then is furthered through the work of gathering and collecting energy in the seat of our being. True intent constitutes a force that can have an impact on the world and ourselves, allowing us to *genuinely* act. Setting a course, making the vow to grow, discovering our aim and striving toward it, is one of the chief characteristics of creative courage. Many things are beyond our control, but we can try to move forward in spite of obstacles, strive to realize our deepest possibilities and grow beyond our perceived and self-imposed boundaries.

Without intent, without an abiding aim, we are lost at sea, drifting without a course or clear direction. Our gifted moments of knowing are glimmers of a larger purpose that sometimes reveal only the very next steps on the path ahead. Often, when I work with the *I Ching*, regardless of the grand scope of my question, the answers give a clear course for only a fairly short distance or limited span of time. We actually need both: a long-term abiding aim, a road map; and clear seeing of the next bend in the road. In other words, we rely equally on both distant navigation beacons and flashlights. What we want, growing from deep within, constitutes our *wish*, which then shapes our *intent*, which then serves our larger *aim*. Our most awakened moments, which cut through the fog of our ordinary mind with uncommon clarity and directness, *can* be trusted. Only in the spacious environment of these moments, with the lights turned on, can we reliably formulate the guiding aim that we may follow willingly, joyously, and gratefully—with unbending intent.

Once we uncover our aim and uncoil the seat of our intent, we should let nothing deter us. One of the chief characteristics of creative courage is perseverance, following our guiding vision with diligence and focus, learning to take distractions in stride. For me and for most, there are large and small, inner and outer, necessary and stray distractions that can knock us off course in the middle of a day, a week, a project, or a life. Perseverance is a forward trajectory; continually growing and moving in the direction of our aims but allowing for corrections, setbacks, and the shifting tides of our circumstances. Our aim can be like a magnet, drawing to us what we need. In the light of our aim, we may begin to see that many distractions that appear at first glance to make us veer us off course actually provide help, insight, and appropriate challenge when we most need it. The driving impulse of our efforts is not found in a forced self-discipline; rather it is discovered through devotion to our genuine aim, the guiding principle that shades our entire existence.

3. *Opening to the Mystery*
    Placing our trust in a deeper order is a risk. We do not know what will happen or what plans are in store for us within this larger framework. We surrender to the mystery, give in to the unknowable fabric of a divine plan. When we stay with the not-knowing, we experience moments of synchronicity, in which we are given glimpses of an implicit order, and unseen forces lend a helping hand. Courage invites a hint of the miraculous, the magic found through opening to a larger perspective—and not through following our mundane selves or the forceful dictates of our ego.

    True courage aligns us between intent and surrender. The ego can be devious. It wants to be in charge at all costs and will assume a false face of confidence, a brittle self-assuredness. It is blind to real dialogue, to the search for truth, and it does not allow itself to be influenced by the viewpoints of others. It is stubborn and believes strongly in its own opinions, rather than embracing the discomfort of open, unanswered questions that leave the process of discovery intact. In its shallowness, the ego is not capable of penetrating the barriers to the voices of intuition and conscience.

It is closed to the insights that arise from deep within, often hiding to avoid the truth. And it is fragile and afraid, it cannot withstand disagreement with its own hastily formed conclusions. We need creative courage to direct the lamp of awareness, placing the ego in question and opening to the deeper sources of knowing and inspiration within.

Another of the ego's identifying features can be seen in its tendency to react rather than truly respond. A reaction is superficial and partial, automatically arising when our deep-seated habits, ill-formed conclusions, and dearly-held emotional patterns are interrupted. A response, on the other hand, involves a moment of relative wholeness; our entire being is activated in a manner that is fresh and unfamiliar. In a response, our bodies, minds, and feelings play an equal role. Each contains an essential form of knowing, integral to gaining an understanding of what may be in front of us.

Through creative courage, we may humbly stand before the mysterious forces that guide us, opening to the everpresent stream of a greater intelligence. We strive for a larger perspective: to heighten our conscious awareness, to encourage the emergence of conscience, to place our faith and trust in a deeper source, and to believe in the possibility of magic.

4. *Striving to Live Within*

In the contemporary world, it is an act of courage to live "within." We have misplaced key ingredients of the creative process: the ability to inhabit the body, discovering its rich source of sensitivity and intelligence; the capacity to awaken the subtle intimations of our feeling nature, opening to empathy and compassion; and the quest to nourish the mind through the discipline of objectivity and impartiality, seeing things from many angles without the distorting lenses of our judgments and opinions.

Without the capacity to stay focused on ourselves and our tasks through attention and concentration, we cannot be fully creative. Increasingly, it seems that all of life conspires to pull us away from ourselves. Our culture promotes and encourages restless inattentiveness. Everywhere we see the erosion of attention spans: in the media's reliance on the sound bite, the ever-increasing pace of modern life, mounting social and professional demands, and the ever-escalating violence and horror in the movies—designed for our jaded sensibilities so that we may feel *something*. Even our educational system has gone too far in prioritizing the development of self-esteem at the expense of the challenges—and therefore, true joys—of learning.

Without question, attention is in short supply, and seems to be shrinking all the time. Yet it is the very thing that we need for our creative energies to emerge and nourish the human spirit. In the face of these obstacles, paying attention to the world around us and within us requires courage and diligence. We do not always see what we want or hope to see. But seeing the truth of our situation is the first step toward a mastery of it.

Attention turns inward as well as outward to discover the world. Staying focused on the point of intersection between the inner and outer worlds through our senses is the key towards a creative response. All of our responses to the world take place within us. Different energies in our being are vitalized as we take in impressions; like a tuning fork, a creative response arises from within as an impulse that is activated by *receiving* impressions through the *whole of ourselves*. All too often, our attention is automatically attracted outward to the source of the impression, not inward to the slate or to the energy created at the intersection, behind our eyes, in our being. Clearly observing how impressions of the outer world strike us serves to deepen and inform our creative expression. What chords within us are sounded? The inner vibrations of these chords reverberate outward defining our deeds and shaping our works.

5. *Cultivating Compassion*

The courage to create depends upon the awakening of our feeling nature, an opening to the sensitivity of the heart—the discovery of our interrelatedness with life.

One of the true sources of creative courage lies in our capacity for compassion—a deep sense of acceptance of ourselves and others, along with a recognition of shared human experience. Through this form of humility, we are called to address the three primary concerns of the creative act: first, to serve our own growth and evolution; second, to help and assist others on their journey; and third, to contribute to society and the world. Through compassion, we cultivate an empathetic relationship with all three elements simultaneously. Deeply internalizing our response to ourselves, to others, and to the planet, brings us to the threshold of conscience, where we are touched by both the pristine order and the excruciating contradiction of what is. Thus moved, we cannot remain indifferent, and this is often reflected in our creative efforts. When our efforts spring from the heart in this way, we become servants of, and participants in, a greater whole.

The Dalai Lama teaches that the greatest impediment to our awakening is self-centeredness. When we begin to perceive the interconnectedness of life, the unity of all things, we draw strength and inspiration from this larger perspective. We are not in this alone. All human beings share many of the same challenges and possibilities. Both courage and compassion derive from the epiphanal recognition of our profound kinship with each other and with all living things.

One of the key elements of the teachings of the Dalai Lama, for what he calls "this age of degeneration," is the development of a kind heart and an altruistic attitude toward all other human beings. Across the planet, we are witnessing unprecedented conditions of change, many of them not for the common good. Many artists and creative individuals are deeply searching for ways to cultivate and preserve empathy for the world and for others, to renew hope, and to revive passionate caring. They sense the danger to our common humanity if any one of us of runs away in fear or panic, becomes cynical or apathetic, or turns a blind eye to the world. In *For Common Things*, young scholar Jedediah Purdy eloquently argues: "Our liberty means unprecedented power to neglect the questions that tradition addresses, and that responsibility to any commons relies upon . . . Whose well-being is in my hands and in whose hands is mine?" This question redirects into our lives the light of the Buddha's teaching, and the purpose of the bodhisattva's great vow: to help all sentient beings and to assist all others on the path by skillful means. It offers a new perspective for caring, intelligent individuals that remains fully aware of human folly, but encourages us to persevere, to bring our wisdom to others with persistence, detachment, and the unshakable conviction that the world is worth saving. Vowing to find creative solutions to our challenges requires courage, and courage is found when we no longer view ourselves as the center of all things, and open our hearts to the fragile, beautiful world that we inhabit.

The Dalai Lama speaks frequently of courage. The three principal tenets of his teaching—establishing empathy, relinquishing self-centeredness, and cultivating compassion—are acts of common bravery and hold important clues to the creative process.

Establishing empathy means thinking of others as of oneself, standing in others' shoes, and understanding them from the inside out. We use our senses and feelings as instruments of discovery, relinquishing some of the boundaries that separate us from our real selves and from others. The creative act helps us discover the wisdom of empathy. Conversely, empathy is one of the fundamental tools of a creative response. When we plant a garden, we empathize with the soil and the seeds. We care for them, sense their needs, and give them our energy and attention. A photographer maintains an awareness of the integrity of his subject and strives to connect with his evolving internal relationship with what he sees. When a painter applies paint to a canvas, she senses and feels the colors, shapes, light, and surface textures, not only as an individual artist, but as a human being responding to the universal language of vibration and form. When a filmmaker makes a film, he expresses aspects of the human condition; an author who writes a how-to or self-help book uses elements of her own experience as a means of assisting others.

Similarly, relinquishing self-centeredness is an action of caring, of directing attention to others, seeing them as equal to oneself, and seeing oneself as part of a larger whole. It means treating others as we ourselves wish to be treated. In writing the self-help book, the author thinks of the others that she may be helping, and focuses on the value of the information rather than on her ego's desire for success or admiration. The courage to release the grip of self-centeredness is found within our own integrity. Most of us believe in the basic goodness of the human spirit—and believe that we can address the real needs of others by staying true to ourselves and maintaining self-respect. Care for others then arises naturally.

Unfortunately, some of us maintain the stubborn attitude that we cannot serve the needs of others until we ourselves are healed, whole, and realized.

Do you expect full enlightenment, godlike completion, and unending success in *this* lifetime? What about now and tomorrow? To me, this attitude smacks of the self-justifying voices of the ego, desperately seeking its greatest desire: that *I* come first. The truth is that we help others as we help ourselves in an ongoing reciprocal exchange. Whether we care to admit it or not, our growth and well-being often *depend* on our relationships with each other. Not only do we offer service in a multitude of ways, but we stimulate, challenge, share, and assist each other's search for meaning and awakening. Self-centeredness is diametrically opposed to the smooth mirror of genuine being, which takes in all of life and reflects it back, deeply serving ourselves, others, and the planet itself.

I believe that we do not have the right to live removed from the realities of each other or our times. Our vast freedoms come with—are predicated on—responsibility. We live in an intricately, sensitively, and mysteriously connected world. Our words, our actions, our thoughts, our feelings, our inner energies, our attitudes, our hidden motivations, as well as our creative works have a profound, tangible, *and* energetic affect on others. Relinquishing self-centeredness grows from assuming responsibility for what proceeds from our person on all levels, either in a conscious or unconscious, willed or involuntary manner. The creative act, regardless of how it takes shape, is one of service and devotion to the world. We are the world, we are its children, all of us.

Cultivating compassion implies the recognition that we are all in this together. Compassion grows in the climate of empathy and relinquishing of self-centeredness. It arises once we have released our conditioned stance of seeing ourselves as separate from others, and let go of our honored position as the center around which all things revolve. Compassion means having the courage to feel—to acknowledge the life around us, the conditions of others, and the state of the planet. As we awaken to life, we naturally grow in compassion and love. In time, and with maturity, the formerly cherished angst of the artist gives way to a seasoned warrior's acceptance of the universality of suffering and a deep recognition of its tempering effect on us. We can take heart, because on the deepest level we are all one. We face the challenge of being human. And this is the universal subject, the binding force, of all art. Creativity calls us to see and feel the reality of self and others, and to express our insights with caring and compassion. We bring hope and promise to an unsettled world. Through compassion, we learn the lessons of how to deal with adversity and setbacks, viewing these challenges through the lens of the universality of the human condition.

> *The oppression and persecution the Tibetans have suffered and continue to suffer under Chinese rule is one of the greatest human tragedies. But just being negative about the situation is not constructive, and losing heart does not help us solve problems. So in the light of the Buddha's teachings, we should develop courage. . . .*
>
> *Even our enemies give us the best training in patience. When we reflect on these holy instructions, in a way we should feel grateful to the Chinese. If we were still living in the same old system, I very much doubt that the Dalai Lama could have become so closely acquainted with worldly reality. . . .*
>
> *It is quite possible that I could have become narrow-minded, but because of the Chinese threats and humiliations, I have become a real person. . . . There is no mental determination or courage stronger and purer than the awakening mind.*
>
> —His Holiness, the Dalai Lama

9

The Second Principle: Right Place, Right Time

Peace and an hour's time—given these, one creates. Emotional heights are easily attained; peace and time are not.

—Edward Weston, *Daybooks*

In the creative act, when we are in the flow, all the elements of the process synchronize into what we experience as a unique sense of "rightness." We are here, now, occupying the moment with all of ourselves. Our energies are fully engaged. It is a form of magic, a finely-tuned sorcerer's dance between ourselves and our materials. We could not be anywhere else. This moment, this place vibrates with a resonant intensity.

The quality of such moments depends on our focus, dedication, sensibility, and the accumulation of knowledge and skill that we have attained with our medium. Much is up to us, yet we need help. An essential ingredient of creativity is the discovery of suitable, supportive, and sometimes appropriately challenging conditions. This second principle—right place, right time—refers to the need for coordinating our schedule and environment to correspond with the demands of the creative process. And, it refers back to Socrates's great admonition: "Know thyself." Here the creative process branches into many tributaries; we must find the circumstances that we need, our sources of sustenance and support, our own allies and places of power.

The question is: What works for you? What conditions, challenges, and influences do you need, that bring you closer to an intimate relationship with the creative impulse? Certain features of our lifestyles make possible our artistic strivings and serve to awaken our creativity. For example, some people prefer to make their living doing something other than their chosen discipline—something that does not require their full attention and all of their energy. When the time comes to approach their creative efforts, they are free of obligation to others and liberated from the demands of the marketplace. Some artists prefer to work in environments close to the rhythms of the natural world, while others cannot imagine being out of the city, even for a day, when it comes to finding the stimulus for their work. Some prefer to work in complete solitude, others find inspiration through group endeavors, shared questions, and mutual discoveries. Some constantly listen to music, others crave absolute quiet, yet others thrive on the chaos and noise of busy surroundings. And some have highly personal and even superstitious habits to help stimulate the flow.

SUPPORTIVE CONDITIONS

In Chinese philosophy, it is said that the superior man or woman can thrive in hell, while the rest of us need supportive conditions to aid our growth and development. The good fortune to live in a free society, with friends and family, space and time for creative work, and sufficient income to support our efforts can contribute greatly to the creative process.

Suffice to say we must be *intelligent* in our choices; building a life that helps, rather than hinders, our creative development. Finding enough free time, sufficient energy, and the "right" inner attitudes and outer environment is a continual challenge for the daimon of creativity, no matter what form it takes. Besides common sense, what are some of the most important features of a support structure for our artistic efforts?

Many will say to the aspiring or established artist: Get a life! Whether we like it or not, the fine arts are rarely valued as highly as business, law, medicine, and many other mainstream occupations. Further, avocational artists' activities are often labeled as "hobbies" or "arts and crafts" or "leisure pursuits," making them seem somehow less important than "professions" or "careers." For example, I am not a professional artist, in the sense that little of my income is derived directly from my art work, yet my life is devoted to the arts. I have often felt that creative individuals face a *triple* challenge: not only do we need to balance time and attention between our occupations and families, but we must add our creative work to this juggling act. And the unfortunate fact is that not all people understand or value our need to measure and save time, energy, and attention for the part of the day or week when a clear path opens for creative work.

Many artists find a significant difference in attitude among their friends and associates. Some are extremely supportive and helpful. Others are an incredible hindrance, seeming always to take energy away, rather than give it. Julia Cameron, in *The Artist's Way*, calls these types "crazy-makers." There are many reasons for this attitude: envy, lack of understanding of the value and purpose of creative work, a view of art as mere self-indulgence, and finally—most difficult of all—fear. Yes, *fear*. People are often afraid of what they do not understand. They may be afraid that you won't be able to support yourself. Or they may even be afraid that you, someone they love and care about, may do something crazy or harmful: cut off your own ear, negatively influence and set a bad example for the children, become highly promiscuous or alcoholic, or end up in an asylum. It is amazing, in today's enlightened and progressive society, how many negative attitudes about artists remain.

There are two ways to approach this challenge. First, surround yourself with friends and family who are naturally supportive of your interests and aspirations, and who respect your need for sufficient working time. In the case of family, we do not always have the luxury of choice. Education is then important. Show them examples of "successful" and "normal" artists. Introduce them to the merits of creative work, and teach them about the value that the arts have for society. Show them examples of creative endeavors, drawn from their own interests and spheres of activity, that they will find reassuring and helpful. And finally, do your own work with dignity, passion, and commitment. That itself will have a major impact and may turn a non-supporter into an ally.

Time management is difficult for most people, and enlisting the help of those closest to us can help immeasurably. When I need large chunks of working time, I often ask my friends and family to understand that I may not be as available as usual. I request support in the daily details of life and learn to temporarily forget about those tasks that can easily wait a week or two—sometimes even a month or two. Others can help us keep on track by respecting schedules, showing up punctually and not wasting our time, and by encouraging us to stay focused. Moral support, the knowledge and feeling that another human being is there, cheering on our efforts, lending an ear to the inevitable challenges, and sharing the joys, is of enormous benefit.

We should not ignore the value of community as a means of sustaining our creative work. When others support my efforts, I always try to do the same, to repay a kindness with a kindness. Many times I have asked others for help and support, and I feel a strong sense of responsibility to give back, to maintain a reciprocal flow in all of my relationships. Many of my friends also pursue lives in the arts, and the mutual gesture of sharing our creative efforts can be highly nourishing and instructive. While creative work often involves a great deal of solitude, a community of artists who understand and support each other's needs, who stimulate each other, respond to each other's efforts, and give due criticism, can bring about a condition in which "the whole is greater than the sum of its parts." Many great works have been created within this type of community, as found in the guilds of the past, in the present-day university, or even around the bar or cafe table.

An entire book could be written on the subject of how to find space and time for creative work in the midst of our busy lives. Each of us must find our own way, but many artists and creative individuals have discovered similar strategies. First and foremost, it can help immensely to have a dependable and stable rhythm in your daily, weekly, or annual schedule. If your time is fragmented, with a highly variable schedule, you may discover a central tenet of folk wisdom: the work expands to fill the time available. This means there will never be enough free time for the kind of experimentation and play that creative work requires. However, within the context of a stable routine you can usually find or create working time. I know many writers, for example, who write for a couple of hours in the early morning or late evening on a highly consistent basis, before or after their day jobs, and photographers who manage to get much darkroom work done during the cold winter months when going outside is not much fun anyway. One of the reasons that so many artists teach, for example, is because of the school breaks during the holidays and spring, and the legendary summer vacations.

There is truth to the axiom that if you want something done, ask a busy person. Busy people tend to know how to organize their time, get things done efficiently, and always seem to have time available—not only for themselves, but for others as well. For example, I have verified repeatedly that during the summer break of the academic calendar, teaching one or two summer classes actually helps me structure my time more effectively than when I am free of *all* responsibilities.

The tempo of today's world does not easily allow for the luxury of the expansive time we need to work through our ideas and artistic concerns. The work often takes on a life of its own, asking that we honor its requirements and let it flow into its natural momentum. We cannot compress the artistic process into stolen moments or coffee breaks. It is an immense and ongoing challenge to maintain a wide margin in one's life, to form the intent of a daily practice of work, and to keep the rest of the world at bay for long periods of time. We learn to take a decisive stand on limiting our activities, social engagements, and recreational activities during periods of intense work.

Another aspect is at work here that we often ignore. Artistic production does not spring full-blown out of thin air. It takes place in the normal flow of time. This is a deceptively simple but easily forgotten concept. If we can create the special conditions—a personal space, a sanctuary—of place and time, and engage in creative work on a daily or weekly basis, the process will expand and take on its own steam. All we need do is *allow*, not force, the evolving process of creativity and our endeavors will develop on their own; with our ongoing participation, but without the neurotically driven, obsessive quality that characterizes many of our youthful efforts. After all, if we write a page a day, in a year we will have written a book. If we expose several rolls of film a week, or sketch, draw, or paint frequently, a body of work will arise naturally within the flow of time available to us. Whoever said that "all things are manifest in time" articulated an all-important reminder for the creative individual.

Impatience is one of the greatest traps of modern life—and a formidable enemy to the creative process. When making love, reading a novel, watching a film, or creating artwork—if we give our attention to looking for the result, the ending, the climax, we lose sight of what is important. The Zen phrase, "wherever you go, there you are," articulates the all-important reminder to stay in the present where the real, tangible confluence of energies resides, as opposed to the illusionary world of our expectations and desires. A novel is experienced in every line and in each sentence, and paintings are viewed with a distanced perspective of the whole combined with careful regard of each color, line, and shape. The products of all artistic work grow out of the nature of the experience itself—of each moment in their making—and out of the quality of attention that we bring to our activities.

Being in the moment, not one step behind or one step in front of it, is where our efforts must lead—and this sense of timing is important in all creative work. A subtle but undeniable signature is present in objects created with the care of placing one's energy and attention *here*, in this place, this time. A palpable presence is experienced through these works—and invites both the maker and the viewer toward a heightened sense of being.

~

What ways of working invite our best creative efforts and encourage our most memorable, sustaining moments? The effort to be present within ourselves that we have explored in preceding chapters can now emanate outward and extend naturally to our physical environment. The action of returning to the organic energies of the body, again and again, creates a special place within— an inner source for our creative efforts, a sanctuary that is less dominated by the noisy turnings of the mind and the urgency of our daily responsibilities. It is our practice, our daily task, to nourish and support this inner move- ment—and to remind ourselves of what we once knew, but have mostly forgotten, about the fluid, responsive energies of the human body.

Through this repeated action of turning inward, an incremental growth occurs that brings a new level of surety and confidence, grace and simplicity to our efforts. As we have noted, some measure of inner and outer silence is required to undertake the subtle, inner work of connecting with, and staying within, the body. The fragile sensitivity needed for this kind of inner work is easily overwhelmed by the busy demands of our lives, so most of us learn to find or create conditions within our own intimate environment that naturally support us. We need a place, a room, a time, or a studio dedicated to our special work—that we can call our own, or in some way, make our own. In *The Power of Myth*, Joseph Campbell points this out: "This is an absolute necessity for anybody today. You must have a room, or a certain hour or so a day...This is a place where you can simply experience and bring forth what you are and what you might be. This is the place of creative incubation. At first you may find that nothing happens there. But if you have a sacred place and use it, something eventually will happen."

Depending on the nature of one's work, this may simply be a desk, or a corner of a room. For works on a larger scale, such as painting or sculpture, we may need an entire studio dedicated solely to our work. Geographic location and level of income often dictate the practical considerations. Even within small apartments or places where it is necessary to make do, we can creatively design our working environment so that it feels right, so that it invites and encourages our deepest aspirations. I have seen many cramped, tight spaces where innovative solutions had been found to maximize the work area, and give a feeling of sanctuary and of retreat from the mundane. The search for and creation of suitable work spaces is an art in itself, and becomes a deciding factor for many creative individuals in choosing where to live or plant one's roots. When I enter an artist's home, or when others enter mine, the first question is often: "Can I see your darkroom or studio?" I often feel that the way in which we honor places of transformational work is akin to genuflecting at an altar upon entering a place of worship. A vibration lingers in the air. The quality and care of the work we perform there is immediately perceivable.

There is simply no substitute for an orderly and well-planned working environment. The sheer joy of entering a well-lit studio and preparing one's paints or darkroom chemicals, or gathering one's materials in a well-stocked kitchen, with ample work space and everything within easy reach, is an enlivening ritual of commencing work. Having to clear one's desk of bills and household paraphernalia, to transform a frequently used bathroom into a darkroom, or to paint in a bedroom or living room does not always support the flow of the creative process. To be sure, having a space of one's own, to manage as one will and to leave in the condition that one's ongoing work dictates, is not absolutely essential—many great works have been produced in abominable conditions—but it certainly helps to get the juices flowing and to keep us on track. The recent interest in Feng Shui, the Chinese system for ensuring a harmonious and life-affirming flow of energy in one's home or working environment, gives evidence of this need for not only suitable working spaces, but for *energetically* supportive conditions.

We cannot underestimate the energetic factor in the process of creation. While this may be a subtle consideration, many artists have perceptively observed that some people, places, and conditions nourish our being, whereas others deplete it. We can (and should) extend this to all aspects of our lifestyle. Each of us must find our sources of energy and inspiration. Minor White wrote in his retrospective monograph, *Mirrors Messages Manifestations*: ". . . there is food unique to the growth of each of the Twelve Disciples." What life conditions serve our need for gathering energy, generating passion for our work—and for feeding our souls? For example, many people take intensive workshops in their field, not only for the instruction and feedback, but for the opportunity to participate in an environment in which risks are supported, regular response is available, and a creative intensity is generated by the "critical mass" of people working in a similar way.

In an energetic sense, the people we surround ourselves with can be a significant source of assistance and help. What do the people in our life call forth, what is stirred through the interaction, and what is awakened within us? Certain people, by virtue of their accomplishments and level of being, have the capacity to teach and inspire, helping us to transcend our boundaries. And through our efforts, we may similarly nourish others and assist them in approaching their potential.

In our relationships with one another, there are two roads that we can take: we can serve as agents of awakening, inspiring and challenging each other toward a deeper presence and greater creativity, or we can be indulgent of each other's unconscious lack of awareness. In giving feedback, for example, it is not enough merely to be supportive. We must be honest. We must aspire to elevate our responses to the level of a creative act, looking deeply within to discover what is evoked by viewing another's efforts and giving support or due criticism where needed. We can employ our intuitive capacity and synthesize our response to another's work, to know when to uphold, when to challenge, and when to stand back and merely observe. In short, we must be willing to give of ourselves and avoid the routine formula, the easy answer.

Through the intensity and care we bring to our own efforts, we are helping others as well. In our individual efforts, attention breeds attention, and perseverance breeds perseverance. When we are present, working with a focused awareness, we reflect and activate the same quality in others, as they do for us. We serve as reminders of each other's search for wholeness of being. And if we wish to awaken our creativity, we must seek influences and people that challenge us, help us reach toward greater heights of expression, and guide us inward toward deeper layers of experience.

Finally, we often take for granted the importance that society has in our creative development; the privilege and responsibility of liberty, of living in a democratic society in which free expression is allowed, indeed even encouraged. Despite my deep concerns about the inequities and disparities that exist in our society, my perspective has broadened. Through recent contact with Eastern European artists, post–Tiananmen Square Chinese art, and artists of rapidly developing Asian nations, I have come to understand and value the very real freedoms that we enjoy in Western society, and the ease with which we work as artists. I have been deeply impressed by the courage of artists working under extremely adverse conditions (where death or imprisonment was a potential penalty for free expression), and overwhelmed by the tempered intensity of their work.

~

Many artists have commented on the highly nourishing or depleting effect that the atmosphere and feeling of certain places has had on their work. Look at O'Keeffe in New Mexico, Gauguin in the South Seas, and Thoreau at Walden Pond. Not only did these locations help unleash their creativity, but the artists' unique relationship to the places themselves helped shape the content of their work. The experience that we have of the vibrations embedded in the environment has been articulated by many authors. D. H. Lawrence wrote an essay called "Spirit of Place," Carlos Castaneda's tales of don Juan frequently refer to "places of power," and Lucy Lippard, contemporary art critic, recently published a book called *The Lure of the Local*, in which she revives the phrase *genius loci*, the guardian deity of a place.

What is the meaning of sanctuary, of sacred places, in the context of our creative pursuits? Are there certain places where life can be lived more fully, that help us in our work, and that contain a field of energy due to the vibrations of the place itself or the discoveries made there? Most of us will admit to the widely varying effects that different places have on our energy and well-being. Though it may be subtle, and we may not be able to identify the precise nature of our response, an inner shift takes place as we enter the energy field of a building, a landscape, a city, or even a country. On a conscious or unconscious level, we often find solace in external environments that correspond to the unique shape of our inner landscape. Every region we encounter *feels* different to our sensibilities, and we seek locales that energetically suit our temperaments and needs.

There are certain locations on earth, and even within our own spheres of activity, that we recognize as special, and which may be considered sacred by virtue of the resonance emanating from them that hints of a living intelligence. Many of us long for contact with these places that have the capacity to help us return to ourselves. We may be attracted to the locations of our childhood; or to cities where there is an enormous reservoir of human nature and activity, such as New York, London, Benares, and Tokyo; or to places where energy is impregnated in the land itself, regions of power and grace, such as Mount Fuji, Canyon de Chelly, Haleakala of Maui, or the Himalayas. Many such places bless this planet.

Or we may be nourished by the sacred places shaped by master builders, men and women who studied the multifaceted laws of life and gave glory to their gods: Chartres and the Gothic Cathedrals, Machu Picchu, Stonehenge, Angkor Wat, the Mayan temples, the Taj Mahal, and other enduring expressions of human endeavor. These places provide sanctuary and renewal. They remind us of the fortitude and unquenchable desire of the human spirit—for relationship with the *otherness* of life.

The *wahi pana* ("storied places") found in the islands of Hawai'i are a profound source of energy and inspiration for those fortunate enough to experience them. Without exception, the important ancient and sacred sites of the islands emanate a palpable presence. The question emerges: Are these places significant because they themselves contain a certain confluence of energy, or did the ancients, in the manner in which they interacted with the land, leave behind a subtle signature of their presence? Or is it both?

For years, I have tried to understand the nature of the Hawaiian experience and its potent effect on my internal efforts and creative work. As I experience the land, people, culture, and traditions, I am consistently nourished and moved.

James D. Houston writes of ancient Hawaiian sites:

The place has a kind of power, which is to say, it releases something in those who experience it. And after enough people have visited the spot, to stand, to pray, to sing, to fast, to chant, century upon century, its original impact has been layered and amplified until the ancestral atmosphere . . . is so rich with what Hawaiians call mana, *you can feel it like a coating on your skin. Later, trying to explain this to myself, I begin to think of sacredness as a kind of dialogue between the human spirit and certain designated places. These sites that call forth reverence and awe and humility and wonder, we make them sacred. It is a way of honoring those feelings in ourselves.*

And when we hear the songs the places sing, we are hearing our own most ancient voices.

Few of us will have the opportunity to experience firsthand all of these special places. But in our own communities, in our own locales, there are places that have the capacity to provide sustenance and spiritual nourishment. Robert Adams writes: "Each of us already knows such places, exceptional in the peace and insight they bring."

We must find and set aside such places: we must honor them, and use them; not exploitatively, but interactively, such that we are sustained by contact with the places themselves. In turn, we will help to sustain and preserve their energy, leaving behind the signature of our energy and creative work for those adventurers to come. We are well counseled by don Juan who cryptically advises Carlos Castaneda to find his "spot," where his body is happy and at home, where he is given strength, and where he can be safe from the discordant energies surrounding him. It is *here*, in places such as these, where we can be free to pursue our own being and our own necessity.

10

The Third Principle: Deepening Connections

Once we allow mystery in nature and in our definition of a person, then we discover that our current technological and therapeutic responses are extraordinarily inadequate. We begin to appreciate the role of the arts, not as entertainment or education, but as servants of deep vision and subtle sensibility. We see the need for piety, an attitude of respect for the vast realm of experience we know little about and can't begin to understand.

—Thomas Moore

We open to the mystery—to a deepening connection with the current of a vast intelligence that pervades all things. This principle reflects a hierarchy in which we come into relationship with a larger whole, with forces greater than those found within our ordinary lives and mundane selves—but which *are* available to our experience. Here we are called to the search, to become more deeply related with the core of our being, with other human beings, with the living culture, and with life itself.

It opens many questions and offers few answers:

In what way does a larger perspective, a deeper connection to the sources of life assist in our search for creativity and authentic expression?

Conversely, in what way does creativity help open the doors of perception? How can it function as a pathway toward the awakening of conscience and consciousness?

In what way does creative expression bring us closer to the sacred dimension of life?

What forces are we related to and aligned with; what energies do we come into accord with through the creative act? Can we become conscious participants in the universal movement of creation? Does the creative process follow natural law, on a level and scope much grander than we can imagine?

What is expression of Self, as opposed to self-expression?

How can artists function as agents of change and transformation for their times?

We are not looking for answers. The questions themselves enliven the mind, activate the heart, and sensitize the body's intelligence. As we approach the questions, they may invite us into greater realms of experience, and help to awaken our search for an ever-deepening flow of creativity and awareness.

ART AND SPIRITUAL PRACTICE

I firmly believe that there is a profound and ongoing relationship between the creative process and the traditional disciplines of the spiritual quest. Aren't artists, first and foremost, seekers of the truth—of the world we live in, of culture and its influence, and of the multidimensional levels of existence, from the sacred to the profane?

∼

Stillness . . . silence . . . the void . . . the field of being . . . vision quest . . . the center . . . the sacred . . .

How often do we read or hear these concepts expressed in a wide range of sources, from traditional sacred texts to New Age essays or books on self-improvement, and even now in magazines, movies, and television? Frankly, these terms have become so cliché that in careless, everyday use their original and essential meaning has been lost. But in my experience, they have definite, even precise, meanings. We must return these ideas to their proper context and place. These concepts collectively represent an action, an inner movement, and an absolutely necessary quest for those of us living at the beginning of the new millennium. The realities of our fragmented selves and fractured world demand that we return to something within us that stands apart from the fray, from the struggle for achievement and the increasing demands of everyday life.

To return to a place within us; to sit quietly and allow the dust to settle; to engage the subtle energies of the body, mind, and feelings; this is not a passive exercise, but an active turning toward the still resonances of the interior world. This movement is an essential means of inner transformation, growth, and change. Do we want or need to change, as individuals or as a society? Why would we aspire today toward this quality of inner silence? Doesn't this go against the very grain of modern life? Most of us are certainly not striving to be Zen monks, have not joined a religious order, and live quite ordinary, even uneventful lives. We simply want to live our lives and do our work. But if we care about personal and collective healing, if we want inner transformation, then we need to find the way home, forging new connections to the deeper parts of our being and the causal realms of existence.

From inner quiet, the right, true action arises—a genuine response. Through the field of silence, we hear the subtle voices of intuition, and open to hints of conscience and moments of greater consciousness. We know what is right and true, and we see more clearly our actual condition, with all of its potential and contradictions. Ordinarily, our thoughts turn constantly, our bodies are rarely still, and our emotional nature distracts us from this moment and from our true purpose. The action of sitting quietly, sensing the body, and quieting the mind allows for the emergence of our true Selves and reveals the essential shape of our own mature form of creative expression.

Many years ago, when I began this practice, a recurring image would emerge: I imagined myself to be akin to a young tree, unable yet to stand on its own and needing the triangulation of cables, attached to its trunk and the ground, that held it upright. The practice of sitting quietly, of returning to the subtle inner sensations, I likened to watering this young growth, giving it nourishment and sunlight, and simply providing the necessary conditions for growth to occur. True spiritual practice does not seek results and can not proceed from forced, self-willed efforts. It proceeds from the search for Self and the gentle but firm effort to engage a contemplative practice. This, and this alone, engenders growth of being, from which results may proceed according to one's temperament. For example, don Juan claimed that his "predilection" was "*to see.*" The seminal work outlined here can be defined by the wisdom found in four simple words from the Christian tradition: *Be still and know.*

Be courageous and discipline yourself . . .

Submit to a daily practice.
Your loyalty to that
is a ring on the door.

Keep knocking, and the joy inside
will eventually open a window
and look out to see who's there.

> —Rumi, translated by Coleman Barks

The principle of deepening connections is an action, an aim, not a definitive destination. The movement into ourselves, as reflected in the Rumi quote, *is* the means of potentially engaging the radiance and wonder of the All. As I understand the process, the way toward unitive consciousness, toward an experiential awareness of the whole, lies within the fulfillment of our passage through self-consciousness, becoming aware of the whole of ourselves. Hence, inner transformative work is the basis, the fundamental means of connection to higher realms, as given by most of the world's great teachings.

~

Art is, or can be, a genuine spiritual practice. It can function as a staircase to the Way, a pathway toward consciousness, when it is aligned with the means and methods of genuine teachings. For many in our society, religious forms of belief have lost currency and meaning. The great wisdom teachings, mostly Eastern in origin, have penetrated deeply into our common spiritual perspective. Yet the question remains whether they adequately address the nature of the Western mind and the complexity of our experience in today's world. We have turned to nature for inspiration and renewal, experiencing her rhythms and organic processes as an expression of the divine. In a world where even mother nature has been dramatically modified and literally threatened with extinction, where do we find the sacred in our lives? A balanced integration between the contemplative Eastern way and distinctly Western mode of action can be found through the practice of art. Certain aspects of the creative act can introduce us to the myriad levels of reality, help open us to the sacred, and offer a way of working toward our lifelong aim of inner growth and development. Here I wish to merely point toward the Way by identifying several paths of action through which art can serve to deepen our connection to the great Work and help us to engage the methods offered by genuine teachings.

1. *A Way of Growth*

Authentic creative expression is a way of encouraging our inner growth, and a means of mirroring the development that takes place. It is a reciprocal relationship. As we engage the creative process, we are thrown into relief and we encounter the particular shape of our psyche and inner energies. Our potential and our limitations reveal themselves. Our demons are called forth, often with a force that shakes loose our reluctance to acknowledge and intimately know them. We are challenged to stretch and grow. We attempt to integrate and transform, but not ignore, our shadow selves—and to move beyond the deep-seated habitual patterns that govern our automatic selves.

The practice of perfecting an art or craft is akin to the practice of perfecting ourselves. This work takes place through two equally important, but different forms of practice. The first is the division of attention between ourselves and the outer task, remembering to stay within, mindful of our own energies and careful to not get swept along by the attractions and seductive draw of the outer world. As don Juan counseled Carlos Castaneda, we learn to view the radical comings and goings in the human sphere as "controlled folly," that we deeply engage in—because we live in a world defined by action—yet we do not identify with our work or its results.

The second form of practice is self-observation. Proceeding from a deeper level than ordinary, mind-based introspection (which is often the mind viewing the mind, or wishful seeing that lends strange colors to our vision), self-observation is impartial, objective, and simultaneous. We observe ourselves in the moment, without wishing to change what we see. Staying in touch with our awareness, we allow ourselves to be, and simply observe what we are. Paradoxically, the more we can stand above and genuinely see, the more we can truly live within, in touch with our genuine presence. The very act of seeing, of cultivating an inner witness that resides in the constant stream of clear awareness, sheds light into the dark places. From true self-observation, a new and heightened perspective may arise that in itself is deeply transformative. Through seeing and feeling our contradictions, and not shrinking from the truth, a subtle, joyful taste of unitive consciousness may, over time, begin to emerge. What obstructs this work also arises from within us: our obstacles, unhealed wounds, and fragmented energies. Creativity may be allied with insanity because it opens us to the realm of darkness. But in turn, it ignites passion, engenders healing, and leads us toward integration. Experience bears out the truth: that creativity, unlike madness, provides a pathway for self-realization, and is a hallmark of the evolving individual.

Our resulting works are mirrors of ourselves. Through examining our work, we encounter ourselves. In painting, writing, photographing, or tending a garden, we are creating an image of ourselves, and our real responses to the world, and seeing a reflection of our own processes of growth and discovery. We can only express that which arises through direct experience. If we wish for a fullness of expression, we must strive toward fullness of being. Expression follows being, not the other way around.

2. *The Way of Balance*

The means and methods of working with an art form are an outer measure of our own energies. Through creativity, we witness our own fragmentation and particular form of imbalance. The body, mind, and feelings; each has its own intelligence and makes its unique contribution to the process. Yet some people are more comfortable with the work of the body, others are far more oriented to the work of the mind, and others prioritize the feelings. Creativity calls us to become whole, and that often means attending to our weaknesses, the component parts of ourselves that are underdeveloped. Here we strive toward an inner balance, with all of our parts working in unison. Cultivating a broad, embracing awareness, we may connect the disparate pieces of the creative act: our tools, ourselves, and the process itself.

The body and the senses know proportion and balance and can sense where sounds, words, or colors resonate within its field of vibration. If we allow for its intelligence, the body often knows the actions necessary for the activity in front of us.

The mind, of course, is given the task of grappling with the implications of content, of analogy and symbol, and sifting through options to bestow a living quality on our expression. The mind listens within, activates imagination and visualization (the capacity for storytelling and mythmaking), and opens to the contents that emerge from the unconscious. The mind focuses our intent, assisting the body and the feelings in staying with the moment, allowing it to organically unfold.

The feelings are a unique instrument of discovery. Through feeling, we perceive nuances and the subtle energies underlying surface manifestation. We make relationships, we understand metaphor and allegory in a manner that extends beyond the mere information provided to the mind. Our feeling nature often provides the particular coloration to our works that makes them distinctively our own.

When the body, mind, and feelings are working in balanced synergy, with each doing the work it was intended for, a channel opens, a conduit appears for the voices of intuition and conscience—which are often the true guiding forces of our creative expression. It seems contradictory, but these simple everyday efforts toward balance and integration will gradually lead us toward clarity and invite the inspired moments of understanding that grace our works.

3. *The Search for Self*

Creative expression encourages the discovery of Self and brings us closer to our essential nature, our original face. It is a means of discovering our place and our true calling. We strive to be open, to become transparent and receptive to the guiding impulses from within. Creative work is a discipline that calls forth the deeper parts of our nature. What we call inspiration or the muse—that which visits us when we are receptive and open—is a manifestation, a lawful result of our efforts with ourselves and our medium.

Working with a craft can be similar to the mindfulness and gathering of attention that takes place in meditation. We begin by turning inward and surveying our inner landscape. Most of the time, our minds are obstinate, distracted by the urgent tasks of the day; our emotions are agitated, reacting to the events of our lives; and our bodies are not still, but filled with nervous movements and stray energies. Yet in the process of quietly attending—watching, waiting, and listening—a movement toward a deeper, fuller state of being incrementally emerges. This work is none other than a search for enlightenment and understanding through creativity.

As we persevere, breathing awareness into ourselves and our work, this movement breeds an active stillness that magnetizes us to the finer energies in the atmosphere and in ourselves. We open to something more than the calls of everyday life. Suddenly, we are being breathed, seemingly by a far greater attention. A deeper intelligence graces our efforts, reveals what we need to express, brings insights in its wake, and nourishes the audience of our works.

The lightness of being that arises through the creative act is simultaneously serious and playful. It requires discipline, yet calls forth innovation and risk-taking. The creative act is one of liberation, once that asks us to go beyond ourselves. When we try to work in this manner, to transcend our perceived boundaries, a new quality of feeling emerges: a joy, a clean sense of satisfaction, a sense of being right and true. When the heart opens in this way, we recognize the possibility of a new, heightened sense of being—one that is limited only by our deep-seated inner attitudes of habitual thinking and reactive emotions.

The rare, illuminating moments that reveal the unity of existence are attracted through our inner work, our creative practice, and our strivings toward consciousness. Ken Wilber calls this perception "One Taste," the experiential recognition of the All. Here we earn hints of unitive consciousness revealing the radiance of what is, which appear through the cracks in our conscious mind—active fissures that are widened through creative work.

Photographer Paul Caponigro writes on the resonating potential of silence:

What about those images not thought out, but made with inner quiet? I am there, not only moving toward creation but toward realization. Knowledge and viewpoint are at the service of what, in me, wants to know. I feel my way. I know and direct up to a point and only so far as nature cooperates to carry out what I feel. . . . In the end, I produce something that is a surprise to me. There are no rules. I only work and say what I have discovered.

Of all my photographs, the ones that have the most meaning for me are those I was moved to make from a certain vantage point, at a certain moment and no other, and for which I did not draw on my abilities to fabricate a picture,

> *composition-wise or other-wise. You might say that I was taken in. Who or what takes one to a vantage point or moves one at a certain moment is a mystery to me. I have always felt after such experiences that there was more than myself involved. It is not chance. It happens often. . . . I cannot deny or put aside these subtle inner experiences. They are real. I feel and know them to be so. I cannot pass it off as wild imagination or hallucination. It is illusive, but the strength of it makes me yearn for it, as if trying to recall or remember an actual time, or place, or person, long past or forgotten. I hope, sometime in my life, to reach the source of it.*

4. *A Way of Devotion*

Unlike purely intellectual pursuits, creativity can be a transformative discipline. As we open to the larger mysteries of existence, resting in the stream of awareness, even for moments, we are transformed: stunningly, gratefully, unforgettably. We give up the dream that we are, take down our shields to the forces that surround us, realizing that the Creative in ourselves *is* ourselves. This begins the Way.

Creativity, then, becomes a path toward the great Way of transformation. It encourages us to stand in front of infinity, not-knowing, slowly simmering into radical openness through our everyday practice and inward efforts. It teaches nonattachment to the ego and nonidentification with the final result. In the words of the *Bhagavad Gita*:

> *You have a right to your actions,*
> *but never to your actions' fruits.*
> *Act for the action's sake.*
> *And do not be attached to inaction.*

Self-possessed, resolute, act
without any thought of results,
open to success or failure. . . .

Creativity enlightens the proper attitude between our actions and our work. We express our initiative and effort, then stand back and allow the process to unfold, aligning ourselves with the flow of life. All activities, when given our full attention, are analogous to the organic processes of growth and development. Through art, we learn about the laws of life and the possibilities inherent in being human.

The creative process unfolds in every moment—in nature, in the earth, in humanity as a whole, and in the cosmos—on a scale and dimension vastly larger than our personal expression. Yet we are not separate from these energies. Through creativity, we become participants in a greater whole; we are a part of it, and it is a part of us.

Finally, creative expression leads us back to the hidden, more essential parts of our nature, our innate vision, our true voice. We know it when it begins to emerge, yet could not predict its sound or coloration without the assistance of a physical medium that reflects our myriad energies. It helps us to discover who we are and brings us closer to ourselves. Through art, we make a vow to grow.

The Silence and Solitude of Consciousness
Certain types of art can transcend art; the connotative function of creative expression gives way to actually depicting higher states of being and deeper levels of reality. There are works of art that vibrate with subtle intensity, that originate through the field of silence, and remind us that impressions of color, voice, and sound, certain expressive movements, subtle combinations

of words, expansive ideas, piercing shapes or tones, and particular qualities of light can evoke transcendent realms within us. Much of what we call sacred architecture, certain kinds of music such as Tibetan or Gregorian chants, Scriabin's *Poem of Ecstasy* and Ravel's *Bolero*, some forms of dance, films such as Peter Brook's *Mahabharata* and *Meetings with Remarkable Men*, and works of literature such as the poetry of Rumi and Rilke or Hermann Hesse's *Siddhartha* and *Magister Ludi*; these works have the capacity to help us open to a greater dimension. Indeed, most were created with the intention of awakening our higher nature and fostering our search for consciousness. When artists reach into the deeper levels of the human experience, their resulting works express an energy, a vibratory tone, that contains within it the potential to help awaken something in us if we seek it. During the premiere of the film *Meetings with Remarkable Men*, Peter Brook, the noted director, stood before the assembled audience and introduced the film in the following way: "This is *not* art, *not* entertainment. Rather, it is the result of one man's search . . ."

Once again, Rilke's phrase, "the grace of great things," describes the language inherent in these works of art and literature that serve to activate our deepest impulses. Throughout history, works of art can be found that transcend their makers, that grow out of a sense of community, that involve the work of generations of individuals, such as the European cave painters, the medieval guilds, the schools of Japanese craftsmen, or the Romantic composers of the nineteenth century. Such art is often produced for the glory of God; it arises from a highly spiritualized impulse, in which the attention and care that goes into the making is both the means *and* the end. Here the work of craft is closely aligned with the effort towards self-perfection of the artist. In the Japanese tradition, as we refine the pot, we refine ourselves. The discipline involved in this form of artmaking provides a means for the active self-development of the individual and, by extension, the society. According to Soetsu Yanagi and Bernard Leach in *The Unknown Craftsman*, many early Japanese and Korean potters found simple dignity in their artistic anonymity and did not sign their works. They felt that it was enough to tune their energies toward listening to the inner music and allowing it to pass through them into the created piece. And Ananda Coomaraswamy, the great Oriental art scholar, found agreement with Stieglitz's answer to the question of why he did not sign his work: "Is the sky signed?"

Many artists from the modernist era attempted, though awkwardly, to achieve this ideal. The vigilance necessary to open toward this inner listening, bypassing the ego, is one of the challenges inherent in using art as a genuine practice. The discipline of synchronizing with the materials of one's craft, allowing something of another order to come through—and gaining the self-knowledge required to distinguish between real intuition and the multitude of other voices clamoring within—is part of the magnificent exercise undertaken through art and creativity. When an artist works in this manner, their own search comes alive for the viewer. We cannot ignore the palpable and highly nourishing energy transmitted through this type of art. Its affect on us is enduring and it feeds our collective soul.

The color field paintings of Mark Rothko and Ad Reinhardt are examples of such work in the visual arts. The paintings have no conventional subjects and are nearly devoid of compositional elements. Rather, both painters used the luminosity of color to penetrate beyond the superficial and pierce through the armor of the self, to reflect the finer quality of energies experienced in our most collected, unified, inner states of being. The mature work of Mark Rothko is, according to Roger Lipsey, "one of the great spiritual realizations of twentieth-century art in any medium." Rothko's own statements confirm his artistic intent. In a conversation with critic Harold Rosenberg, Rothko said, "I don't express myself in my painting. I express my not-self." And in his last major public statement, "The dictum 'Know thyself' is only valuable if the ego is removed from process in search for truth." Rothko's friend, art critic Dove Ashton, reported him as saying that art was not self-expression as he had thought in his youth, that "a work of art is another thing." Ashton also recalls a moment during a studio visit, with the lights dimmed, when Rothko asserted, "They are not pictures." For the viewer, they make visible the silence and solitude of consciousness.

Ad Reinhardt's work is even more subtle and deeply mysterious. Using only shades of black and barely discernible forms reminiscent of the Christian cross to divide the flat spaces of his canvases, he created a vocabulary of silence. Roger Lipsey comments on the experience of viewing Rothko's and Reinhardt's paintings: "One could feel again that there *is* a modern spiritual, and these works demonstrated it. One responded to their simplicity and quietness by becoming like them."

As we move beyond the strict conditions of postmodernity, where all experience is relative and based upon one's upbringing, conditioning, and cultural background, we are witnessing a rebirth of interest in our essential humanness and shared truths. Maya Angelou, when teaching a class, begins by writing a quote on the blackboard: "I am a human being. Nothing human can be alien to me." Defying the deeply ingrained attitude of defining ourselves by our differences, we can maintain hope for a widespread embrace of the human context that we all share, a return to empathy and compassion, and a renewed search for the sacred dimension of life.

The heroic quest is nothing more, but nothing less, than the search for an authentic life, a life lived from within—and it is a holy task. The journey of the hero or the heroine in myth and legend is the role of the artist today.

We need our artists. We need to be perpetually reminded of the possibility of a life lived *authentically*, of a life lived to transform and transmit those forces and energies that exist within us, pass between us, and come down to us from another source.

Sing Through Me, O Muse

The works of art with the most lasting impact, which have influenced generations and brought something of another order into the world, give the feeling—and there is often anecdotal or documentary evidence to support this—that the artist was merely the vehicle. "Sing through me O muse," begins Homer in the *Odyssey*. What we call a miracle or an ecstatic creative vision is often the manifestation of the energies and laws of one realm descending into another.

In the *involving* universe, where energies of the Absolute or God descend into matter (coming to meet us, as it were), at least several stages of energy manifestation take place before they reach the level of our physical realities. Ken Wilber believes that through long, transformative inner work, our consciousness can access the four major levels of transpersonal awareness: psychic (the unity of the physical world, nature mysticism), subtle (mythic or "conscious" forces, deities), causal (emptiness, formlessness), and non-dual (integral, the All). All of these realms, nested in the Great Chain of Being, vibrate at increasingly finer levels. While I don't know with certainty where artistic inspiration comes from, it is well-established that when we raise our level of vibration, like a tuning fork, we magnetically attract influences from higher realms. At this higher level of the creative process, the artist can become a transparent vehicle for another order of intelligence to pass through *fully formed*.

This is not a vague concept or a mystical conundrum as many would think. It is a lawful result. The artist has prepared the ground, developed his or her craft with rigorous intent, and struggled with the question of content, often for years. It is through these conditions of a sustained commitment that something may clearly pass; from our unconscious, from a transcendent source, from our own deeper nature, or (as some are disposed to believe), from the energies that pass between us as human beings. Some of Rilke's greatest and most mature poetry arose unexpectedly as he was composing a business letter. The lines of verse just appeared in his mind fully formed. He simply wrote them down, making few changes in the poems that arose spontaneously in a short period. His friend Princess Marie von Thurn und Taxis-Hohenlohe reported that he whispered: "What is that? What is coming?" And after their swift arrival, "he knew that the god had spoken."

In the preceding chapters, we have explored the creative process as a means of serving our own individual growth and development. Now the creative currents use our talents, our efforts for their own mysterious purpose. Here the stream widens from receiving fragments of intuitive revelation to the potential of becoming a willing, gracious host for the transmission of forces and energies much larger than we are, originating from cultural, collective, transpersonal, or spiritual realms. I think Ken Wilber is absolutely right when he says: "Humans do not create Spirit, Spirit creates humans!"

The implications of this phenomenon are enormous. Simply stated: The gods speaks to humanity through art. What has been called "conscious" art is a means of giving expression to the voices of the deeper realms for the purpose of transmitting collective or transpersonal truth. All peoples of the world have offered their unique gifts, increasing our perspective of the human condition—and these insights are often left behind in the form of works of art. Many works that have endured express something well beyond the artist's personal experiences. Examples of sacred architecture, the Pyramids and the Sphinx, much Hindu art, the fine arts and crafts of indigenous cultures, even some contemporary art and film, contain truths discovered by a culture, not just an individual, and represent a transmission of ideas and values.

Here we acknowledge that the human organism is the same the world over. The vibration of color and form, sound and light, and carefully crafted words have universal implications. The language of myth, allegory, and symbol can speak across the barriers of time and environmental conditioning. Through the language inherent in art, we may elevate thought, voice our deepest truths, and communicate our most profound experiences. Many, for example, are touched by a sense of the sublime in experiencing the space, light, and symbolic expression found in the Gothic cathedrals of Europe. The sacred geometries and the conscious use of proportion and symbol have been richly explored by scholars over the years. And many find a resonance with their own paths through life in reading Homer's *Odyssey*. The trials of Odysseus in his great journey home after the Trojan Wars closely parallel the universal stages of the hero's journey as outlined by Joseph Campbell and others. Admittedly, this form of expression does require a high level of skill and knowledge, and is generally seen only in the mature work of a creative individual.

A. R. Orage writes: "Minor art is concerned with self-expression. Major art is an effort at conveying certain ideas for the benefit of the beholder; not necessarily for the advantage of the artist." Gurdjieff refers to this form of art as *objective art*, in which the artist studies color, form, music, or word patterns and examines their measurable and specific effect on the viewer. From this exploration, the artist then attempts to intentionally convey the truths that they have discovered, with great precision. The effects of this form of art are often designed to awaken higher states of consciousness, uncover the long-buried voice of conscience, and uplift the viewer into new realms of experience. We see this kind of expression in allegorical tales and mythology, in the world's sacred texts, and in certain musical forms, such as Tibetan chant, Indian ragas, and some classical compositions such as those by Bach and Ravel. In contemporary art, many artists, with varying levels of success, aspire to this form of expression.

We are only beginning to recognize that the energetic expression of a work of art or literature—that which underlies the surface level of meaning—is of equal or greater import than the overt content. In this context, art is a physical manifestation of energy and an expression of consciousness.

At the beginning of the twentieth century, one of modernism's greatest voices was Wassily Kandinsky, who attempts, in *Concerning the Spiritual in Art*, to examine and restate for this century the function of art as a precise language.

Color . . . form. Two great signposts pointing toward a great end... Consciously or unconsciously, artists are studying and investigating their material, weighing the spiritual value of those elements with which it is their privilege to work . . . they are obeying Socrates' advice: "Know thyself". . .

Every serious work resembles in poise the quiet phrase: 'I am here.' Like or dislike for the work evaporates; but the sound of that phrase is eternal . . .

Color is the keyboard, the eyes are the hammers, the soul is the piano with many strings. The artist is the hand that plays, touching one key or another purposively, to cause vibrations in the soul.

Works of art resound in our being in a manner that transcends pure subjectivity. It is a fruitful field of exploration to observe where in the body particular colors or musical compositions strike us, how they interact with our emotional nature, and what forms of thought they evoke. Ken Wilber, in *One Taste*, describes the effects of certain forms of music on the chakras or centers of energy in the human body. He observes that rock music definitely strikes the lower chakras, the best of jazz, the middle chakras, and the great romantic composers, either the heart chakra or the upper chakras, depending on the specific composer and work. Wilber states: "You can actually feel your attention gravitate to various bodily centers (gut, heart, head) as these musical types play."

The impressions that we receive and take in through the senses constitute a precise and powerful language that can convey truths and concepts extending beyond literal description and subjective commentary. Through art, we may express universal elements of human experience: our aspirations, discoveries, and cultural, psychological, or spiritual conditions.

One of the strongest impressions I have ever received of genuine conscious transmission through art came from a hula performance, *Holo Mai Pele* ("The Myth of Pele"), performed by *Halau O Kekuhi* at the Maui Arts and Cultural Center, the first performance of this particular hula in more than two hundred years. The members of the *halau* (gathering of dancers) have danced together for many years and publicly perform only in very selected venues. This performance of *hula kahiko* (ancient hula) was theatre and dance, mythology and historical drama, integrated in an extraordinary two hours. It was the transmission of the beliefs of a people, and was both an individual and communal effort. It was, in essence, a form of prayer. From the very first moment, my partner and I were transfixed.

I felt a palpable energy, an undeniable grace, and a hint of the miraculous. Conscious forces permeated the atmosphere and passed through the performers as they aligned their efforts to become vehicles for ancestral voices. The dancers seemed to be working in a very particular manner, emanating an inner presence and fluidity. They were highly attentive to their movements, to their voices, and to each other. Each dancer maintained his or her own part, clearly expressing individual strengths and unique styles. Yet they were all synchronized with the deeper, intended meaning of the epic hula.

The dance was in their very blood, and there could be no question that the soul of the Hawaiian people was transmitted through the dance in a way that brought the entire experience to a higher realm. As the narrator introduced each dance and chant, he emphasized the desire of the performers and the *Kumu Hula* (hula teachers), Pualani Kanaka'ole Kanahele and Nalani Kanaka'ole, to bring this special experience home, and to reintroduce this epic poem to their community, the people of *Hawai'i ne* ("beloved Hawai'i").

In this dance, the balance between these two forces, these two modes of expression—the genuine, authentic expression of the individual, and their embrace of the communal movement in which the whole is much greater than the sum of its parts—was sheer poetry. It provided a new model for my own understanding of the resonating potential of collaboration and partnership, in which each individual adds their own imprint to the evolving whole. When two or more are gathered together, so much more is possible—more energy is attracted than each individual could hope to find solely from his or her own initiative.

What is even more remarkable about this performance, offering a profound lesson to us all, is that the dancers were, without exception, ordinary people. Though highly committed, they danced on a part-time basis, busy with jobs and families in the other parts of their rich, full lives. In many traditional cultures, the art forms and rituals that define worship and expressions of beliefs are available to all members. The living quest for excellence, for experiencing the passage of larger forces and transmitting shared truths, is open to everyone, not limited to professional artists or performers.

As I left the theatre, the lingering thoughts that haunted me for weeks centered around the question of what is in *my* blood, or in our blood as people of European ancestry and modern American culture. What has our common cultural heritage given us? Not MTV and Madonna, Burger King and John Wayne? But deeply embedded in our commonality is art, literature, music, and film. In these forms of expression we, like those dancers, may discover and transmit our own truths, and seek to become a conduit for the passage of energies within and through us.

Halfway up the Mountain

In any form of spiritual practice, there is a right relationship that must be maintained. The discipline of searching for a state of inner quiet, of silence, is not to be approached with the goal of becoming a better artist—or even, for that matter, a better person. Although greater confidence and greater effectiveness in life may also result in the course of inner development, these are beside the point. The real aim, and the only worthwhile goal of this practice, is true growth of being. Perhaps the greatest danger found in the proliferation of contemporary writings on self-improvement and New Age wisdom is the potential for losing sight of this lawful and proper hierarchy. In *Halfway up the Mountain: The Error of Premature Claims to Enlightenment*, Mariana Caplan presents compelling evidence that some contemporary spiritual teachers and students have partial awakenings to a deeper level of consciousness but misappropriate its use for selfish and highly personal ends. Growth of being is organic and must be predicated on a fundamental integration of the whole of ourselves, accompanied by a healthy psychological, sexual, and emotional development.

We use the process of living and of creating art to move toward greater understanding, toward greater consciousness, toward becoming willing servants of that which needs to pass through us from a deeper source. It is a path, a way toward inner development. In Zen it is said that the finger pointing toward the moon should never be confused with the moon itself. Our aim is not to focus on or serve the finger, the path; it is to serve the luminance that creates the moon. In other words, we engage these practices in order to serve life, to serve the higher manifestations both within and without, to serve our real Selves, and to serve others. Life does not exist to serve our egos, our social personalities, our residual childhood complexes, or our material aspirations. Nor do conscious forces exist to support our petty desires and earthbound selves. The higher should never be used to serve lower ends. The lower should always stand in service of the higher. This is a subtle but important distinction if we are to use artmaking in a respectful manner.

In our most profound moments—of beauty and radiance, of great pain or trauma, of love and awakening, of seeing and feeling the sublime—we also sense our mortality. Everything that is born must die. All the manifestations of life that we are privileged to experience are temporal and mortal, and will pass from this earth. The Greeks have given us a word for this: *pathos*, which represents the duality present in rare moments of awareness, when joy is intertwined with sadness, and hope is tempered by reality. Pathos, I believe, is seen in many works of art in which we feel simultaneously a living, radiant presence and a recognition of the sometimes painfully acknowledged facts of our existence. Indeed, in many of the greatest works we find a search for wholeness of spirit, for redemption, and for eternal values expressed through the transitory moments and ephemeral circumstances of our lives. Beethoven's Ninth Symphony, written when he was almost completely deaf; the later works of Edward Weston from Point Lobos, photographed after learning that he had

Parkinson's disease; Rilke's later work, the *Sonnets to Orpheus* and the *Duino Elegies*; all contain this admixture of joy and sadness, this tempering of darkness with transcendent light, and express, as Theodore Roethke put it, "the intolerable sadness that comes when we are aware at last of our own destiny."

What Roethke may be referring to as his personal destiny, we cannot know. But it is in our lot as human beings to maintain this tenuous balance between the unrestrained joy of being alive and the absolute certainty that we, like all living things, will someday die—that our lives on this planet are temporal and short.

This quality of pathos is, I imagine, the source of such phrases as "struck by awe" and "wounded by beauty." Awakening exacts a price, and real seeing acknowledges both the life force present in all things and the concrete realities of living and dying. It acknowledges our highest and best possibilities as well as our most conflicting elements and greatest obstacles.

Don Juan recounts to Carlos Castaneda:

For me the world is weird because it is stupendous, awesome, mysterious, unfathomable; my interest has been to convince you that you must assume responsibility for being here, in this marvelous world, in this marvelous desert, in this marvelous time. I wanted to convince you that you must learn to make every act count, since you are going to be here for only a short while; in fact, too short for witnessing all the marvels of it.

—Carlos Castaneda, *Journey to Ixtlan*

NOTES TOWARD THE FUTURE

I stand among the many who have been deeply touched by the views of earth in photographs taken from space. The solitary blue planet—the one round ball, unencumbered by divisions of nations, peoples, and ideologies. This is probably the single most monumental visual image to have ever entered our collective consciousness. Our beautiful, fragile world—our home.

These photographs from space are beyond art, beyond science. They represent a new paradigm, one that is nearly impossible to ignore, and a new challenge for those of us fortunate enough to live in these times, with the extraordinary intersection of forces and events taking place at the beginning of the twenty-first century. We have this image of the single, isolated planet Earth seen amidst the black vastness of space, showing at least the potential for a vision of global unity, contrasted with the plethora of events, challenges, complex issues, technological achievements, and scientific discoveries that make up the world we live in. If we are the least bit sensitive, then all of these phenomena have entered our souls, compete for our attention, and cause much questioning and consternation within us. The challenge is to move this questioning beyond the mind; to embrace the question that does not contain words or concepts or have an answer, but presents an opening, a doorway to a deepening sense of experience, one that includes the body, mind, feelings, and soul. To ask the question with our entire being: How can we live a human life, one filled with integrity and shaped by conscience?

Ultimately, the creative process is not about making objects. It is about the rediscovery of ourselves and the remaking of the world; about becoming an artist of the very act of living. The quest for genuine creativity, in whatever form, is none other than the search for the awakening of consciousness and the gradual uncovering of the long-buried voice of conscience. If consciousness is the higher and truer function of the real mind, then conscience is the higher and truer function of the feeling nature. However, due to the conditions of our upbringing and the discordant conditions of modern life, we are often exiled from the transforming influence of conscience. A thick, inert crust has grown over it, separating us from its unifying potential. Conscience begins to make its appearance when we relinquish the shields that hide us from feeling and knowing the truth of our situation, replete with inner fragmentation and contradiction. Even our rational minds know that to achieve unity we must first embrace, and then go beyond, the region of duality in which contradiction resides.

The masks that hide us from ourselves are often deep-seated filters that block our entrance into the subtle, causal levels of reality. Don Juan recounts to Carlos Castaneda:

> The things people do are the shields against the forces that surround us; what we do as people gives us comfort and makes us feel safe . . . We never learn that the things we do as people are only shields and we let them dominate and topple our lives . . .
>
> The world is incomprehensible. We won't ever understand it; we won't ever unravel its secrets. Thus, we must treat it as it is, a sheer mystery!
>
> An average man doesn't do this, though. The world is never a mystery for him, and when he arrives at old age he is convinced he has nothing more to live for. An old man has not exhausted the world. He has exhausted only what people do. But in his stupid confusion he believes that the world has no more mysteries for him. What a wretched price to pay for our shields!
>
> A warrior is aware of this confusion and learns to treat things properly. The things that people do cannot under any conditions be more important than the world. And thus a warrior treats the world as an endless mystery and what people do as an endless folly.

Losing self importance, giving up the illusion of what we believe we are and the false security of what we think we know, opens us to the path of knowledge.

Seeing, feeling, and deeply engaging the mysteries of the world brings us closer to the joy of consciousness. Seeing and feeling the contradictions within ourselves and witnessing those very same contradictions reflected in the world brings us closer to the sorrow of conscience.

It is important to keep in mind at every turn that we are microcosms of the larger universe. Everything that we observe in the world, that we react to, and that we see externally also exists within us—our culture is nothing more than a reflection of our collective state of being. And everything that we observe in ourselves, our contradictions as well as our potential unity, is manifested in the world. If we wish to affect a change in the world, to make sense out of the fractured conditions of our collective existence, we must begin with ourselves. If we wish to awaken from the dream that we are, we must refine and transform our experience, and strive toward a state of inner unity and wholeness of being.

George Santayana writes: "The great function of poetry . . . is precisely this: to repair the material of experience . . . and then out of that living but indefinite material to build new structures, richer, finer, fitter to the primary tendencies of our nature, truer to the ultimate possibilities of the soul." Repairing the material of existence might, then, be seen as a suitable and true role for the artist. This suggests transformation, a refinement of our energies and our way of seeing, and the possibility of an experience that takes place in two directions simultaneously. It begins with a deepening awareness of ourselves, a lowering of gravity into our still center, the eye of the storm. Then, like a wave arising from deep within, the creative impulse compels us back into life with new realizations, new forms built on the more human foundation of our centeredness. The principle of deepening connections takes us both downward and inward, and upward and outward. I believe that this is one of the laws governing our planetary existence. The farther that we can penetrate the depths of ourselves, the more that our vision and experience can extend outward, to the whole of the world and the cosmos.

In preceding chapters, we observed that the creative impulse locates itself between and integrates both of these directions. It fountains from deep within (the active, upward-reaching force) and comes down to us from above (the descent of Spirit into the body) through an open receptiveness to the subtle energies that surround and permeate us. We are the meeting ground, the transforming agent, the expressive medium for these dual energies to be made manifest. And both, our aspirations and our egoless receptivity, are essential. Forsake one, forsake the other. Ken Wilber writes that "a strong repression against id will also tend to block out God, simply because both id and God can threaten the ego, and a defense against one helps defend against the other." Creativity, then, means simply standing out of the way, developing our skillful means, our craft, to allow the myriad energies of life to move through us, creating objects, genuinely responding to others, and offering our experiences and understandings back to life. A phrase given by Laura Sewall in *Sight and Sensibility* continues to reverberate in me. She claims that we are "receptacles, vessels, and transformers" of the vast energies (of life, nature, and culture) that surround us.

This magnificent view of planet earth as one integrated whole, our blue planet: the realization of this vision of connectedness will only be possible for humanity when the search for wholeness, for integration, and for a connection to the deeper voices takes place in each and every one of us individually.

Artists and creative individuals can, and I believe must, take the lead. In many cultures, highly creative people have assumed the role of shaman, interpreting the forces and energies passing through and between us, encouraging a deeper vision of reality, and sharing those insights with their community. I am reminded of Black Elk of the Oglala Sioux, who had a series of prescient visions at nine years of age, delineating the fate of his people. In his vision, he saw his people as a sacred hoop, which was merely one of many hoops, "that made one circle, wide as daylight and as starlight, and in the center grew one mighty flowering tree to shelter all the children of one mother and one father. And I saw that it was holy." A vision of hope, of the true nature of the peoples of earth, of interlocking sacred hoops, with one flowering tree in the center, available to all.

Black Elk also saw the terrible trials that would come to pass for his people in the years ahead. He saw the oncoming wave of greed and materialism that tamed the American West and destroyed the lands and the spirit of his people. His nation's hoop was broken, his people were dying, and the holy tree was gone, lost amidst the rising tide of the white man's exploitation. As an old man, Black Elk understood the need to tell the story of his great vision to the world. When the writer John Neihardt was first granted an introduction and visited Black Elk in the early 1930s, he had the distinct impression that the elderly man had been waiting for him. During their first visit, Black Elk acknowledged: "There is so much to teach you. What I know was given to me for men and it is true and it is beautiful. Soon I shall be under the grass and it will be lost. You were sent to save it."

The search for wholeness, to repair the material of experience, to unify our fractured sense of self, to come into direct contact with the sources of knowing and guidance within, must become a new paradigm for the artist. Our culture needs it perhaps as never before. The age has long passed for which the ideal of the tortured, neurotic, angst-ridden artist, isolated from the community on some romantic but self-destructive quest, is appropriate and desirable. Unfortunately, in the arts, in the music and the entertainment communities, abuse of drugs and alcohol, and lifestyles built on ego and excess are still tolerated and often sensationalized. In the worlds of business and government, we have numerous examples of highly exploitive attitudes and abuses of personal power. The events of September 11, 2001 tragically demonstrate beyond a doubt the immense danger to the common good of any highly obsessive ideal, self-aggrandizing agenda, or unflinching religious fervor that clouds conscience and furthers the pain or suffering of others.

Whether for God or country or satisfaction of the ego, extreme imbalance in any form cannot be seen as a suitable example for the present age— and for the children who must inherit the massively problematic world that we will pass on. Turn on the television any night of the week and the message is clear: it is cool and OK to embrace greed and the pursuit of success by any means possible; to be shallow, self-serving, and neurotically obsessed with the petty personal details of one's own life. And the ever-escalating violence— whether on the part of the good guys or the bad guys—is perceived as a titillating element that sells movies or advertising time.

Even those individuals on whom we should reliably be able to depend for psychic nourishment, greater perspective, and life-changing insights— often found in the art and literary communities—are in no way immune from the vulgarities of ego and indulgent excess. It is regrettable that some artists are deeply infected with the insistent drama of the career game and the pursuit of the elusive vagaries of fame and fortune. Many artists seem to care more about their own success than they do about what they are actually communicating, and don't bother to address the kind of impressions that they are serving up to their brothers and sisters. As long as their efforts are deemed "successful" by the market-driven art community, they simply do not consider their responsibility to their audience, in terms of what is being expressed and what attitudes are being promoted. Compounding the difficulties for the public at large, some segments of the art world are marked by arrogance and a desire to deliberately distance their work from any potential audience other than smug and elitist peers. This can result, at times, in work that is appallingly indulgent, mean-spirited, and agenda-ridden. A. D. Coleman, the noted media critic, in a review of work found in a Whitney Museum of American Art exhibit, questions why anyone would be moved to make art so filled with alienation and cynicism: "The show's reply, by contrast, is short and sweet: you make art nowadays so as to get rich and famous. Ours is not the first culture to find itself in decline, but I know of no other that has enticed so many artists to wallow in its decay. . . . in the truest, deepest sense of the word, much of the work in this show is not healing but diseased."

The way up is the way down, and I believe that the way to reach the life-affirming values that I am espousing is through an unfiltered seeing and acknowledgment of the contradictions and self-seeking in some quarters of the art world today. Recognition of the problem is the first step toward real change. If we can provide new models for the young people who might fulfill our cherished hopes for the future, and help destroy their illusions about the gods of ego and excess, then shouldn't we try with all of our might and passion to do so?

Many artists have simply not taken responsibility for seeing the larger picture, for becoming the shamans of our age, or for endeavoring to assist in the necessary process of healing ourselves and the world. Genuine creativity brings a palpable force into the collective atmosphere. It can literally help heal the world. To be creative is to participate in the ongoing process of making our world anew, of searching for innovative solutions, and offering a vital, special energy to our planetary existence. Jeanne de Salzmann, Gurdjieff's successor, in observing how the vibrations of our world have been deeply affected, brought down, by the energies and actions of humanity, said simply: "The earth needs our work . . . now." If humanity has helped lower the level of vibrations, then humanity can help raise it once again. William Segal, also a student of Gurdjieff, perceptively regards the conditions of our time in *The Structure of Man*: "Power potentials have been released which threaten to upset cosmic balances. Ironically, the more gigantic and astonishing our manipulation of these energies, the more puerile and insignificant our understanding of them. Philosophers and scientists are coming to agree that not only do we need a deep alteration in the present state of mankind, but that this radical shift depends solely upon our relationship to consciousness—the invisible, fundamental energy behind phenomenal existence."

If our age is to be healed, we must heal ourselves. It is not enough to simply work through our residual problems, what our mothers or fathers may or may not have done to us when we were young. We must come to know ourselves fully: our strengths, weaknesses, potentials, and the purposes of our lives. And we must know ourselves in context, with others, in a culture, and on the earth with six billion other beings. In short, the search for consciousness forms the foundation of our discovery of the role that we are called to play in the drama of life, and guides our enactment of it. We have within us an inner measure of integrity, the experience of conscience. When we step off the bridge of alignment with our true Selves and enter into a situation unbecoming (in the words of the *I Ching*) of a "superior" man or woman, we feel remorse. And this sorrow, this care for ourselves, can eventually create an inner fusion, a solidifying that leads toward a wholeness of being containing hints of the joy and liberation of consciousness. When we see and feel that we are not whole and indivisible, we are on the path of becoming. Like a clay pot, we are fired in the kiln of suffering, with our inconsistencies and our many conflicting selves, until we gradually fuse into a new level of integration.

Our world is fractured, as are we. I believe that one of the core meanings of the word "legion" in the Christian gospels refers to the many different roles in the human makeup, which we identify with and call "I' or "me." We are not one. We lack inner unity and wholeness. At one moment, in one situation, certain parts of ourselves are called forth. In another moment, quite another part asserts itself, and these parts scarcely know one another. We have many selves: some sad, some happy, some confident and strong, some self-effacing and weak, some sane, some disturbed, some peaceful, some violent, some compassionate, and some completely self-centered. We are angels; we are human. The experience of conscience begins when we loosen the walls that hide our different parts from each other.

In a truly groundbreaking book, *Conversations Before the End of Time*, art critic Suzi Gablik, in response to a question about whether art and artists can help turn around some of the apocalyptic conditions in the world today, says:

At this point . . . I myself am unclear as to what can and cannot be turned around. I do think that living in the reality and truth of our situation is one small step towards mastery of it . . . Living in the truth of our situation is related, I believe, to really contacting the grief that one would feel at the loss of this beautiful life that we have here on this planet, or the inability of the human race to sustain itself. Somehow or other, that grief has to be experienced fully, devastatingly, before we will actually make the necessary changes.

What concerns me . . . is a kind of blind participation in the norms of the art world that is soul-destroying and abrasive . . .

> *I think we're living in a transitional time, when the values and way of life we've been taught to live by in our culture have to be seen as toxic. That brings up issues of healing, and of transformation. It seems as if there is a spiritual and social obligation to participate in this process of healing our world, however one can.*

Living the truth of our situation, to use Suzi Gablik's phrase, brings home the experience of conscience. This form of self-inquiry, which is not based in the mind but rather grounded in the deep emotional realization that our lives could end before we uncover our true estate, leads to our becoming more whole and helps us become compassionate toward ourselves and others. So, too, with the planet. When we live the reality of our situation in this fragile, beautiful world, we are one step closer to assisting the positive change and evolution of our species and environment. And we might well ask: How do we approach this vague yet essential task of awakening? All of the world's great teachings point the way. One of the most encouraging features of modern life is the help and nurturance available through teachings that we can find in our own backyard.

As I have suggested throughout these pages, art encourages the awakening of conscience and consciousness. Artists may, at times, function as the conscience of the world. We see and feel the contradictions within ourselves and in our society. We see our own fragmentation and the fractured state of the world. Many artists have expressed a vision of what they feel are the apocalyptic conditions of our age. Indeed, much contemporary art reflects what the writer James Agee saw in the photographs of Walker Evans: "the cruel radiance of what is."

In *The Courage to Create*, Rollo May asserts that "genuine artists are so bound up with their age that they cannot communicate separated from it . . . For the consciousness which obtains in creativity is not the superficial level of objectified intellectualization, but is an encounter with the world on a level that undercuts the subject-object split. 'Creativity,' to rephrase our definition, 'is the encounter of the intensively conscious human being with his or her world.'" Artists have provided many insights that express the spirit and challenges of our age: questioning difficult societal conditions, outworn conventions, and accepted standards in media, advertising, and entertainment. What kind of world would it be without the indispensable checks and balances gifted us by artists? Art can serve as a thundering reminder of what we have lost of our common humanity, or what we may yet strive for.

What about visions of hope, of healing, of the interconnectedness of life, of a true relationship to oneself and others? These are lacking in much contemporary art. Such themes can somehow be a source of embarrassment to the modern artist, viewed as saccharine and sentimental; or, worse, as inauthentic and irrelevant to the present time. Perhaps the most symptomatic condition that underlies our problems, causing the rifts of the modern age, is our lack of connection to the spiritual dimension; conversely, the search for this dimension may provide the only real solution.

The tragic fact is that any depth of inquiry, or evidence of interests that run counter to the accepted, secularized values of Western culture, is often ridiculed—sometimes even from within the artistic community. What we lack is a durable connection to a larger dimension—artistic, social, historical, psychological, or spiritual—and the discipline required to achieve that kind of perspective. Current thinking in segments of the arts and education communities strenuously challenges the credibility of the heroic quest, the sustained lifetime commitment to an ideal, and the paradigm of the artist as a seeker or purveyor of spiritual awakening, cultural identity, or moral truth, treating these aims as the residual vestiges of modernism, and outdated artistic or culturally elitist modes of interaction.

There are problems with the old models, it is true. Certainly, the notion of the heroic male genius, the great white hope, no longer functions as an appropriate role for the artist today, as that model historically excluded or marginalized the voices of minorities and differing cultural views. We need a new model based on our interrelatedness, on collaboration and exchange. One that supports, rather than denies, our inherent connectedness and the need for continuing dialogue with a sharing of mutual discoveries. Toward this end we must continue to embrace those remaining bright and true elements of the modernist era: the passionate search for meaning; the potency of individual vision, meaningful to oneself and others; and the age-old quest for a genuine connection to the sacred.

In an issue of the *Paris Review*, the writer Edna O'Brien was asked: What do you think the future has in store for literature? She answered:

As you know, the future itself is perilous. What would be wonderful—what we need just now—is some astonishing fairy tale. I read somewhere the other day that the cavemen did not paint what they saw, but what they wished to see. We need that, in these lonely, lunatic times. . . .

What the world needs from us is a vision of hope, of renewal, of the sanctity of life and the sacredness of experience. If we genuinely care about the future and the legacy that we will leave behind, we must actively seek to be agents of change, and reassume our rightful role of midwifery, giving birth to new understandings and the poetry of insight that so desperately needs to come into the world today. We must strive to become whole, self-actualized human beings, capable of listening to the voices in the subtle realms within and without, which pass through our world unseen and unacknowledged in our present state. We must become "shadow catchers" once again, offering and receiving the oracles of the future, giving to and taking from each other, in whatever way that our talents and capabilities dictate and demand.

~

Certain artists impress us with the enormity of their chosen task and the boldness of their vision. We are inspired by their uncommon bravery in sharply revealing their incisive observations, filtered through genuine compassion and deep caring. Often risking personal happiness, they become the conscience of the age, the lens through which the living culture resolves its contradictions. The painter Anselm Kiefer personifies in his work the past, present, and future of Germany. By assuming this collective karma through his art, Kiefer demonstrates his belief in the possibility of redemption for the sometimes illustrious and deeply troubled past of the German people. Employing metaphors such as fire and straw, and numerous symbols and allegorical myths, his work addresses the entire scope of the German national heritage and encompasses, according to Mark Rosenthal, "an enormous sense of mission and ambition—the wish to grasp great regions of human history within the boundaries of his art."

Another example is Judy Chicago, whose *Dinner Party* celebrates the achievements of notable women throughout history, symbolically collecting their wisdom and contributions in one single, monumental gesture, with place-settings for each of the individual women at a communal dinner table. Richard Misrach's continuing saga, *Desert Cantos*, speaks eloquently and passionately about the fragility of the land and the destructive intrusions of modern culture, through photographs of the California-Nevada desert.

I recently viewed an exhibition of the work of prominent French artists at the Contemporary Museum in Honolulu. Christian Boltanski's work, from the series *Les enfants de Dijon* and *Monuments*, was startlingly moving. Not much art has the capacity to make me weak at the knees, but Boltanski's work most assuredly did so, and brought me nearly to tears. The installation consists of the graduation photos of a class of students from a private Jewish school in Vienna in 1931. The faces, like many graduation pictures, are filled with life, hope, and the joyous sense of potential reserved mostly for the young. The images are enclosed in shrinelike simple handmade frames, and lit with small lightbulbs around each. Otherwise, the gallery is dark. Although it is not stated, the implied reference to the Holocaust is self-evident. A sense of sadness permeates the room; one cannot escape the question of what may have happened to these young people. It is enough for Boltanski to simply give us their faces; we infer the rest from the perspective of history. Yet while the installation is profoundly disturbing and expressed in the nature of an elegy, an aura of the sanctity of life prevails.

On a collective level, the AIDS quilt and the Vietnam Memorial are broadscale gestures, artistic in their origin and deeply social in their message and content. These, and all of the aforementioned works, grapple with very large themes and are undeniably moving in their epic quality. Though some of the works contain an element of critical commentary as part of their essential message, without exception they all inspire healing, express a deeply felt form of caring, and respond to a collective need expressed through the individual insight of particular artists—with a large measure of both courage and compassion.

~

The whole is greater than the sum of its parts. We need each other. We must strive to recognize our relatedness if we are to make sense of the world that we inhabit, and if we are to generate sufficient force and insight to make a difference. One of the principal maladies of the present time is our stubborn stance of isolation and our inability to fully recognize the enlarged potential that can be found in dialogue and shared creative response.

Since the Renaissance, Western culture has glorified the individual, giving primacy to our subjective perceptions and our inherent personality apart from the tribe or society. Though we are grateful for the opportunity to unfold our sense of self and seek our particular calling, perhaps we have we gone too far to one extreme. We have learned well the lessons of our *independence*, now we must learn the wisdom of *interdependence*. In this respect, we are fortunate today to have a global perspective within our grasp, with literature, art, and music available from the corners of the earth. Creativity offers a universal form of communication that can reach out across continents or centuries to expand our world view and place our lives in perspective. We have much to learn from each other. If identity politics—as found in many quarters of academia—means that black women can only find relevance in works by other black women, or Latin Americans can only relate to the experience of others of like kind, then clearly something is wrong, just as it was when the canon of art and literature almost exclusively reflected the dominant white male. Our rich cultural differences exist within the ground of a common humanity. Among the great lessons of art is the cultivation of empathy and compassion. "Unitas Multiple"—universal pluralism, the many contained within the One—is an idea that has been emphasized in the writings of Ken Wilber and could be the right credo for the arts and culture of our age, cultivating openness, universal understanding, and broad tolerance; a recognition of our profound similarities with an acknowledgment of our real differences. Paul Theroux writes of this: "There is a paradox . . . the deeper I have gone into my own memory, the more I realized how much in common I have with other people. The greater the access I have had to my memory, to my mind and experience . . . the more I have felt myself to be a part of the world." He goes on to speculate about the political dimension of the creative process, seeking the ground of our common human heritage and trying to identify the size of the plot in which are we genuinely, unambiguously different. He echoes the feeling of many that the recognition of our shared conditions and our individual variations contribute equally to the dialogue of our times.

What grows out of our interactions with others? Through exchange and mutual sharing—and through our differences—we move toward deeper understandings and an expanded point of view, one that would be impossible to reach alone, in our isolated, subjective ponderings. Together, we attract energy and discover creative solutions in a manner we cannot accomplish by ourselves. This forms the true ideal of the classroom, the tavern, the town meeting, and of any gathering of individuals with shared interests or common aims. My own views of life and art, my understanding of myself and others, have opened up and significantly evolved due to my exchanges with others.

As a teacher, I have serious concern over the prevailing trend in education, in which an overreliance on subjective thinking and the premature development of an individual point of view takes precedence over the discipline of objectivity and the ability to see things from many angles. Like the creative process itself, education is ultimately a paradox. We must remain committed to our own evolving point of view and have the courage to vigorously express our convictions, yet we must remain unbiased—a formidable challenge—and be willing to look beyond ourselves and hear the ideas of others. Is this not the real meaning of dialogue? The openness to a rich exchange helps us to understand the world and ourselves that much better, with greater insight, empathy, and compassion.

We have an unfortunate tendency in our society to believe too strongly in our own opinions, to have a fixed standpoint or, worse, a passionate, unflinching agenda, one that cannot be influenced by the viewpoints of others. Witness the cultural wars currently underway, with conservatives pitted against liberals and traditionalists against revisionists, with each side scarcely hearing the other. Truth often resides in the middle of a conflicting encounter, and everyone, regardless of their standpoint, has genuine insight and wisdom to offer.

In the closing paragraphs of *The Scandal of Pleasure: Art in an Age of Fundamentalism*, Wendy Steiner writes:

For art's relation to reality is paradoxical. It serves to open thought rather than close it down. It helps us entertain possibilities—enriching or threatening—which may "bring newness into the world." It dramatizes to us what we like and care about, and how we relate to others who are moved the same way or not . . . It appeals to our freedom and individualism and in the process to our investment in collectivities . . .

Maintaining an openness to such contradictions, instabilities, and psychic challenges is a test of each person individually and of the culture as a whole. It takes candor to acknowledge the self-revelation in our own interpretations, and generosity and respect to open ourselves to the interpretations of other people. The presence of art in a democracy always involves this kind of stress. . . . Unfortunately, the "trials" surrounding art have been rather too literal of late. We must learn to respond with more subtlety, tolerance, and pleasure to the paradoxes art poses.

My question here is a simple one: Will polarization, and the actual violence inherent in adhering to a fixed position, bring about positive change and evolution for humanity? I cannot believe that unflinching agendas or reactionary points of view further the aims of education and the arts, or that they can resolve the highly complex social and ecological issues facing us today.

A group of people, however gathered together—as students in a classroom, as faculty in a department, as artists in a neighborhood bar, as partners in a workplace, or as members of a larger community—contains a potential that is amplified well beyond their individual capabilities. The image of the circle, each person representing a point along the circumference, some next to each other, some fully opposed across the diameter, is a fitting symbol of the potential for dialogue and collective understanding. The more points that exist around the circle, the greater is the possibility of seeing the entire contour, not just our small part. And any solution, any meaningful response, will arise through seeing, with greater clarity, more of the shape of the whole. When we gather together, energy increases and understanding is enlarged. Our point of view widens and expands. Something does pass between us as human beings, in our energy exchanges, that is integral to the creative process.

In my daily practice of sitting quietly, I find a notable difference between being alone and being with others similarly engaged. When I am alone, the struggle to still my body and mind often lacks sufficient force or direction. I can frequently sense the difference between my fragmented energies responding to the calls and demands of daily life, and something deeper within. But my attention may not be focused enough to reliably penetrate the veils that separate me from the true integrity of my inner life. Sitting with others, a very different quality is present. At times, when two or more are gathered together for this kind of work, a resonating silence combined with the palpable vibration of finer energies permeates the surrounding atmosphere. And this is a great source of help in renewing my connection with myself and collecting my own energies. While each of us does bring something to the process through our own efforts, what we receive is not commensurate with what we contribute. What we take away is usually much greater than what we bring. When gathered together, there is an additional force available, and a finer quality of energy is attracted and experienced by all.

We can see this also in creative work. In communal song and dance, in collaborative projects and group endeavors, in the process of giving and receiving feedback, we feel enriched and enlarged, as if we are participating in a larger whole. The process of sharing, of collaboration, is often more important than the specific nature of the activity. It is in the gathering together itself—in the search for dialogue and for exchange—that we find help in moving toward genuine creativity, toward our real Selves and authentic visions, and toward greater understanding and collective solutions.

∾

With all of the preceding pages behind me, I can now acknowledge my deep reservations and enduring doubts about the future. Art may be an expression of human consciousness, but I don't know if it will solve our problems, right any wrongs, or effect positive change in the world. That depends on each one of us. Without a doubt, the only real agent for change in this world is the individual, multiplied into societies, nations, and cultures. The power of creativity remains within the reach of us all, yet our individual and collective fate lies in the hands our god-given free will. The will to respond to the song of the world and the call of conscience is within our grasp, right here, right now.

A Bach cello suite, Van Gogh's *Starry Night*, a Shakespeare sonnet, the stunning choreography of Martha Graham, or the best efforts of a plethora of younger artists, writers, and performers—these are all opportunities for experiences in which we find ourselves deeply moved, inwardly healed (perhaps for a moment, perhaps longer), skillfully taught, profoundly awakened, rudely challenged, and downright shaken loose from our brittle ego-encapsulated boundaries. The power of art will not let us forget the greatness of our humanity.

~

Robert Adams, photographer and eloquent spokesperson for the integrity and ethical responsibility of the artist, writes:

Photography ought to start with and remain faithful to the appearance of the world, and in so doing record contradictions. The greatest pictures would then—I still believe this—find wholeness in the torn world . . .

As defined by hundreds of years of practice—I think this history is vitally important—art is a discovery of harmony, a vision of disparities reconciled, of shape beneath confusion. Art does not deny that evil is real, but it places evil in a context that implies an affirmation; the structure of the picture, which is a metaphor for the structure of Creation, suggests that evil is not final . . .

Art does not in fact prove anything. What it does do is record one of those brief times, such as we each have and then each forget, when we are allowed to understand that the Creation is whole.

When I was young, and the Vietnam War was in progress, many of my friends who were not drafted were deeply involved in the antiwar protest movement. Being against the conditions of that (or any) war, I briefly joined the ranks of the protestors. But as I saw at Kent State, direct social action in that manner did not work for me. At its best, protesting served to awaken our leaders to the fact that the American people were divided on the issue of this war. At its worst, protesting fostered divisiveness, polarization, and another form of violence.

I had a growing awareness that something else was needed. I began to feel that evolution of human consciousness was the only real answer—and represented the only possible solution to the problems of the modern age. We must strive to see more, feel more deeply, and awaken to the deeper levels of consciousness inherent in our human potential. True awakening—of consciousness and conscience—is the only agent of change that can make a difference in our lives on this planet, as individuals and nations. And in this search for awakening, art and creativity can help; they provide a pathway for personal and social evolution.

For many years, I felt alone in this way of seeing, even amid my peers, other artists and photographers. It wasn't until the past decade that I found my attitudes and beliefs corroborated in the public domain, in one of the most significant and stirring speeches that I have ever heard, by Václav Havel, the playwright and President of the Czech Republic, in an address to the joint session of the U.S. Congress in March, 1990:

> *The salvation of this human world lies nowhere else than in the human heart, in the human power to reflect, in human meekness and in human responsibility . . . Without a global revolution in the sphere of consciousness, nothing will change for the better in the sphere of our being as humans, and the catastrophe toward which the world is headed—be it ecological, social, demographic or a general breakdown of civilization—will be unavoidable. If we are no longer threatened by world war or by the*

danger that the absurd mountains of accumulated nuclear weapons might blow up the world, this does not mean that we have definitely won. We are still incapable of understanding that the only genuine backbone of all our actions, if they are to be moral, is responsibility. Responsibility to something higher than 'my family,' 'my country,' 'my company,' 'my success'—responsibility to the order of being where all our actions are indelibly recorded and where and only where they will be properly judged.

I can only wish that we, as artists, students, educators, and other creative individuals, might begin to understand and feel the meaning and challenge of these powerful words and ideas.

SOURCES

Adams, Robert. *Beauty in Photography: Essays in Defense of Traditional Values*. Millerton, NY: Aperture, 1981.

———. *Why People Photograph*. New York: Aperture, 1994.

Angelou, Maya. *Even the Stars Look Lonesome*. New York: Random House, 1997.

Bayles, David, and Ted Orland. *Art & Fear: Observations on the Perils (and Rewards) of Artmaking*. Santa Barbara: Capra, 1993.

Bhagavad Gita. Translated by Stephen Mitchell. New York: Harmony Books, 2000.

Boleslavsky, Richard. *Acting: The First Six Lessons*. New York: Theatre Arts, 1933.

Brady, Frank B. *The Art of Seeing with One Eye*. Oradell, NJ: Medical Economics, 1979.

Brook, Peter. "The Secret Dimension." *Parabola*, vol. 21, no. 2, (summer 1996).

Cameron, Julia. *The Artist's Way: A Spiritual Path to Higher Creativity*. New York: Tarcher/Putnam, 1992.

Campbell, Joseph. *The Power of Myth*. New York: Doubleday, 1988.

Caponigro, Paul. *Paul Caponigro: An Aperture Monograph*. New York: Aperture, 1967.

———. "Writing with Light." *Parabola*, vol. 26, no. 3 (1991).

Carnwath, Squeak. *Squeak Carnwath: Lists, Observations & Counting*. San Francisco: Chronicle, 1996.

Cartier-Bresson, Henri. *The Decisive Moment*. New York: Simon & Shuster, 1952.

Castaneda, Carlos. *The Teachings of Don Juan: A Yacqui Way of Knowledge*. New York: Ballantine, 1968.

———. Journey to Ixtlan: *The Lessons of Don Juan*. New York: Simon and Schuster, 1972.

Charlot, John. *Chanting the Universe: Hawaiian Religious Culture*. Honolulu: Emphasis International, 1983.

Coleman, A. D. *Critical Focus: Photography in the International Image Community*. Munich: Nazraeli, 1995.

Coomaraswamy, Ananda, K. "The Use of Art." *Parabola*, vol. 26, no. 3 (1991).

Csikszentmihalyi, Mihaly. *Creativity: Flow and the Psychology of Discovery and Invention*. New York: HarperCollins, 1996.

Dalai Lama, H. H. *Awakening the Mind, Lightening the Heart*. New York: HarperCollins, 1995.

Daumal, René. *Mount Analogue*. Boston: Shambhala, 1959.

Dillard, Annie. *The Writing Life*. New York: Harper & Row, 1989.

Dooling, D. M. *A Way of Working*. New York: Anchor Press/Doubleday, 1979.

———. *The Spirit of Quest: Essays and Poems*. New York: Parabola, 1994.

Emerson, Ralph Waldo. *The Portable Emerson*. Edited by Mark Van Doren. New York: Viking, 1967.

Fremantle, Christopher. *On Attention*. New Jersey: Indications, 1993.

Friedman, Bonnie. *Writing Past Dark: Envy, Fear, Distraction and Other Dilemmas in the Writer's Life*. New York: HarperCollins, 1993.

Gablik, Suzi. *The Reenchantment of Art*. New York: Thames and Hudson, 1991.

———. *Conversations Before the End of Time*. New York: Thames and Hudson, 1995.

Ghiselin, Brewster. *The Creative Process: Reflections on Invention in the Arts and Sciences*. Berkeley: University of California, 1952.

Gogh, Vincent Van. *Dear Theo: The Autobiography of Vincent Van Gogh*. Edited by Irving Stone. New York: Plume, 1995.

Goldberg, Natalie. *Writing Down the Bones: Freeing the Writer Within*. Boston: Shambhala, 1986.

———. *Wild Mind: Living the Writer's Life*. New York: Bantam, 1990.

Hale, Constance. *Sin and Syntax*. New York: Broadway, 1999.

Hammarskjöld, Dag. *Markings*. New York: Knopf, 1964.

Herrigel, Eugen. *Zen and the Art of Archery*. New York: Vintage, 1971.

Hillman, James. *The Soul's Code: In Search of Character and Calling*. New York: Random House, 1996.

Hlobeczy, Nicholas, C. *Seed To the Fertile Soil: Selected Poems 1980–83*. Cleveland: Reflections, 1984.

Houston, James, D. "A Pilgrim's Kisses." *Manoa*, vol 1, nos. 1–2 (1989).

The I Ching, or Book of Changes. Translated by Richard Wilhelm and Cary Baynes. Princeton: Princeton University, 1967.

Jung, Carl G. *Memories, Dreams, Reflections*. New York: Vintage, 1961.

———. *Man and His Symbols*. New York: Dell, 1964.

Kandinsky, Wassily. *Concerning the Spiritual in Art*. New York: Wittenborn, 1947.

Keyes, Ralph. *The Courage to Write: How Writers Transcend Fear*. New York: Holt, 1995.

Klee, Paul. *Paul Klee Notebooks: The Thinking Eye/The Nature of Nature, Vols. 1 & 2*. Translated by Ralph Manheim; edited by Jürg Spiller. Woodstock, NY: Overlook Press, 1992.

Lippard, Lucy. *Lure of the Local*. New York: New Press, 1995.

———. *Pink Glass Swan: Selected Feminist Essays on Art*. New York: New Press, 1995.

Lipsey, Roger. *An Art of Our Own: The Spiritual in Twentieth Century Art*. Boston: Shambhala, 1988.

Lusseyran, Jacques. *And There Was Light*. New York: Parabola, 1987.

———. "Blindness: A New Seeing of the World." *Parabola*, vol. 5, no. 3 (1980).

Lyons, Nathan, ed. *Photographers on Photography*. Englewood Cliffs, NJ: Prentice-Hall, 1966.

Mander, Jerry. *In the Absence of the Sacred*. San Francisco: Sierra Club, 1991.

Maslow, Abraham. *Toward a Psychology of Being*. Third Edition. New York: John Wiley and Sons, 1998.

May, Rollo. *The Courage to Create*. New York: W.W. Norton, 1975.

Meyerowitz, Joel. *Cape Light*. Boston: New York Graphic Society, 1978.

Misrach, Richard. *Desert Cantos*. Albuquerque: University of New Mexico, 1987.

Moore, Thomas. "The Soul's Religion." *Parabola,* vol. 21, no. 2 (1996).

Needleman, Jacob, ed. *Speaking of My Life: The Art of Living in a Cultural Revolution*. New York: Harper & Row, 1979.

Neihardt, John G. *Black Elk Speaks*. Lincoln, NE: University of Nebraska, 1961.

Nin Anais. *The Diary of Anais Nin*. Edited and with a preface by Gunther Stuhlmann. New York: Harvest/HBJ, 1977.

Norman, Dorothy. *Alfred Stieglitz: Introduction to an American Seer*. New York: Duell, Sloan and Pearce, 1960.

O'Keeffe, Georgia. *Georgia O'Keeffe*. New York: Viking, 1976.

Orage, A. R. *A.R. Orage's Commentaries on G.I. Gurdjieff's All and Everything*. Edited by C. S. Nott. Aurora, OR: Two Rivers, 1985.

Ouspensky, P. D. *In Search of the Miraculous: Fragments of an Unknown Teaching*. New York: Harcourt, Brace, 1949.

Purdy, Jedediah. *For Common Things*. New York, Knopf, 1999.

Reeve, Rowland B., comp. *Kahoʻolawe: Na Leo o Kanaloa*. Honolulu: ʻAi Pohaku, 1995.

Reinhardt, Ad. *Art as Art: The Selected Writings of Ad Reinhardt*. Edited by Barbara Rose. Berkeley: University of California, 1991.

Rilke, Rainer Maria. *The Selected Poetry*. Translated by Stephen Mitchell. New York: Vintage, 1984.

———. *Letters to a Young Poet*. Translated by Stephen Mitchell. New York: Vintage, 1986.

———. *The Notebooks of Malte Laurids Brigg*. Translated by Stephen Mitchell. New York: Vintage, 1990.

———. *Diaries of a Young Poet*. Translated by Stephen Mitchell and Michael Winkler. New York: Norton, 1997.

Roethke, Theodore. *Straw for the Fire: From the Notebooks of Theodore Roethke 1943–63*. Selected by David Wagoner. Seattle: University of Washington, 1980.

Rosenberg, Harold. *The De-Definition of Art*. Chicago: University of Chicago, 1972.

Rosenthal, Mark. *Anselm Kiefer*. Chicago: Art Institute of Chicago, and Philadelphia: Philadelphia Museum of Art, 1987.

Rumi. *The Essential Rumi*. Translated by Coleman Barks. New York: HarperCollins, 1995.

Segal, William. *Opening: Collected Writings of William Segal 1985–1997*. New York: Continuum, 1998.

Sewall, Laura. *Sight and Sensibility: The Ecopsychology of Perception*. New York: Tarcher/Putnam, 1999.

Shapard, Robert, ed. "The Self in Contemporary American Short Fiction: Who Are We?" *Manoa*, vol, 1, nos. 1–2, (1989).

Steiner, Wendy. *The Scandal of Pleasure: Art in an Age of Fundamentalism*. Chicago: University of Chicago, 1995.

Stewart, Frank, ed. "To Repair the Material of Experience: Symposium on Writing and Spirituality." *Manoa*, vol. 7, no. 1 (1995).

Strunk, William Jr. & E. B. White. *The Elements of Style*. 4th ed. Boston: Allyn & Bacon, 2000.

Tao Te Ching. Translated by Stephen Mitchell. New York: Harper & Row, 1988.

Theroux, Paul. *Fresh Air Fiend: Travel Writings 1985–2000*. New York: Mariner, 2001.

Thurman, Robert A. F. "The Fullness of Emptiness: An Interview with His Holiness the Dalai Lama." *Parabola*, vol. 10, no. 1 (1985).

Tracol, Henri. *The Taste for Things that Are True*. Rockport, MA: Element, 1994.

Vaysse, Jean. *Toward Awakening: An Approach to the Teaching Left by Gurdjieff*. London: Routledge and Kegan Paul, 1980.

Wertenbaker, Christian. "The Nature of Consciousness: An Interview with Oliver Sacks." *Parabola*, vol. 22, no. 3 (1997).

Weston, Edward. *The Daybooks of Edward Weston, Vol. II: California*. Edited by Nancy Newhall. Millerton, NY: Aperture, 1961.

White, Minor. *Mirrors Messages Manifestations*. Millerton, NY: Aperture, 1969.

Whitman, Walt. *Complete Poetry and Selected Prose*. Edited by James D. Miller, Jr. Boston: Houghton Mifflin, 1959.

Yanagi, Soetsu and Bernard Leach. *The Unknown Craftsman: A Japanese Insight into Beauty*. New York: Kodansha, 1972.

Zaleski, Jeffrey P. "Echoes of Infinity: An Interview with Seyyed Hossein Nasr." *Parabola*, vol. 13, no. 1 (1988).

— COPYRIGHT ACKNOWLEDGMENTS —

OTHER BOOKS FROM
BEYOND WORDS PUBLISHING, INC.

Spiritual Writing
From Inspiration to Publication
Authors: Deborah Levine Herman with Cynthia Black
$16.95, softcover

Spiritual writers are drawn to the writing process by a powerful sense of mission. But that call to write is often at odds with the realities of publishing and the commercial needs of publishers. In *Spiritual Writing*, writer and literary agent Deborah Levine Herman and publisher Cynthia Black show writers how to create a book that both remains true to their vision and still conforms to the protocols of the publishing industry. Written with the intention of guiding and informing writers on their journey to publication, the book includes journaling exercises, tips on finding an agent and publisher, guidelines for writing query letters and proposals, a glossary of industry terms, and a comprehensive database that provides specifics on "spirit-friendly" publishers and agents.

Conscious Seeing
Transforming Your Life Through Your Eyes
Author: Roberto Kaplan, O.D., M.Ed.
$14.95, softcover

In *Conscious Seeing*, the reader learns that no eye problem is independent from our experience and perceptions. It is the first book that explains in depth how the mind elaborates on the sense of sight. By being guided to look at their eyes beyond the diagnosis of a problem, readers will come to understand that their visual symptoms are valuable messages through which they can be more aware of their true nature. If an eye problem exists, a person can gain the skills to modify his or her perceptions. As the author asserts, looking is trainable when people see consciously.

PowerHunch!
Living an Intuitive Life
Author: Marcia Emery, Ph.D.; Foreword: Leland Kaiser, Ph.D.
$15.95, softcover

Whether it's relationships, career, balance and healing, or simple everyday decision-making, intuition gives everyone an edge. In *PowerHunch!* Dr. Emery is your personal trainer as you develop your intuitive muscle. She shows you how to consistently and accurately apply your hunches to any problem and offers countless examples of intuition in action, covering a wide spectrum of occupations and relationships. With its intriguing stories and expert advice, *PowerHunch!* gives you the necessary tools and principles to create an intuitive life for yourself.

The Intuitive Way
A Guide to Living from Inner Wisdom
Author: Penney Peirce; Foreword: Carol Adrienne
$16.95, softcover

When intuition is in full bloom, life takes on a magical, effortless quality; your world is suddenly full of synchronicities, creative insights, and abundant knowledge just for the asking. *The Intuitive Way* shows you how to enter that state of perceptual aliveness and integrate it into daily life to achieve greater natural flow through an easy-to-understand, ten-step course. Author Penney Peirce synthesizes teachings from psychology, East-West philosophy, religion, metaphysics, and business. In simple and direct language, Peirce describes the intuitive process as a new way of life and demonstrates many practical applications from speeding decision-making to expanding personal growth. Whether you're just beginning to search for a richer, fuller life experience or are looking for more subtle, sophisticated insights about your spiritual path, *The Intuitive Way* will be your companion as you progress through the stages of intuition development.

Celebrating Time Alone
Stories of Splendid Solitude
Author: Lionel Fisher
$14.95, softcover

Celebrating Time Alone, with its profiles in solitude, shows us how to be magnificently alone through a celebration of our self: the self that can get buried under mountains of information, appointments, and activities. Lionel Fisher interviewed men and women across the country who have achieved great emotional clarity by savoring their individuality and solitude. In a writing style that is at once eloquent and down to earth, the author interweaves their real-life stories with his own insights and experiences to offer counsel, inspiration, and affirmation on living well alone.

Seeing Your Life Through New Eyes

InSights to Freedom from Your Past
Authors: Paul Brenner, M.D., Ph.D., and Donna Martin, M.A.
$14.95, softcover

Seeing Your Life Through New Eyes is in a hands-on workbook format that helps you create a diary of self-discovery and assists you in resolving any misunderstood relationships. You can learn how to uncover unconscious patterns that define how you love, what you value, and what unique gifts you have in life. This book reveals those obstacles that too often interfere with loving relationships and creative expression, and it includes diagrams to use for your personal exploration and growth.

Your Authentic Self

Be Yourself at Work
Author: Ric Giardina
$14.95, softcover

Working people everywhere feel that they lead double lives: an "on the job" life and a personal life. Is it possible to live a life in which the separate parts of our personalities are united? In *Your Authentic Self*, author Ric Giardina explains that it is possible, and the key to achieving this integrated existence is authenticity. By honoring your authentic self at the workplace, you will not only be much happier, but you will also be rewarded with better on-the-job performance and more fulfilling work relationships. With straightforward techniques that produce instant results, this practical and easy-to-use guide will empower you to make the shift from seeing work as "off the path" of personal and spiritual growth to recognizing it as an integral part of your journey.

To order or to request a catalog, contact
Beyond Words Publishing, Inc.
20827 N.W. Cornell Road, Suite 500
Hillsboro, OR 97124-9808
503-531-8700 or 1-800-284-9673

You can also visit our Web site at *www.beyondword.com*
or e-mail us at *info@beyondword.com*.

BEYOND WORDS PUBLISHING, INC.

OUR CORPORATE MISSION

Inspire to Integrity

OUR DECLARED VALUES

We give to all of life as life has given us.

We honor all relationships.

Trust and stewardship are integral to fulfilling dreams.

Collaboration is essential to create miracles.

Creativity and aesthetics nourish the soul.

Unlimited thinking is fundamental.

Living your passion is vital.

Joy and humor open our hearts to growth.

It is important to remind ourselves of love.